FOUNDATIONS OF MULTILITERACIES

Using the concept of multiliteracies and multimodality, this book provides foundation knowledge about the new and continuously changing literacies of the 21st century. It details the five semiotic systems (Linguistic, Visual, Audio, Gestural and Spatial) and how they contribute to the reading and writing of increasingly complex and dynamic texts that are delivered by live, paper or digital technologies.

One of the main tenets of the book is that social, cultural and technological developments will continue to give rise to changing literate practices around texts and communication, requiring a rethinking of classroom practices that are employed in the teaching of literacy. Therefore, the role of talk, together with traditional lesson structures, is examined and the concept of dialogic talk is introduced as a way of moving towards an effective pedagogy for the teaching and learning of multiliteracies and multimodality.

The book also demonstrates that children's literature can provide a bridge between old and new literacies and be an effective vehicle for introducing the five semiotic systems to all age groups. Comprehensive and accessible, this book addresses the issue of translating complex theories, research and concepts into effective practice by providing the reader with four avenues for reflecting upon and implementing the ideas it contains:

- Reflection Strategies that enable the reader to gauge their understanding of key concepts;
- Theory into Practice tasks that enable the trialling of specific theoretical concepts in the classroom;
- Auditing Instruments provide specific tasks related to assessment of student performance and evaluation of teacher pedagogy;
- QR Codes immediately link the reader to multimodal texts and further references that illustrate and enhance the concepts being developed.

Dr Michèle Anstey is co-director of ABC: Anstey and Bull Consultants in Education and formerly an Associate Professor at the University of Southern Queensland, Toowoomba, and a teacher in Victoria, NSW and Queensland. She provides professional development in literacy, children's literature and pedagogy throughout Australia and New Zealand. She also conducts tendered research, commissioned writing, speaks at conferences, prepares professional development packages for trainers and advises on curriculum.

Dr Geoff Bull is co-director of ABC: Anstey and Bull Consultants in Education and formerly an Associate Professor at the University of Southern Queensland, Toowoomba. He provides professional development in literacy, children's literature and pedagogy throughout Australia and New Zealand. He also conducts tendered research, commissioned writing, speaks at conferences, prepares professional development packages for trainers and advises on curriculum.

FOUNDATIONS OF MULTILITERACIES

Reading, Writing and Talking in the 21st Century

Michèle Anstey and Geoff Bull

LONDON AND NEW YORK

First published 2018
by Routledge
2 Park Square, Milton Park, Abingdon, Oxon OX14 4RN

and by Routledge
711 Third Avenue, New York, NY 10017

Routledge is an imprint of the Taylor & Francis Group, an informa business

© 2018 Michèle Anstey and Geoff Bull

The right of Michèle Anstey and Geoff Bull to be identified as authors of this work has been asserted by them in accordance with sections 77 and 78 of the Copyright, Designs and Patents Act 1988.

All rights reserved. No part of this book may be reprinted or reproduced or utilised in any form or by any electronic, mechanical, or other means, now known or hereafter invented, including photocopying and recording, or in any information storage or retrieval system, without permission in writing from the publishers.

Trademark notice: Product or corporate names may be trademarks or registered trademarks, and are used only for identification and explanation without intent to infringe.

British Library Cataloguing in Publication Data
A catalogue record for this book is available from the British Library

Library of Congress Cataloging in Publication Data
Names: Anstey, Micháele, author. | Bull, Geoff, author.
Title: Foundations of multiliteracies : reading, writing and talking in the 21st century / Micháele Anstey and Geoff Bull.
Description: Abingdon, Oxon ; New York, NY : Routledge, 2018. | Includes bibliographical references.
Identifiers: LCCN 2017041975 | ISBN 9781138079915 (hbk) | ISBN 9781138079908 (pbk) | ISBN 9781315114194 (ebk)
Subjects: LCSH: Literacy–Social aspects. | Language arts. | Computers and literacy.
Classification: LCC LC149 .A65 2018 | DDC 374/.0124–dc23
LC record available at https://lccn.loc.gov/2017041975

ISBN: 978-1-138-07991-5 (hbk)
ISBN: 978-1-138-07990-8 (pbk)
ISBN: 978-1-315-11419-4 (ebk)

Typeset in Interstate
by Apex CoVantage, LLC

CONTENTS

	List of Figures, Tables and QR Codes	vi
	Preface	ix
	Acknowledgments	xi
1	The rise of multiliteracies: Global trends and practices that change literacy	1
2	Being multiliterate: A repertoire of practices	44
3	Communicating through multimodal texts and semiotic systems	80
4	Teaching and learning multiliteracies: Examining classroom pedagogy and practices through a focus on teacher talk and dialogic talk	127
5	Exploring literature: Engaging with multimodal texts and new literacies	169
6	Assessment and evaluation of pedagogy, practice and planning in the multiliterate and multimodal classroom	197
	Full Bibliography	224
	Glossary	236
	Index	240

LIST OF FIGURES, TABLES & QR CODES

Chapter One

Tables

1.1	A summary of the functions of language proposed by Halliday and Smith	7
1.2	Comparing traditional literacy and literacy as social practice	15
1.3	Relationships among multiliteracies, changing workplace characteristics and pedagogy	27
1.4	Relationships among multiliteracies, changing technology and change in social, cultural and civic settings, and pedagogy	37

Figure

1.1	A visual concept of the origins of the term *multiliteracies*	17

QR Codes

1.1	Movietone news archives on YouTube	5
1.2	A list of movies set in the 1950s	5
1.3	Trailer for *Hidden Figures*	5
1.4	An article on Google as a workplace where organisation of space encourages creativity	19
1.5	An article that discusses how the availability of different workplace settings (use of space) facilitate different work practices	19
1.6	An article in which the professor who led the team that created Nadine discusses the implications for workplaces and employment in the future	24
1.7	Commonly known network sites ranked by number of users in January 2017	30
1.8	Photoshop turns pizza into woman	33
1.9	Photoshop has gone too far in CollegeHumor Originals	33
1.10	The Five Laws of Media and Information Literacy (MIL)	38
1.11	A community response to change	40

Chapter Two

Table

2.1	Comparing Standard English (SE) and Non-standard English (NSE)	53

Figure

2.1	The concept of literacy identity	68

Chapter Three

Tables

3.1	A metacognitive view of the process of consuming a multimodal text	100
3.2	A metacognitive view of the process of producing a multimodal text	104
3.3	Introductory list for the codes and conventions of the Visual Semiotic System	118
3.4	Introductory list for the codes and conventions of the Audio Semiotic System	120
3.5	Introductory list for the codes and conventions of the Linguistic Semiotic System	121
3.6	Introductory list for the codes and conventions of the Gestural Semiotic System	121
3.7	Introductory list for the codes and conventions of the Spatial Semiotic System	123

Figures

3.1	Text and design: Encouraging talk about texts as dynamic rather than static	85
3.2	Early comparisons of the writing and reading processes	90
3.3	Consuming and producing multimodal text in a multiliterate world	91
3.4	Resources that may be drawn upon when producing or consuming (designing) a multimodal text	107

QR Codes

3.1	Shaun Tan's website	99
3.2	A website that provides metalanguage for talking about the web	114
3.3	Advice to teachers regarding the writing test for NAPLAN	116

Chapter Four

Tables

4.1	Functions of teacher talk	151
4.2	Phases of lessons	156

Figure

4.1	Mapping the phase structure of a lesson	157

Chapter Five

Tables

5.1	Characteristics of postmodern picture books and how they might be realised	174
5.2	A group of books that explore the concept of picture book	177
5.3	A model for engaging with multimodal text	185

QR Codes

5.1	Link to 'It's not all Black and White'	179
5.2	Discussion about making the picture book *The Lost Thing* into film	182
5.3	Matt Ottley talks about composing images and music	183
5.4	Three links to cartoon and puppet versions of *The Three Little Pigs*	189

1. The original 1933 cartoon version 189
2. A 2008 version 189
3. A puppet version in French to a Lady Gaga song 189

Chapter Six

Figures
6.1 The monitoring cycle 199
6.2 Understanding by design and backward design 209

PREFACE

Our professional development work and research with teachers and students across all education systems since we wrote *Teaching and Learning Multiliteracies: Changing Times, Changing Literacies* (2006) and *Evolving Pedagogies: Reading and Writing in a Multimodal World* (2010) stimulated the ideas that inform this book. We found that it was not only necessary to reconsider what constituted reading, writing and text as teachers and students began to engage with new and changing literacies, but that there was a need to change pedagogy. Therefore, issues around classroom talk, planning and practice needed to be addressed. It was also necessary to understand the factors that have brought about these changes, and the continuation of them, in order to make literacy teaching and learning relevant to students' present and future lives.

We are firm believers in looking back in order to look forward. Education is littered with bright ideas, courses and approaches that are adopted and abandoned as the next best thing comes along. Therefore, we have approached this book in terms of what has come before and is seminal in informing current and future approaches to literacy teaching and pedagogy. It is our belief that the concept of multiliteracies is a sound basis, but that there is much additional research and methodology that can be drawn upon to inform its implementation.

As a consequence of our findings from working with teachers and leaders and from our research, we have written two complementary volumes. *Foundations of Multiliteracies: Reading, Writing and Talking in the 21st Century* provides a comprehensive introduction to multiliteracies and the ideas and concepts that inform it, together with information about the changes to classroom talk, planning, pedagogy and practice that are necessary as a result of adopting a multiliterate pedagogy. The complementary volume, *Elaborating Multiliteracies through Multimodal Texts: Changing Classroom Practices and Developing Teacher Pedagogies,* builds upon the previous volume by embedding an action learning model throughout the book, encouraging readers to explore classroom practice around multiliteracies, collect data about their practice and enact change. Its aim is to concurrently build a more refined and in-depth understanding of literacies, multiliteracies and multimodal texts and develop a multiliterate pedagogy, thus addressing the issues that informed the writing of these books.

Designing the books

Throughout the books we refer to writing and reading as a process of designing and redesigning text in order to convey or make meaning, that is, to fulfil a particular communicative purpose. Therefore, we have designed this book around five intertwined themes:

- the origins and development of the concepts of multiliteracies and multimodality
- the five semiotic systems (linguistic, visual, audio, spatial and gestural) that underpin today's texts

- the examination of classroom talk as a tool for enhancing the teaching and learning of multiliteracies and multimodality
- the use of dialogic talk as the vehicle for teaching and learning multiliteracies and multimodality
- literature as an essential component for developing multiliteracies and multimodality

As always our overarching goal is to blend theory and practice and provide readers with the opportunity to reflect upon and develop their own understandings, as well as apply this knowledge to the educational setting in which they are based. Therefore, we have also designed particular features to help the reader in these endeavours:

- Graphic Outlines for each chapter are designed to orient the reader to the concepts contained in the chapter and the relationships among them
- Reflection Strategies provide activities and tasks that enable the reader to gauge their understanding of key concepts
- Theory into Practice tasks provide ideas and activities that enable the trialling of specific theoretical concepts in the classroom
- Auditing Instruments provide specific tasks related to assessment of student performance and evaluation of teacher pedagogy
- QR Codes are used to address the multimodal and digital nature of new literacies. They immediately link the reader to multimodal texts and further references that illustrate and enhance the concepts being developed
- A Running Glossary enables the reader to immediately access definitions of key concepts.

ACKNOWLEDGMENTS

As with all our work the focus of this book has been informed by our discussions and engagement around multiliteracies and multimodality with teachers and teacher leaders throughout Australia in recent years. We thank them for their willingness to share their thoughts and ideas with us. In doing so they have revealed their passion for teaching and learning and their deep commitment to the education of their students.

Thank you also to the many people associated with Taylor & Francis who have supported and advised during the process. In particular, we wish to thank Lucinda Knight, Matt Bickerton, Emma Sudderick, Rebecca Wise and Nicola Lennon for their guidance and assistance.

1 The rise of multiliteracies: Global trends and practices that change literacy

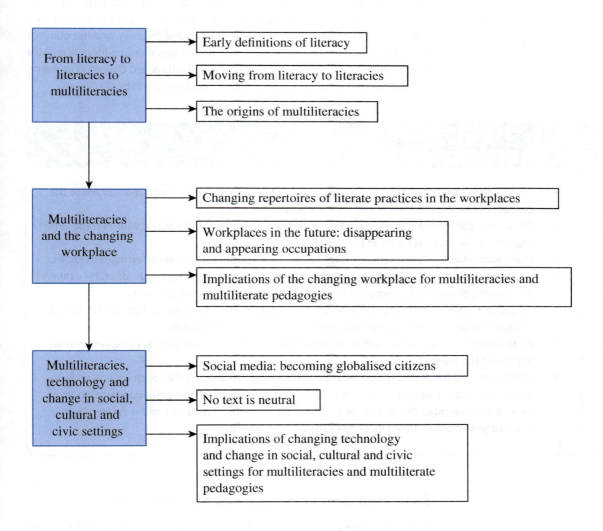

This chapter provides the historical, sociocultural and educational basis for using the term *multiliteracies* to describe literacy. It commences with a section in which the reasons for continuously evolving definitions of the term *literacy* are explored, concluding with the emergence of the term *multiliteracies*. The implications for education and pedagogy will be discussed in relation to the evolving definitions of literacy, literacies and multiliteracies.

The remainder of the chapter will establish the relevance of, and necessity for, using the term *multiliteracies* and its associated pedagogies in current and future educational settings. This will be addressed through the concept of continuous change as the new constant of societies across the world, focussing on increasing globalisation, social and cultural diversity, and use of developing technologies. The impact of continuous change on the literacy and the literate practices of workplace, leisure, social, cultural and civic environments, together with the implications for literacy pedagogy, will be discussed.

REFLECTION STRATEGY 1.1

- The purpose of this Reflection Strategy is to identify your current understandings about the concepts of literacy, literacies and multiliteracies.
- Before you commence reading the next section of this chapter, think about your current perceptions of literacy, literacies and multiliteracies.
- Using your reflections, write your own definition of each term: literacy, literacies, multiliteracies.
- You can express these definitions in whatever way you feel best conveys your ideas, for example, a series of dot points, complete sentences, a flow chart, table or diagram.
- As you read this chapter and come across ideas that are new to you or cause you to change or modify your definitions, go back and revise your original definitions.
- Write your revisions into a new definition each time, separate to the previous one, rather than modifying the original.
- The reason it is suggested that a separate and new definition be written each time is because this will provide a way for you to reread all your iterations of the definition, tracing your developing understanding of the terms. It will also provide a good source for reviewing your knowledge and understandings of this chapter when you finish it.

From literacy to literacies to multiliteracies

In the educational context, definitions of literacy have been used to shape curriculum, specifying the desired outcomes of literacy education and the knowledge, skills and understandings that need to be taught. Definitions of literacy can also be found in civic documents at the local, state, national and international level to explain and justify social, economic and education policy or provide benchmarks for the measurement of literacy.

Logically, when definitions are used to shape the content of curriculum it would be assumed that they would also shape the teaching and learning of literacy, that is, the pedagogy. However, as Gardner (2017) pointed out in a comparative analysis of the current primary English curricula in the U.K. and Australia, this is not always the case. As will be discussed later in this chapter, one of the reasons the concept of multiliteracies was originally proposed was to address the gap between evolving definitions of literacy and literacy pedagogy. Therefore in this chapter, and the whole book, there will be a focus on the implications of evolving definitions of literacy, literacies and multiliteracies for literacy pedagogy.

Early definitions of literacy

It is useful to look at definitions of literacy over time, as they provide insights into how and why perceptions of literacy and being literate have changed. Kalantzis et al. (2016, p. 6), suggest that education is about creating 'kinds of people' and therefore definitions of literacy and literacy education are about the knowledge, skills and understandings that have been identified as necessary to participate in the work, public and community life of a society. Therefore, such definitions implicitly (and sometimes explicitly) tell us about the current views of society and the desirable characteristics of people in that society. Because of the relationship between literacy and all aspects of society it is understandable that definitions of literacy will change as societies change.

The following definition from a UNESCO document in 1957 provides a good example of how analyses of a definition can provide such insights into society at that time and what literacy skills were perceived as important. It also helps to reflect upon whether such a definition would be adequate today.

> [L]iteracy is a characteristic acquired by individuals in varying degrees from just above none to an indeterminate upper level. Some individuals are more or less literate than others, but it is really not possible to speak of literate and illiterate persons as two distinct categories.
>
> UNESCO (1957, p. 18)

This statement about literacy does not suggest what skills, knowledge and practices constitute literacy but it does assert that it is acquired at various levels and some individuals might be less literate than others. What these levels are and what constitutes achievement at these levels is not stated. It tells us little about what global documents in society at that time specified as literacy, but it does recognise degrees of literacy and it infers that defining literacy and illiteracy is difficult – '…not possible to speak of literate and illiterate persons as two distinct categories.'

Just a few years later, in recognition of the impact of illiteracy on human rights and discrimination, UNESCO launched an Experimental World Literacy Program (EWLP). A 1962 UNESCO document cited by Oxenham (1980, p. 87) provided a definition with a more detailed picture of how literacy and literate practices were viewed in this period.

> A person is literate when he has acquired the *essential knowledge and skills* which enable him to engage in all those activities in which literacy is required *for effective functioning in his group and community*, and whose attainments in reading, writing and arithmetic make it possible for him to continue to *use those skills toward his own and the community's development*.

Examination of the italicised sections of this definition indicate a belief that there is a finite set of skills and knowledge that are unique to a group or community and that acquisition of them is a prerequisite to being able to function and develop oneself and one's community. The apparent gendered nature of the definition (use of him) reflects the language of the times and does not necessarily preclude other genders.

Most of us cannot picture the world in 1957 or 1962; our perceptions and experience are mediated by old movies, film or TV shows from those times, or those made more recently to depict the period. Therefore, it is difficult to picture a society in which these definitions would function. At the time in Western English-speaking countries such as the U.K., U.S.A., Canada and Australia, the skills and knowledge necessary were language dominated as communication in work, public and community life was largely transacted through words on paper, and oral communication in person or by phone. Phones were fixed and had to be used in an office, home or telephone box. As publishing in colour or reproducing photos and images was very expensive, images in print-based material were minimal. Television was in its infancy; colour was only just beginning to become widely available. In some countries owning a television was still the province of the rich. Therefore, the movie theatre was the main source of entertainment through film or moving images. It was also a source of world news in documentary style newsreels that were played before the main film, for example, Movietone News. If you wish to get a picture of life and news in the 1950s, the following QR codes give access to Movietone News archives and lists of movies that are set in the 1950s. However, as you access them and view them, remember that these depict one group's perceptions of life at this time. The third QR code is a link to the trailer for the film *Hidden Figures*, which was released in December 2016 and is set in the early 1960s. This link is included because it gives insight into the technologies of the period, as well as the social values the producers of the movie chose to highlight. It depicts NASA and the early space launches and the use of human computers. The job of the human computers was to do the mathematical computations necessary to predict things like the orbit of space capsules, prior to the introduction of the technology that became non-human computers. These calculations were done using pencil and paper or chalk and a blackboard, slide rules and basic adding machines.

QR Code 1.1 Movietone news archives on YouTube (https://www.youtube.com/channel/UCHq777_waKMJw6SZdABmyaA)

QR Code 1.2 A list of movies set in the 1950s (https://en.wikipedia.org/wiki/Category:Films_set_in_the_1950s)

QR Code 1.3 Trailer for *Hidden Figures* (https://www.youtube.com/watch?v=RK8xHq6dfAo)

Most people left school and stayed in one job for life and, while a few might move towns, it was rare to move states or countries for work. Travel by plane for work or leisure was expensive and therefore limited to those who had the means to pay for it. Education often encouraged the early filtering of students into occupations through academic and manual streaming and exit points that encouraged early identification of career into manual labour, apprenticeships, office work, professionals or university. For example, in England the Tripartite System was used from 1944 to 1976 and the 11 Plus exam at the end of primary school determined whether students should attend a grammar school, a secondary modern or a technical school. The idea was that students' performance in the test indicated their ability to enter particular careers and these three different types of schools provided the skills and knowledge appropriate for entering those careers. In Australia in the 1960s Scholarship, Junior and Senior exams screened students firstly for entry to secondary school, secondly for entry into apprenticeships or trades and finally entry to university. Very few attended university, firstly because of the school filtering process and entry requirements and secondly because it required the ability to pay fees and the funds to move and live away from home. Literature of the dominant society was most valued and there was an accepted canon of 'good quality' literature reflecting writers identified as the 'great writers' of previous generations. Knowledge of such literature was seen as prestigious, an indicator of a fine mind and education.

What are the implications for literacy education in such a period? If communication is language dominated then understanding the rudiments of grammar, spelling and punctuation and comprehension are essential requirements for both reading and writing. If jobs are for life, then the set of communication skills and knowledge necessary for those jobs is finite and identifiable. If you do not travel then the groups and cultures you encounter will be those of your own society and community, so there is no need to know about how to communicate with people who may not share your beliefs, culture or ways of communicating or who may challenge yours. As access to media such as television or film was limited and largely for leisure there was no need to understand how to make meaning of film or how to make it.

The education and literacy of this period has been characterised as old basics (Luke 1995), (Luke and Freebody 1997), traditional (Anstey and Bull, 2004, 2006), and heritage-based (Kalantzis et al. 2016). That is, at this time the goal of education generally was to pass on and maintain one's heritage and the literacy skills needed to maintain it. Literacy was language dominant, as language was the most powerful tool for use with the available communication technology (paper and phone). Therefore, the teaching practices or pedagogy of this period were content and rule based (grammar, phonics, punctuation and spelling), test oriented (to check mastery), and encouraged passive learning where the teacher was the holder of all knowledge. A society of hierarchical workplaces where jobs were held for life required well-disciplined people and these teaching practices encouraged such behaviour. Luke (1995) referred to this as providing a basic toolkit, which is an appropriate analogy given the social context and technologies of the time.

Interestingly, in the Western English speaking countries previously identified, post-World War 2 immigration meant that people from other cultures (largely European) were now entering these societies. For example, 1.25 million people immigrated to Australia between 1949 and 1959, over half of whom were from Europe, the rest British. At the time Australia's population rose from 8 to 10 million. The cultural and linguistic diversity of Australia was changing, yet the traditional, old basics, heritage model of literacy and education was dominated by Australia's British heritage. The United Kingdom not only had an influx of European but also Indian immigrants, after India gained its independence from Britain and was no longer a British colony. The U.S.A. also had an influx of European immigration, as did Canada, though as a proportion of their total populations it was smaller than Australia's and not as diverse as the United Kingdom's. It is appropriate to ponder whether a heritage based model of literacy and education generally was becoming less appropriate at this time.

REFLECTION STRATEGY 1.2

- The purpose of this Reflection Strategy is to re-examine your initial definitions of literacy, literacies and multiliteracies in terms of the information about early definitions of literacy that have been presented.
- Do your definitions reflect any of the trends described in the traditional, old basics, heritage based model?
- Are your definitions influenced by the culture and other characteristics of your society, group, country and/or place of work? If so, how are they influenced and, if not, why did you exclude these aspects from your definition?
- Do you wish to revise your definitions? Explain the reasons behind your decision.

Moving from literacy to literacies

Definitions of literacy that focussed on skills and knowledge that could be used to participate in society, that is, in workplace, leisure, social, cultural and civic environments, led researchers to try and categorise the ways in which language was used to complete transactions and communications. It marked a change in the way literacy was perceived: as researchers were now focussing on the practices associated with literacy, literacy was beginning to be constructed as more than a set of language skills and knowledge. It was also about how language was used in **social practice**. One of the first researchers to suggest this was Michael Halliday, who proposed seven purposes for the use of language by children in order to make meaning (Halliday 1973). Smith (1983, p. 53) later expanded on these purposes. Table 1.1 presents Halliday and Smith's functions of language (adapted from Anstey and Bull 2004, p. 24).

Social Practice
The recognised, agreed upon and accepted behaviour (acting and interacting), talking and valuing among a social or cultural group. The social or cultural group will use these ways of behaving and talking in particular contexts. They may have a shared language (for example, slang) and ways of dressing or ways of wearing clothes. They may also share ways of viewing or acting toward particular social or cultural groups.

Table 1.1 A summary of the functions of language proposed by Halliday and Smith

Function	Explanation
1 Instrumental: 'I want.'	Language as a means of getting things, satisfying material needs
2 Regulatory: 'Do as I tell you.'	Controlling the behaviour, feelings or attitudes of others
3 Interactional: 'Me and you.'	Getting along with others, establishing relative status. Also 'Me against you' – establishing separateness
4 Personal: 'Here I come.'	Expressing individuality, awareness of self, pride
5 Heuristic: 'Tell me why.'	Seeking and testing knowledge
6 Imaginative: 'Let's pretend.'	Creating new worlds, making up stories, poems
7 Representational: 'I've got something to tell you.'	Communicating information, descriptions, expressing propositions
8 Diversionary: 'Enjoy this.'	Puns, jokes, riddles
9 Authoritative/contractual: 'How it must be.'	Statutes, laws, regulations, agreements, contracts
10 Perpetuating: 'How it was.'	Records, histories, diaries, notes, scores

(N.B. Halliday's original seven functions are contained in the shaded rows.)

In 1983 the seminal work of Shirley Brice Heath heralded a further change in beliefs about what constituted literacy and consequently, definitions of literacy. Heath researched the language use and behavioural patterns of African American communities who worked in textile mills in the south eastern United States. By following the children into the classroom, it was found that the language and behaviour of their home and community differed markedly from the expected language and behaviours of the classrooms of the school. The classroom behaviour and language were essentially white middle class and were unfamiliar to the African American students. Consequently, their ability, confidence and desire to participate in the literacy practices of the classroom was affected, as often their use of language and behaviour was seen as inappropriate or wrong, despite it achieving its communicative purpose. As one parent observed:

> My kid, he too scared to talk, cause nobody plays by the rules he know. At home I can't shut him up.
>
> Heath (1982, p. 107)

Because Heath's research focussed on language and behaviour it broadened the previous definitions of literacy that focussed only on language. She recognised that literacy is a set of social practices that vary according to culture and context. The African American students were literate in their own culture and community but they did not have the set of social practices for school, as they were those of a different social group and culture. For example, when asked to deliver a report about something they had been doing they would exaggerate pitch and tone, use a lot of facial expression and gesture, and engage with word play (rhyming, making up words for fun), because sharing information in their community was not only about giving the information, but entertaining. This research challenged the idea of literacy being one basic toolkit focussing on language that was transferable to any situation. It indicated that there were many literacies associated with different social groups and cultures that they were embedded in social practice.

By 1986 Heath's ethnographic research enabled her to conclude that there were a number of functions of literacy related to everyday life, but they might be practiced differently among social and cultural groups. While her functions still focussed on language her research had encompassed all aspects of these communities and therefore these functions look at language in a variety of social settings, once again broadening the definition of literacy, constructing it as social practice. These practices can be summarised as instrumental (e.g. reading price tags, paying bills), social interactional (e.g. writing letters or sending postcards) news-related (e.g. reading the newspaper), memory supportive (e.g. writing a shopping list), substitutes for oral messages (e.g. leaving a note for a family member), provision of permanent record (e.g. registering a business or completing tax returns) and confirmation of ideas (e.g. finding further information about policies of a political party) (Heath 1986, p. 21).

The work of Halliday, Smith and Heath heralded a significant change in views and knowledge about literacy, as investigations into how it was practiced led to changes in how it might be defined. Similar work was constructed by Street in the U.K. who wrote extensively about the emerging concepts of literacy as social practice and literacies (Street 1984). Together these researchers' work had emphasised that literacy had different functions; that is, it was used for different purposes, and the way in which it was used to achieve these purposes was influenced by culture and social settings. Therefore, it became evident that there were multiple ways of using literacy and these related to purpose, and social and cultural context. Moreover, it was necessary to be able to change one's **literate practice** in order to achieve one's purpose. These ideas and their work on literacy in Nicaragua led Lankshear and Lawler to state that because literacy is a social practice and practices vary among groups, culture and social settings, it was more appropriate to think of literacies rather than literacy (Lankshear and Lawler 1987, p. 43).

Acknowledgement that in any society there are a variety of literacies and contexts in which they might be used led researchers to examine the relationship between literacy and power. Heath's work had already highlighted the fact that not understanding or being able to perform in the dominant literacy (that is, the accepted literacy of school) could influence students' understandings about, attitudes toward, and achievement in, literacy and learning. Researchers now investigated whether access to and the ability to use the literacies deemed appropriate to different social settings and contexts could assist in the acquisition of money, power and status. Conversely did a lack of access to some literacies deprive or alienate people? Issues of access and power can range from being able to carry out basic transactions such as ordering food in a restaurant as opposed to a fast food outlet, to participating in a formal meeting or an interview at work, or being able

Literate Practice
The ways in which literacies (for example speaking, listening, reading or writing) are used in a particular social or cultural group. This includes, the purposes for using literacy, the ways of using literacy and the contexts in which literacy is used. Membership of a particular social or cultural group may influence what aspects of literacy are valued most (for example oral language over written language, images over words).

REFLECTION STRATEGY 1.3

- The purpose of this Reflection Strategy is to focus on the concept of literacy as social practice and to consider exactly what that means in your world and the implications for literacy pedagogy.
- Re-examine the functions of langauge in Table 1.1 and the list of functions and literate practices identified by Heath in the preceding paragraph.
- Think about your day and how many different ways in which you used literacy.
- List the purposes for which you used literacy and the contexts in which you used it.
- Did any of these require particular behaviours or skills and knowledge in order to achieve your purpose? These are your social and literate practices, your literacies.
- Continue to record them for a few days and start to look for the most common purposes and settings in which you engage in literacy. What are they and why do you think you used some more than others?
- Did you struggle in any of these situations – were your literacies adequate, did you know the appropriate behaviours?
- Discuss your findings with others and compare similarities and differences and explore reasons for the similarities and differences.
- Now go back to the original and revised literacy, literacies and multiliteracies definitions you completed in Reflection Strategies 1.1 and 1.2. Complete any further revisions.

THEORY INTO PRACTICE 1.1

- The purpose of this Theory into Practice strategy is to explore the social and literate practices of your students through discussion. In this way, you will get to know more about your students' literacies and it may also help the students to broaden their understanding of literacy and literate practice.
- Ask your students to keep a literacy diary for a few days in which they identify every time they engage in a literacy task, what they were doing or trying to get done at the time and where they were doing it.
- They should also note any specific social behaviours they needed to use in order to get the task done and whether they struggled with any of the tasks and why.
- Depending upon the age of your students you may need to model the task, possibly sharing your findings from Reflection Task 1.3 and how you completed it.
- It may be useful to work with the students to prepare a method for recording the diary, for example, setting up a table and completing a few examples from their current day.
- When completing this task, students will sometimes only include reading and writing tasks associated with school and not include things that involve oral transactions or things that occur out of school. This immediately gives you insight as to their perception of literacy and how and where it is practiced. Monitoring and discussing their diaries and findings over the next few days may help expand these concepts and generate more useful data for discussion.
- Ask the students to discuss their findings with one another and compare similarities and differences and explore reasons for the similarities and differences.
- Generate a summary of the class findings that classifies the purposes and settings in which literacy is practiced and the unique knowledge, skills or behaviours associated with them. Discuss what their findings mean for their literacy learning. What do they need to know and be able to do in order to participate successfully in all aspects of their lives?

to participate in a formal learning situation such as a classroom. See Luke (1993) for a particularly comprehensive discussion of literacy as a social practice, access to literate practices and the defining of literacy practices. McConnell (1992) examined the issues of access to literacies and power in the context of adult literacy and Bee (1990) examined them in terms of gender and immigration. Others, Gray (1980a, 1980b) and Bull and Anstey (1997, 2009), looked at how the literate practices of particular cultures could actually prevent them from participating in, or using, certain practices of the dominant culture that are required in particular settings, particularly in schooling. For example, many people in the Pacific region regard the asking of direct questions as extremely impolite and some cultures regard direct eye contact with a 'superior' as inappropriate or rude. Consider the implications of these two cultural issues for the classroom where interaction and learning are dominated by the asking and answering of questions and direct eye contact with the teacher is a way of indicating attention to learning.

These two examples also indicate that literacy is more than listening, speaking, reading and writing language; it also includes particular behaviours and these behaviours may or may not be shared within a society that includes a variety of social and cultural groups.

One of the most compelling and easily understood ways of thinking about the necessity for having access to, and being able to use, a range of literacies was provided by Lankshear et al. (1997, pp. 66-7). They used the analogy of learning foreign languages. They suggested that the literacy that is dominant in your culture and community is your first language. You then acquire literacies in other social settings and learn where and when to use them. These become your 'second languages'. The more second languages or literacies you have the more access you have to education, social equity and power.

As people began to investigate literacies and schooling, the concept of discipline literacy began to be explored. Researchers began to identify specific language forms and literate practices associated with disciplines or subject areas. As early as 1981 Applebee had written about writing in the secondary school, with particular attention to the different ways in which discipline areas structured writing. Davies and Greene (1984) investigated the specific literacies students of science needed to be taught and trialled specific pedagogies. In Australia in the early 1990s the exploration of the specific characteristics of discipline literacy became an influential force in both primary and secondary education, often referred to as the 'genre movement'. For example, Martin (1993) and Martin and Rothery (1993) suggested the explicit teaching of the genres and functional grammar of specific disciplines was necessary in order to provide equity for all students in discipline area studies during secondary school education.

In summary, the basic literacy toolkit of the 1950s and 1960s, though necessary, was no longer seen as sufficient. Investigations by researchers indicated that literacy was used in different ways and for different purposes in a variety of contexts. Furthermore, the ways in which people used literacy depended upon the social and cultural context in which literacy was being used and the social and cultural background of those who were engaging in the literate practice. In other words, literacy and literate practice is shaped by society and society shapes literacy. Therefore, one set of language-based knowledge and skills was not sufficient to successfully participate, negotiate and succeed in all these contexts and for all these purposes. Literacy was now defined as a social practice that required the acquisition and use of a variety of literacies and the associated behaviours, to be used in various social and cultural settings. Moreover, being literate required the ability to identify the literate practices and behaviours necessary to achieve the desired purpose in a particular context, and then employ them appropriately. Therefore literacy also encompasses an element of critical thinking: being able to analyse a situation and take appropriate action.

REFLECTION STRATEGY 1.4

- The purpose of this Reflection Strategy is to examine a task that has the same purpose, but is carried out in two different contexts. The task is to identify the similarities and differences among the literacy knowledge, skills and associated behaviours involved in each context. A task has been selected that is part of most adults' experience. Therefore much of what you do will be automatic and you may not remember the first time you encountered this situation and had to do this sort of analysis. This is one of the problems teachers, as experts in literacy, literacies and literate practice, have when teaching. Because most of the skills, knowledge and practices are completely automatic it is more difficult to break down a task in order to model or teach it. Completion of this task should reinforce:
    - the concept of literacy as social practice and the concept of literacies.
    - that being literate means being able to analyse the context in which you are trying to achieve your purpose.
    - that being literate means being able to use your previous literacy knowledge and experience to identify the appropriate literate practices that will help you achieve your purpose.
- Role play with someone else ordering food in a fast food outlet such as McDonalds and ordering food in a formal restaurant where a waitperson provides a menu and takes your order.
- After role playing describe and compare the two experiences and discuss the similarities and differences. The following questions may assist your analyses:
    - Upon entering the context how did you know what to do in order to get food?
    - Where did you go – e.g. did you line up, wait to be seated?
    - How did you know what food was available and what oral and written language skills were needed to work this out?
    - How was the oral interaction with the person or people who served you similar or different?
    - What were the literate behaviours unique to each setting?
    - What literate behaviours were the same?
    - Where did you eat the food? Were there options? How did you make your decision?
    - How did you negotiate payment – were there specific behaviours and knowledge necessary?
    - What would your purpose be in selecting one or other of these settings to obtain food – would it be different?
- These questions may seem exhaustive but their goal is to identify how much the social context and the socially accepted behaviours associated with that context influence literate behaviour. They also show the number of decisions about the oral and written interaction and behaviour used in each of these contexts – in what seems on the surface to be a very simple task.
- Consider how difficult these tasks would be if you had never before encountered a restaurant or fast food outlet, spoke English as a second language, and/or came from a different culture. While you may consider it unlikely that this would be the case in a Western, largely English-speaking country, think of the many other tasks that are encountered daily in workplace, leisure, and civic settings that are far more complicated than this, and require very specific literacy knowledge and experience.

THEORY INTO PRACTICE 1.2

- The purpose of this Theory into Practice task is to help students broaden their understanding of literacy to include more than reading, writing, listening and speaking language. The purpose is to reinforce the idea that literacy and literate practices (or behaviours associated with literacy) vary depending upon purpose and context and that part of being literate is adjusting your literacy and literate practices appropriately.
- Repeat the task you did in Reflection Strategy 1.4, using either the same scenario or one that your students identify. That is, it must be a task with a similar purpose that is completed in a different context. It can be done as a whole class or group activity. You may need to provide a retrieval chart for them to make notes about their analysis or you may do it as a report back and call out, while you collate their findings. You may wish to model the analysis of the task.
- Focus your final discussion on:
  - The similarities and differences in the oral and written interaction and behaviours between the two contexts.
  - Whether knowing how to behave, and interact in the different contexts would help achieve the purpose of the task.
  - Whether the students can think of other situations or contexts where they had to adjust their oral and written language and/or their behaviour in order to achieve their purpose.

The implications of the evolving broader definition of literacy and literacies for education and literacy pedagogy were, and still are, significant. Clearly, experience with, and ability to use, a range of literacies influences one's access, equity and power in society. As Gee (1992) pointed out, if the scope of a student's literacies is related to their social and cultural background and experiences, then while students may come to school literate and ready to learn, not all students will arrive with the same literacies and approaches to learning. Bourdieu (1986) referred to the knowledge and experiences students bring with them as 'cultural capital', that is, the economic, cultural, social and linguistic knowledge they have acquired before they come to school, which has helped them to make sense of and operate successfully in their life (their specific social and cultural context). However, if their knowledge and experiences are not those of the dominant culture (the culture that influences the ways in which school operates), there is the potential for alienation and disempowerment in the classroom, which will ultimately affect their attitudes toward, and success in, learning. These evolving definitions of literacy and literacies indicated that teachers need to know more about their students to understand, acknowledge and value the literacies the students have, and then use this knowledge to inform their teaching.

The following definitions of literacy, while not using the term *literacies*, encompass the concept of literacies and the notion of literacy as social practice that involves critical thinking and decision-making:

> Effective literacy is intrinsically purposeful, flexible and dynamic and involves the integration of speaking and listening and critical thinking skills with reading and writing.
>
> Dawkins (1991, p. 5)

> Literacy, then, suggests a state of being and a set of capabilities through which the literate individual is able to utilize the interior world of self to act upon and interact with the exterior structures of the world around him in order to make sense of self and other.
>
> Courts (1991, p. 4)

THEORY INTO PRACTICE 1.3

- The purpose of this Theory into Practice task is to consider the implications of the concept of literacies, literate practice and literacy as social practice for your teaching practices.
- In Reflection Strategy 1.3 and Theory into Practice 1.1, you investigated your own literate practice and literacies, and those of your students. Review what you found out during these investigations. Identify what those investigations have told you about the following:
    o The relationship of your literacies to the dominant culture – similarities and differences.
    o The relationship of your literacies to those of your students – similarities and differences.
    o The relationship of your students' literacies to the dominant culture – similarities and differences.
    o The relationship of your students' literacies to your literacies – similarities and differences.
    o The range of literacies among your students.
- Summarise what you have identified and think about the implications for teaching in your classroom – how will you change your teaching practices to accommodate the characteristics and experiences of your students?
- What can you do to demonstrate that you value their experiences and literacies and to extend them?
- How will you demonstrate and involve them in trying out new literacies in new settings and developing understandings about the need to use different literacies to achieve different purposes in different settings?

It is useful to pause at this point and consider how definitions and perceptions of literacy changed between the 1950s and the early 1990s. Table 1.2 provides a summary of the traditional, basics or heritage approach to literacy of the 1950s and 1960s and the concept of literacy as social practice and the notion of literacies that emerged by the 1990s.

Table 1.2 Comparing traditional literacy and literacy as social practice

Traditional literacy 1950s and 1960s	Implications for teaching	Literacy as social practice (literacies)	Implications for teaching
• Literacy as preparation for work and maintenance of society • Language focussed • Emphasis on reading and writing • Focus on spelling, punctuation & grammar • Values literature of dominant culture	• Content based • Rule based • Test oriented • Passive learning • Teacher as expert	• Literacy still language focussed • Reading, writing, listening and speaking all important • Thinking skills an important part of being literate • Not everyone has same literacies • Access to literacies provides empowerment and equity • Literate practices are a product of social and cultural practices • Purpose and context influence literate practices	• Acknowledgement that students come to school with different literacies • Knowing students' social and cultural background and experiences can enhance literacy teaching • Teaching literacy involves teaching about how purpose and context influences choices of language and behaviour, as literacy is a social practice • Language content (spelling, grammar, phonics and punctuation) is necessary. • Listening and speaking must be taught because they are part of literate practice. • Teaching thinking skills is an important part of literacy teaching

The origins of multiliteracies

In 1994 a group of international literacy educators from the U.K., U.S.A. and Australia met in New London, New Hampshire, U.S.A. They had vastly different interests and specialisations in literacy education, which was to their advantage as their goal was confronting and required knowledge and experience from many areas to explore it thoroughly. They wished to re-examine literacy and literacy pedagogy in terms of the rapid changes in society: increasing globalisation, technology and social diversity (Cope and Kalantzis 2000, p. 3).

They were particularly concerned about how literacy teaching should respond to increasing social and cultural diversity as the world grew smaller and more mobile, and language was now only one of many communication channels as technology became more sophisticated and accessible. They suggested that literacy was now multimodal; that is, rather than being language dominated it now included other modes, conveyed through the visual, audio, gestural and spatial meaning making systems. Therefore in order to be literate students needed to be able to understand and use all these modes and their meaning making systems, in order to read and create the texts that technology now produced (for example, film, images and sound).

Their discussions began by focussing on what constitutes 'being literate' in this new and changing world and then focussed on the pedagogies necessary to achieve it. The result of their discussions was the term *multiliteracies* and a paper entitled *A Pedagogy of Multiliteracies: Designing Social Futures* (New London Group 1996). It is now over 20 years since this paper was published and much has been written about multiliteracies since then. While the underlying concepts of multiliteracies remain the same, more recent research and writing has explored its application to specific areas of schooling and the workplace. Issues explored included how multiliteracies might help teachers address the diversity and inequities of classrooms; how to teach about texts that use multiple modes and are delivered by traditional and new and changing technologies; how multiliteracies applies across the curriculum and specific ways for planning and teaching multiliteracies (Unsworth 2001; Anstey and Bull 2006; Baker 2010; Cole and Pullen 2010; Mills 2011). The original authors themselves have researched, revised and rewritten about the concept of multiliteracies, a multiliterate pedagogy and its implementation in the classroom many times (Cope and Kalantzis 2000; Kalantzis et al. 2016).

However, it is important to remember the origins of the term and in particular the original title of the paper. *A pedagogy of multiliteracies* reminds us that multiliteracies is as much about pedagogy as it is about literacy. *Designing social futures* reminds us of the focus of our educational endeavours: to prepare our students for social and cultural futures in which they actively participate and influence the trajectories of their working, civic and private lives; that is, where *they* are the designers of their social future.

The New London Group's work is even more relevant today, as will be demonstrated in the remainder of this chapter, where the specific concerns of The New London Group will be re-examined in terms of the current and future social, cultural and technological landscape. Change is constant and it is impossible to predict the life trajectories of our students, except to say they will be very different from today. As will be explained, the social fabric of society will continue to change; technology will not only change the ways and modes of communication, but it will also influence our notions of self and our expectations. Many of the jobs currently available will disappear and others that are not yet thought of will appear. Therefore the challenges of equipping students for the future are even greater than in 1996. However the notions of being multiliterate and being able to cope with change are still highly relevant.

The preface to the New London Group paper described their two goals for literacy learning as:

> creating access to the evolving language of work, power and community and fostering the critical engagement necessary for designing social futures and achieving success through employment.
>
> New London Group (1996, p. 60)

Today we might add 'in a world, the characteristics of which, we cannot yet imagine.' It is this addition that makes our work as literacy educators today and in the future particularly challenging and the ideas behind **multiliteracies** and multiliteracies pedagogy so useful.

Figure 1.1 provides a visual image of the concerns and concepts underpinning multiliteracies. Together with the definition in the Running Glossary and the introductory information about the origins of the term *multiliteracies*, it should provide a context for reading the next sections of this chapter and exploring how the terms *multiliteracies* and *multiliteracies pedagogy* currently fit in the world generally and in literacy education in particular. Their current and future relevance will be explored in these two contexts.

Multiliteracies
A concept of literacy as being multimodal rather than language dominant, being made up of multiple literacies and multiple literate practices that continuously evolve as local and global society, culture and technology change the contexts in which literacy is practiced. Multiliteracies enable capacities to cope with change and effectively participate and contribute to all aspects of society: workplace, leisure, social, cultural and civic environments.

Multiliteracies and the changing workplace

Previously the characteristics of workplaces in the 1960s were discussed as being largely hierarchical. Each person had a specialised set of tasks that required a specific set of literacy skills. As people usually stayed in the same job or workplace for life they were seldom required to complete tasks that required a broader range of literacy skills or the adaptation and use of current skills in new ways. Only those in

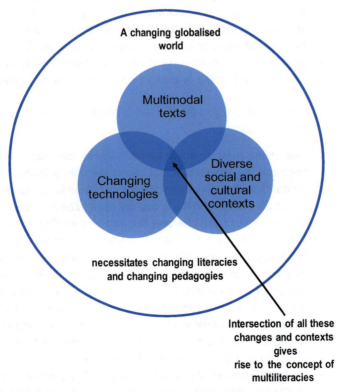

Figure 1.1 A visual concept of the origins of the term *multiliteracies*

higher or executive positions would normally interact with interstate or international clients, largely through phone or letter, and only occasionally travelling to meet person-to-person. Consequently, there was little need to understand much about other cultures, and how social and cultural practices might affect communication and negotiation, because there was less globalised business. Furthermore, the available communication and travel technologies meant that they rarely had to deal with clients and colleagues directly or face-to-face.

For some time researchers have been discussing the effects of globalisation and technology on workplaces and working lives and the literate practices necessary to succeed in the workplace (The New London Group 1996; Cope and Kalantzis 2000; Anstey and Bull 2006). In fast capitalist cultures, such as the U.S.A., U.K., Canada and Australia, workplaces have become less hierarchical organisations, and teamwork and multi-skilling are required. Employees work together as a team on tasks, collaborate, strategise and problem-solve in order to get the job done. Oral communication skills, the ability to listen productively and critically, negotiate, use higher order thinking skills and co-operate are now as important as the ability to read and write with traditional (paper and pen) and digital technologies. These changes mean that workplace literacies have many dimensions to them. Apart from identifying the specific literacy knowledge and skills and the literacies associated with the technology, there is a need to document the complexities of literate practices in the workplace in order to better understand them (Mikulecky in Baker 2010). This information will help prepare students for entering the workplace, assist the preparation of professional learning of those already in the workplace and inform the retraining of workers whose job or workplace no longer exists.

The changing repertoires of literate practices in workplaces

One of the most common trends, already identified in the preceding paragraphs, is the expectation that people will work in teams. The practices associated with working in groups are not just about language: they are multimodal. Those participating in the group will need to be able to employ a repertoire of practices to use and interpret the meaning making systems of all the modes. These may include understanding that oral communication can be mediated by pitch, volume and intonation and that sometimes sounds that are not words may convey meaning. For example, a 'humph!' can express being fed up or disagreement. In addition, gestures and facial expression need to be read and used. Even clothing can indicate a role, expertise or status, which may influence the interpretations of messages in particular contexts. For example, in a scientific or medical workplace a white coat may be associated with a scientist or doctor and lead some participants to accord that person higher status in the team. Alternatively, scruffy or dirty clothing may be associated with undesirable character traits, which may mean people pay less attention or accord less importance to that person's message – depending on whether that dress is appropriate to the context of the teamwork. While it could be argued that people already *automatically* use and interpret the meaning making systems of all modes, the issue when working in a group is about the *conscious* use and processing of all the information provided through these modes.

Finally, the use of space can be interpreted with regard to expected ways of participating; for example, a round table with chairs around it, enabling everyone to hear and see each other, can be interpreted as facilitating and encouraging open dialogue where everyone is equal. The use of space in workplaces is becoming increasingly important as employers look at the best ways to organise space to facilitate the type of work and outcomes they desire. Researchers in the areas of architectural design and behavioural psychology have examined how the organization of workspaces can affect workers' perceptions of the organisation's culture and identity, flexibility, and ability to work as an individual and team member (Varlander 2012; Waber, Magnolfi and Lindsay 2014). Large companies like Google and Apple are often featured in articles about links between use of space in the workplace and productivity. More recently even more conservative industries like banking are beginning to approach workspaces in more thoughtful ways in order to encourage worker comfort, satisfaction, creativity and output and the flexibility to work in teams and as an individual. Further general reading about this is available through QR codes 1.4 and 1.5 which have links to recent online articles that discuss these trends and their advantages and disadvantages. As you read them, reflect on the variety of literate practices and behaviours these different spaces encourage or discourage.

QR Code 1.4 An article on Google as a workplace where organisation of space encourages creativity (https://www.theguardian.com/careers/2016/feb/11/is-googles-model-of-the-creative-workplace-the-future-of-the-office)

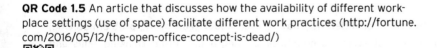

QR Code 1.5 An article that discusses how the availability of different workplace settings (use of space) facilitate different work practices (http://fortune.com/2016/05/12/the-open-office-concept-is-dead/)

While changes in the ways workplaces operate mean that the literate practices of the workplace are multimodal, oral communication, used in combination with the audio, gestural, visual and spatial, is rapidly becoming a dominant mode. Almost all face-to-face interaction, be it via video technology or in person, will involve oral interaction. Therefore, effective listening and speaking when working in groups is an essential literate practice in today's workplace. Some researchers suggest that it is through the use of spoken language that people are able to think creatively and productively together. Littleton and

Mercer (2013, p. 1) suggest that in these contexts people do not simply use talk to interact, but to interthink. They go on to state that not all talk is productive and in order to ensure successful outcomes, we need to understand why that is the case. There is a need to learn the literate practices of productive oral interaction when problem-solving or creating in the social and communicative processes of working in a team – to become effective at the literate practice of interthinking. (For more on interthinking see Chapter Four.)

As workplaces change with an increase in teamwork, job sharing, part-time work, outsourcing and self-employment (Australia's Future Workforce? 2015) there are increasing demands on the workers' social and behavioural skills and practices. These changes to the work place will mean contact with, and working with, people from diverse social groups. Workers in these settings will require an ability to understand, tolerate and work with a range of personalities, cultural and social groups and communicative styles.

THEORY INTO PRACTICE 1.4

- The purpose of this Theory into Practice is to reflect upon the current teaching practices you use when getting students to work in groups.
- Think about why you use group work.
  - What are your teaching and learning purposes – your desired learning outcomes?
  - Are they content or process focussed or both? Think about why this is so.
  - Do you talk to your students about why you are getting them to work in groups?
- How do you go about teaching students to work in groups? What literacy skills, processes and behaviours do you teach about working in groups?
- How do you teach specific listening and speaking skills and discuss the role of talk in clarifying thinking and problem-solving?
- What social skills and behaviours do you discuss and teach?
- How does the concept of group work being multimodal influence your current teaching practices?
- What would you do the same or differently having read about team work, problem-solving, collaborating, co-operating, strategising negotiating, using higher order thinking skills and the role of oral language and other modes in the workplace?

Outsourcing of specific tasks to another workplace, or bringing together a team of specialists from a range of other places is another trend identified by those researching the characteristics of workplaces of the future. This situation has arisen because of a significant increase in self-employment and working from home. Australia's Future Workforce? (2015, p. 182) reports that recent research indicates that across 29 countries in Europe, North America and the Asia/Pacific 20 per cent of the workforce is self-employed.

Bringing together a team of people who have not worked together previously can exacerbate the issues previously discussed regarding the literate practices of teamwork. In addition, this team may often be based in another state or country and connecting digitally through video communication, webinars or online conferencing, introducing a range of dimensions to communication and literate practices not previously encountered. All of these technological options provide the opportunity to participate in a meeting in real time over the web. The sophistication of the technology available for use in these virtual meetings means the choice of software and hardware technology influences the number of modes available for communication and the repertoire of literate practices used. It can expand or limit the ability of team members to discuss, problem-solve and communicate ideas effectively. For example, if it includes video as well as audio communication, items can be held up, manipulated and discussed for all to see and facial expression and gesture can be used to interpret and communicate. Even a person's dress can become part of the communication. Using audio technology only restricts the available modes as only pitch, volume and intonation can be used to interpret a person's oral communication. Removing audio and video, with participants typing in comments and reactions, restricts things further, as only the written word can be interpreted and messages can be influenced by participants' typing skills or ability to quickly and accurately convey thoughts in a written message. The effectiveness of communication, teamwork, discussion and decision-making in these virtual meetings across workplaces is very much linked to the available modes, and consideration would need to be given to the purpose and desired outcome of the meetings, and the modes necessary to facilitate it before choosing the technology and software to be used. The luxury of choosing the best technology option may not always be available. Understanding the links between the modes available, the literate practices participants have and need, and the achievement of the desired outcome when using technology to facilitate teamwork is a new dimension for many workplaces.

Changing organisational structures, definitions and nature of work, job requirements, workplace design, and workforce demographics and capabilities, have changed the ways in which companies search for and select workers. Experts in industrial and organisational psychology have identified the need for additional selection criteria that are more to do with the organisational requirements than job requirements (Holman et al. 2005; Carson and Stewart 1996; Landy, Shankster-Cawley and Moran 1995; Sanchez 1994). Companies want people with a similar philosophy to that of the organisation, capable of growing the company and growing and changing with the company – for example, they may want innovators who suit the company philosophy, attitudes and values. Therefore, there is an increase in the use of personality tests, integrity tests, and value-based selection systems together with more sophisticated interview techniques. These selection practices mean companies are

THEORY INTO PRACTICE 1.5

- The purpose of this Theory into Practice task is to consider how the availability of different modes influences the effectiveness of communication in achieving the desired purpose.
- Consider what you explicitly teach and discuss about tasks such as preparing reports with students.
- What is the balance of information and teaching you provide about:
    o the genre and structure of the writing
    o the technology via which it will be delivered and how that might affect the modes to be employed, and
    o how to make decisions about the best modes of communication that might be employed, for example, visual, images, diagrams, flow charts, oral or written explanations, gesture, facial expression.
- Once you have considered these questions re-examine your planning for a task like this that you will teach in the near future and think about anything you might change.

conducting far more rigorous and careful analysis of the repertoire of literate and social practices and behaviours that best suit the company profile when identifying selection criteria and the best ways of assessing them.

The impact of technology in office-based settings has been discussed in some detail. However technology has had impact in settings that would previously have been technology free and where workers' literacy skills did not need to be particularly high. Anstey and Bull (2006) discussed the changing literate practices of rural industry in Australia, where higher levels of literacy are required as technology and environmental protection influences agronomy. Farm machinery is computerised and programmed using global positioning technology to enable the most efficient ploughing and planting of seed for maximum yield. For example, in cotton growing areas in Queensland, Australian farmers are required to have their fields levelled using global positioning systems to minimise the run off of chemicals into the water table. An unexpected outcome of this requirement was that farmers could use the global positioning knowledge with the computers in their tractors to ensure that the tractor always travelled the same path and the same soil was compacted rather than the planting area being compacted, which would impede growth. It was even possible to ensure that the seed drills occurred in exactly the same place and increases the yield because the roots were able to grow more easily in this already loosened soil. The tractors could also be programmed to work without a driver, leaving the farmer free to do other tasks, employing fewer workers.

In many countries, the transport of goods by road is a huge industry, and one that is changing. Being a long-haul truck driver used to be considered a low literacy job, for those with little success at school. However, government regulation regarding environmental protection and driver safety now requires various levels of certification and computer literacy in order to maintain a job in this industry. For example, in Australia, drivers who haul dangerous goods, such as chemicals, gas and fuel, must complete a dangerous goods course that requires two days of face-to-face work. Some of the knowledge and tasks they need to acquire include:

- examination and knowledge of the Australian Dangerous Goods Code and relevant State/Territory dangerous goods regulations
- knowledge of risks associated with the transporting of dangerous goods by road and related precautions to control those risks
- the ability to read and interpret information on transport documentation, including consignment/manifest sheets
- the ability to apply all this knowledge in order to plan appropriate transport routes and appropriate rest stops and
- knowledge of procedures that would enable putting into place a plan of action should a leakage or other emergency occur when transporting dangerous goods

As can be seen the literacy skills for this course require reading quite dense documents about policy and then translating and applying that knowledge in practice. For example, balancing a load between a prime mover and two tanker trailers to ensure that the weight is distributed across the axles is quite complicated, requiring the use of specific computer software. Once distribution of the load is accomplished, an order of destinations for unloading needs to be planned. This ensures the remaining load remains balanced for safe driving as compartments are emptied en route. (If sloshing occurs it can make the trailers unstable and cause an accident.) In addition, the route has to be worked out in relation to the routes along which dangerous goods are allowed and required rest stops. Recently there is a move to make driver log books digital, another advance in required literacy skills. But what is the future of long haul truck drivers with the advent of driverless cars? Many of the large trucks and other equipment in the mining industries are already operating without drivers, controlled by a central computer system.

Workplaces in the future: disappearing and appearing occupations

In the two examples regarding the impact of technology on workplaces discussed in the preceding paragraphs, one of the outcomes identified has been the disappearance of jobs in these settings. Education is predominantly about enabling students to participate in all aspects of life, that is, in workplace, leisure, social, cultural and civic environments. Identifying what those environments will look like in the future and the literate and social practices and behaviours necessary to participate successfully in them is one of the major challenges for literacy education. Employment, which leads to being economically independent, is essential to being able to participate in social, cultural and civic environments. Therefore, understanding more about the future of employment and workplaces is essential to planning appropriate literacy education.

Two reports on the influence of technology on employment in the future, particularly computerisation and Artificial Intelligence, provide some confronting statistics. A report to CEDA, Australia's Future Workforce? (2015) concluded that more than 5 million jobs, that is, almost 40 per cent of Australian jobs that exist today, have a moderate to high likelihood of disappearing in the next 10 to 15 years due to technological advancements. In some parts of rural and regional Australia in particular there is a high likelihood of job losses being over 60 per cent. Frey and Osborne (2013) examined the impacts of future computerisation on the United States labour market, analysing the number of jobs at risk and the relationship between an occupation's probability of computerisation, wages and educational attainment. They concluded that about 47 per cent of total United States employment was at risk. Globally, manufacturing has, and will, continue to be impacted by computer technology and automation. For example, the shipyard industry in Denmark and the automotive industry in Australia have declined and considerable effort has had to be put into transitioning workers out of declining industries.

The impact of Artificial Intelligence (AI) is often referred to as the Fourth Industrial Revolution. Initially it was thought the influence of AI on the workplace would occur over the next 20 years but predictions are now suggesting it will be much sooner. In 2017 various news outlets reported the development and employment of a robot receptionist called Nadine at Nanyang Technological University in Singapore. Nadine can remember faces, express mood and emotion and conduct a conversation. Nadine also looks human and life-like, rather than robot-like. The application of such technology in fields of health and care occupations is regarded as imminent. QR code 1.6 provides a link to an article in which the professor who led the team that created Nadine discusses the implications for workplaces and employment in the future.

QR Code 1.6 An article in which the professor who led the team that created Nadine discusses the implications for workplaces and employment in the future (http://www.channelnewsasia.com/news/singapore/this-born-in-singapore/2894522.html)

Technology is not the only global influence on the disappearance of jobs. Global environmental issues that have led to globalised collaborative responses among countries on setting environmental targets, such as emissions targets, have meant significant change to particular industries. In Australia, the coal industry has been significantly affected as cleaner sources of energy are sought, not only in Australia but also overseas. Some entire towns and communities have found the major source of employment disappear. Similarly, the timber industry has been affected as the world endeavours to retain or regrow large areas of forest in order to assist in the reduction of carbon dioxide in the atmosphere. Many countries are encountering similar changes in industry.

So what types of jobs will survive and what are the literate practices required of them?

According to Frey and Osborne (2013) the most vulnerable occupations are those that require a low degree of **emotional and social intelligence** and are predominantly made up of tasks for which computer algorithms can easily be developed. One example is that of a court clerk because most searches can now be done by computer. Similarly, some aspects of retail employment can become automated, and this is already evident in supermarkets where customers can scan, pack and pay for their items with no human contact.

At present developments in Artificial Intelligence have been unable to simulate the 'common sense' aspects of human intelligence, so jobs that require a high degree of social intelligence, for example, a public relations specialist, are less likely to disappear. Frey and Osborne (2013, p. 31) predict that occupations that are least likely to disappear would be in the professional, technical and creative areas that involve problem-solving, complex perception and manipulation, persuasion, negotiation, care and a high degree of emotional and social intelligence. The examples they give are in the areas of specialist health care workers, surgeons (although they are now using robotics and lasers, they still require social and emotional intelligence and problem solving), the arts and design.

In Australia's Future Workforce? (2015, p. 15) the notion of career trajectories is discussed. People will change occupations many times as workplaces and occupations evolve; therefore, employees will need to be highly skilled, able to work globally and highly mobile. As a result the report asserts that their skills cannot be firm specific, based on the retention of specific knowledge; rather, they must be broader competencies that incorporate analysing and designing. Simply being able to use technology is no longer sufficient. To be globally relevant there is a need to be able to be a creator of ICT (Information Communication Technologies) – architecting, designing and analysing. Balanskat and Engelhart (2015, p. 6) report that by 2020, Europe may experience a shortage of more than 800,000 professionals skilled in computing/informatics. They go on to report that as a consequence 16 countries have decided to integrate coding into their curriculum at the national, regional or local level: Austria, Bulgaria, the Czech Republic, Denmark, Estonia, France, Hungary, Ireland, Israel, Lithuania, Malta, Spain, Poland, Portugal, Slovakia and the U.K. (England). Australia has also commenced the introduction of coding into the curriculum. While the introduction of coding skills to the curriculum may seem more related to mathematical

Emotional and Social Intelligence
The competencies linked to self-awareness, self-management, social awareness and relationship management, which enable people to understand and manage their own and others' emotions in social interactions. The ability to get along with others and facilitate co-operation.

literacy, if consideration is given to how coding is applied in the workforce, the relationship to literate practices and literacy is immediately apparent. Coding can be used to program robots, which, for example, are increasingly used to provide companionship and basic assistance to the elderly in their homes or in healthcare institutions. In order to write appropriate coding there will need to be collaboration between health care experts, geriatric specialists, coding specialists, robotic specialists, etc. In other words it will require a very disparate team to work together, as has been described in the previous discussion of changes to the workplace. The literacies and literate practices of teamwork have been discussed in full previously and do not need to be reiterated here; however, the act of coding itself also involves many of these literacy skills and practices. As Balanskat and Engelhart (2015) assert, the development of coding skills helps students to understand today's digitalised society and fosters 21st century skills like problem-solving, creativity and logical thinking.

Implications of the changing workplace for multiliteracies and multiliterate pedagogies

In July 2017, The Foundation for Young Australians published the *New Work Smarts* report which identified the skills that would be required of workers by 2030 and the implications for schooling. The report identified the following:

- workers will spend 100 per cent more of their time involved in problem-solving
- 41 per cent more time on making judgements and engaging in critical thinking
- 77 per cent more time using science and maths skills
- 17 per cent more time engaging in verbal communication and using interpersonal skills (*Future Skills Report*, 2017, p. 4)

The report also indicated that workers will spend 30 per cent more time learning while working, indicating the need for an ability to cope with change and be oriented toward lifelong learning. Overall the conclusion of this report was that workers would need to be strategic, able to solve complex problems and think creatively. The indications of this report clearly indicate the need for a multiliterate pedagogy.

Table 1.3 provides a summary of the relationships among the key characteristics of multiliteracies, the changing literate practices of the workplace and the implications for pedagogy. Examination of the literate practices of changing workplaces, future trends in workplaces and the types of work available, together with the need to retrain and transition workers into new jobs, indicates that the concept of multiliteracies, as a way of preparing students for the future, is highly relevant. The implications for pedagogy are also compelling as traditional approaches to literacy education would be inadequate when developing multiliteracies.

Table 1.3 Relationships among multiliteracies, changing workplace characteristics and pedagogy

Characteristics of multiliteracies	Changing literate practices in the workplace	Implications for pedagogy
• Multimodal rather than language dominant • Made up of multiple literacies and multiple literate practices • Will continuously evolve as local and global society, culture and technology, change the contexts in which literacy is practiced • Enables capacities to cope with change and effectively participate in and contribute to all aspects of society: workplace, leisure, social, cultural and civic environments	• Increase in teamwork • Teams drawn from within and across workplaces • Increasingly working with diverse social and cultural groups • Conscious and strategic use of multimodal work practices (audio, visual, gestural, spatial, linguistic) • Using talk effectively – listening and speaking important to teamwork • Use of technology to work in virtual teams • Require high degree of social and emotional intelligence • Recruitment to suit organisational philosophies – need for increased self-awareness • Increase in use of technology – few technology free workplaces • Increase in teamwork requiring ability to collaborate, co-operate, negotiate, problem-solve, use higher order thinking skills, be flexible • Disappearance of industries and occupations will necessitate the ability to cope with change, retrain and transition occupations • Ability to work globally • Necessity to be mobile.	Develop pedagogies that: • involve students working collaboratively on authentic tasks • teach the literate practices of working in a team – emotional and social intelligence (e.g. ability to collaborate, co-operate, negotiate, problem-solve, use higher order thinking skills, be flexible) • develop students' ability to problem-solve and create through talk • involve students in teamwork that involves familiar and unfamiliar team members • develop students' ability to work with socially and culturally diverse groups • actively teach about paper, live and digital multimodal texts • actively teach the conscious and strategic use of all modes • use technology in a variety of ways and involve students in making decisions about the most appropriate technology for a task • develop an understanding of the global nature of work and that workplaces and occupations will change

REFLECTION STRATEGY 1.5

- There are two purposes for this Reflection Strategy. The first is to review your previous definitions of literacy in terms of the preceding discussion about changing workplaces and consider whether you feel your definitions are appropriate or adequate or need further refinement. The second is to reflect upon your current teaching practices in terms of the section on changing workplaces.
- Consider your definitions of literacy, literacies and multiliteracies in terms of changing workplace literacies, changing workspaces and the rise and fall of particular occupations. Do your definitions address these changes?

- Re-read Table 1.3, focussing on the implications for pedagogy. Consider your current teaching practices and whether they address some of the identified needs for workers in the future, how you currently address these needs and how you might address them in the future.
- What would be the major foci of any changes and why?

Multiliteracies, technology and change in social, cultural and civic settings

The preceding section discussed the ways in which technology and globalisation has changed and will continue to change the workplace. However, technological change has influenced all parts of life and linked individuals more closely to the global community and its influences. This section will look at how changes in technology have influenced literacies and literate practices, and potentially, beliefs, attitudes and values in the social, cultural and civic settings of lives.

As with the workplace the most significant aspect of the impact of technology in social, cultural and civic settings, is the availability of multiple modes. Rather than being language dominated, technology can facilitate many ways of shaping the message. Text delivered via technology can include linguistic, audio, visual, gestural and spatial modes; words may be accompanied by sound effects, music, still or moving images. The use of a screen rather than a page means that the organisation and use of space on the screen may vary considerably from text to text. In addition reading screens requires additional skills to reading the page as, for example, information may not be chronological as one moves between screens navigating links creating a hypertext of one's own.

The ability to understand the ways in which the different modes may convey meaning, both individually and in combination, is one of the essential changes to literacy and literate practices. A person must be literate in all modes and capable of understanding and conveying meaning via multimodal texts delivered live, or via paper or technology. Understanding one's preferences for, and abilities with, different modes is also a key aspect of literate practice with technology. Personal preference, possibly influenced by cultural or social group, can mean that an individual pays more attention to messages via particular modes, for example, preferencing the visual over written word, or listening over reading. These preferences could shape the meaning one makes of the text as some information may be omitted from particular modes or provide contrasting views – for example, an image may provide a different meaning to the words.

The purposes for using technology in social, cultural and civic aspects of life vary considerably. Some are personal, for example, shopping online or contacting friends or groups with similar interests via various apps and software available through the internet. The increased ease with which downloading from the internet can occur with the introduction of smart technology to television, tablets and smartphones has rendered DVDs and iPods almost obsolete. Young people who have never known anything but being able to download songs, movies, TV programs and apps, and who conduct almost all forms of interaction via the internet, expect speed, choice and instant connection. This makes for a fast-paced world that may not require long periods of attention.

Increasingly government and business prefer individuals to complete forms and transactions via the internet. While not yet compulsory, individuals find increasing pressure to do so, as offices and branches enabling personal face-to-face contact close or become centralised. Technology also provides users with a degree of choice and independence, with access to services such as booking travel and accommodation, managing finances, ordering take away or booking a restaurant.

However, all these trends raise issues of equity for those who do not speak English as their first language, are not 'internet literate' or do not have access to the internet. While most devices allow internet access (for example, smartphones, tablets, laptops, smart TVs), the user still has to have an internet account with a provider with the attendant costs. Access to the internet and technology that is up to date is an increasing issue in terms of equity, as schools have found when doing surveys of students' access to technology and the internet to complete homework, submit work and access school materials online. Many schools have found that they have made erroneous assumptions about student access: firstly that they have technology that is compatible with school requirements and software, secondly that it is available to the student to use, and thirdly that there is an internet connection that is available and reliable. This is particularly the case in low socioeconomic areas in towns and cities and rural/isolated areas.

REFLECTION STRATEGY 1.6

- The purpose of this Reflection Strategy is to consider how well you know your students in terms of their use of, and access to, technology.
- Survey your students in terms of:
  o the technology only available in their home and the mobile technology available
  o whether the technology is compatible with school requirements and software (i.e. how up to date is it?)
  o what technology (range of devices) is available to the student to use and where and how often is it available?
  o what internet connection is available where and on what devices, and
  o its reliability in all those settings

- Survey your students in terms of their reasons/purposes when using technology (for example, shopping, messaging friends, downloading music), their favourite apps and websites (for example, social networking apps and websites)
- Discuss with your students what they like and dislike about using technology
- After compiling the results consider what you have learned about your students and if, and how, that will influence the ways in which you approach the teaching of literacy (in all disciplines)

Social media: Becoming globalised citizens

Technology enables participation in global events either directly or vicariously. Even if unable to travel to different parts of the world to experience other cultures and events, individuals can experience them via technology. Satellites, the internet and Wi-Fi enable exposure to events as they occur in real time, through live feeds on tablets, smartphones, laptops and desktop computers. In addition, virtual reality kits are now becoming commercially accessible for a similar cost to a smartphone, which means virtual reality may be used to experience activities as diverse as gaming, **social media**, virtual lives, virtual conferences, live music concerts and pornography (Sutton 2017).

The proliferation of social media provides access to a wider range of social and cultural groups and individuals, together with the ideas, interests, beliefs, opinions and information they wish to share. Contact with an increasingly diverse community across the globe, rather than only within one's own community, means shared community values and connections are challenged. Such global contact raises awareness of global events and trends and also has the potential to shape attitudes and behaviour.

Users of social media do so for many different purposes and the types of information shared takes many forms, for example blogs, business networks, forums, photo sharing, social gaming and virtual worlds. QR Code 1.7 provides a link to the most commonly used network sites in 2017 and provides a picture of the number of users around the globe. It reinforces the notion that technology, in particular, access to social media, has the potential to influence users' lives, their behaviour and values and attitudes.

QR Code 1.7 Commonly known network sites ranked by number of users in January 2017 (https://www.statista.com/statistics/272014/global-social-networks-ranked-by-number-of-users/)

The behaviours associated with the use of technology, particularly mobile technology, have led to evolving rules and etiquette. The use of mobile phones on public transport has led to 'quiet areas' or 'quiet carriages', where talking

Social media
Websites and applications (apps) that enable users to develop online social networks and communities to share ideas, information, personal messages and interests, for example, Facebook, Twitter, Snapchat and LinkedIn. They facilitate user-generated content.

on mobile phones is banned so passengers are not disturbed. Restaurants often ask people to go outside to answer phones and some offices (particularly medical) require mobile phones be turned off or put on silent. Mobile devices have modified the practice of meeting people face-to-face to talk over a meal or coffee. It is not uncommon to see people sitting together without speaking as they constantly check messages, email or Facebook. Time spent using technology has increased dramatically in the last 10 years. Hoh (2017) reported that the Roy Morgan Young Australian Survey (2017) indicated that children aged six to thirteen spend almost 12 hours a week on the internet. This is almost double the time spent online in 2008. Interestingly, the same study also found that students now spend more time online than watching television. Consequent changes in social behaviour and literate practice have occurred as families have developed rules about where and when technology might be accessed, monitored sites and imposed filtering mechanisms to ensure online safety. In addition the increase in students' having personal mobile phones and tablets has meant that schools have had to develop policies around students' use of mobile phones and tablets in school.

The ways in which grammar, spelling and language are used in different messaging forms has also evolved and will continue to do so as technology evolves. When text messaging (SMS) began, there was much controversy as people transferred the abbreviations and slang used in this context to contexts in which it was inappropriate. The conventions of language use had to be developed for different settings and the contexts and people with whom messaging occurred, for example, email, SMS and other messaging apps such as Viber or Snapchat. For example, in email, if capital letters are used it is considered the equivalent of shouting. Many of these behaviours and etiquettes associated with technology are global and demonstrate the evolving nature of literacy conventions and the level of decision-making available to users to engage them as technology continues to change in all aspects of life. For example, the user may consider whether it is appropriate, if not coming in for work, to text the boss using the slang and abbreviations normally used in a text to a friend, or whether it would be better to convey the information more formally via a phone call or formal email. Similarly, in social and work settings people have to consider whether there are some messages or actions that should be done in person or via a messaging app, for example, dropping a girlfriend or boyfriend, making arrangements to meet friends or sacking someone.

Social and cultural traditions around significant events such as religious festivals, marriage, funerals that once included the use of greeting cards associated with sentiments of that event have also changed with technology. Greeting cards are often replaced by messaging via Facebook or various apps and virtual cards available via websites. The events themselves may include displays of images via technology accompanied by music, display of pre-recorded messages or live connections for those unable to physically attend, for example using Skype. The event may also be relayed via commercial social media or via individuals attending it. Once again these changes require changes in literate practices and behaviours. It is necessary to understand the influence of context and the social and cultural expectations of behaviour. It is also necessary to be able to make decisions about the appropriate use of available technology.

Some aspects of the changes that technology has wrought on literate practices and behaviours can be seen as potentially negative and once again these are global trends. Psychologists in schools and general practice are reporting an increase in addictive behaviours among users of mobile devices and gaming. Such behaviours result in negative effects, such as ignoring live interaction in favour of virtual interaction and virtual lives online. Other behaviours include the compulsion to constantly check one's social networking apps for updates (described as 'fear of missing out' or FOMO) or for a sense of fulfilment from seeing increasing 'likes'. Some countries report the issue as so pervasive and severe that treatment centres have been set up to combat the addiction (Wallace 2014). Initially it was termed 'internet addiction', but psychologists now point out that the internet is the delivery mechanism through which potentially addictive activities are delivered (Starcevic 2013). Recent studies suggest that the internet facilitates environments, particularly through social media, that are rewarding because they provide escape, a contrast to students' real worlds and a way of building a social profile different to reality. This reward can become addictive, hence the overuse of social media, or addiction.

Recently other negative social behaviours have emerged in social media, for example, cyber bullying, often related to appearance, but also in reference to gender issues, culture and race. The influence of how gender and culture are constructed in media and texts has long been examined by academics (see, for example, Luke 1993). Young people who have been influenced by images of models and high profile individuals, who fulfil the 'ideal' image of beauty on television, in magazines and in social media may bully those who do not fulfil this ideal. Conversely, those who do not feel they fulfil this ideal can develop low self-esteem and eating disorders that are exacerbated by the bullying. The tendency to post images of oneself on social media to show such things as engagement in social activities, new clothes, use of make-up and poses to achieve a 'look' can exclude those who cannot (or feel they cannot) conform to these idealised images. Many of those who view these images do not realise that they are not real, that they have been enhanced to look more ideal through the use of software packages, such as Photoshop, which enable photographic images to be changed. The use of software such as Photoshop was recently ridiculed in a short video that implied that no images were real and that Photoshop and other software could be used to create an image of a beautiful girl out of a slice of pizza. It was posted on YouTube by several groups and further manipulated and commented upon. It is interesting to view the different groups' postings and the comments (see QR Code 1.8 and QR Code 1.9). Many did not realise that it was possibly a hoax to draw attention to the use of software to enhance photographic images and that Photoshop may not actually have been used. Others were incensed at what they saw as the negative portrayal of Photoshop software and disregarded the issue of whether images should be enhanced or changed by software completely. Regardless of the views of those who posted it and those who commented on it, it is a useful way to start a conversation about how social media, images and software combine to shape beliefs, attitudes and behaviour around the portrayal of beauty. Critical reflection about who posts images, why they post them, the authenticity of the image and how what you are viewing and posting on social media affects you, is a necessary aspect of being a multiliterate person.

QR Code 1.8 Photoshop turns pizza into woman (https://www.youtube.com/watch?v=9j656_RiO0k)

QR Code 1.9 Photoshop has gone too far in CollegeHumor Originals (https://www.youtube.com/watch?v=Hnvoz91k8hc)

In a recent issue of *National Geographic* that focussed entirely on what they termed 'the gender revolution', the issues of positive and negative aspects of social media were discussed, '…because social media – a factory for the mass production of insecurity – is transforming everything about adolescence' (Rosenberg 2017, p. 122). While the negative issues of idealised beauty and conformity were identified, the positive point was made that social media could help those who could not find a 'place', group or 'village' in their local real world to find a place online. The example was given of a 15-year-old girl who found that her 'village' was nerds who liked video games and musicals.

Apart from the obvious negative personal and social implications of these addictions, the implication from a literacy education perspective is that individuals need to be more critical and aware about their purposes in using the internet, including social media, and the role of the internet and social media in society. The definition of multiliteracies states that they enable capacities to cope with change and effectively participate in and contribute to all aspects of society: workplace, leisure, social, cultural and civic environments. These capacities would therefore include understanding the potential power of social media and being able to evaluate the types of social media available and their potential for influencing and changing social behaviour, beliefs, values and attitudes. For example, a multiliterate individual would have the capacity to explore and critically evaluate the concept of friendship and whether friending someone on Facebook is the same. Critical thinking skills, problem-solving, evaluating information, comparing and contrasting would all be part of this type of exploration. These literacy skills and literate practices were previously identified as important in changing workplaces. Clearly they are also relevant to other social, cultural and civic aspects of life.

No text is neutral

Increasing use of the internet means that individuals have access to a plethora of sites and texts. The sites are created for particular purposes. An individual may wish to share information, beliefs or opinions, as may non-profit organisations or groups of activists. Businesses and advertising groups want to sell 'things' rather than ideas or beliefs, but may choose to do so by creating a concept or style around that 'thing' that appeals to the beliefs, ideals or lifestyle choices of specific groups of consumers. The texts created for these sites may contain a combination of various modes realised through images, sound effects, music, gestures and facial expression and words. Every one of the texts on those sites was created with a purpose in mind and was therefore shaped in a particular way to expedite fulfilment of that purpose. Therefore none of those texts is neutral. Even a government website that is providing information about a service and the facility to fill in forms to engage that service, will be encouraging participation and use of the service because it is based on a policy that is being implemented. The success of that policy (and re-election by constituents who support that government policy?) is dependent upon its successful implementation through such things as the website. Therefore, those texts have a purpose: to persuade and facilitate participation by the target audience. For example, the addition of an attractive photo depicting the outcome of accessing the service is designed to encourage participation by the potential user of such a site.

The user of the site will bring their social and cultural background to the text or site they are viewing and using and will filter the text through their associated beliefs, attitudes and knowledge. They may use this self-awareness and knowledge to investigate such things as the authority of the site, its sources and the background of the authors, as part of a process of accepting or rejecting all or part of what the texts of that site have to offer. Users of technology must have the skills, knowledge and processes to be critical consumers of all texts if they are to be capable of managing their futures.

In addition to understanding that no text is neutral, users of the internet need a knowledge of how the internet works, including understanding that everything it facilitates is designed or used as part of a business. This knowledge will assist students to understand the ways in which aspects of the internet may be subtly influencing and changing their social and cultural behaviour, attitudes and beliefs. Businesses, advertising agencies, in short, any group that wishes to know how particular groups feel about topics or what people are interested in, will examine social media (for example, Twitter) for trends and topics that people are accessing frequently. Twitter is just one social media app that facilitates social networking. At its simplest level people can tweet about what they are doing to their followers (the equivalent of friends on Facebook). However, users can also elect to follow topics or people that interest them. If people find a topic, person or tweet that interests them they may retweet it and that tweet multiplies as a topic, becomes more prominent and more people may retweet it. As a result, as it gains momentum it may become identified as a trend. Sometimes when this happens in unusually large numbers it is referred to as going viral. If the person tweeting has high status, for example, a close and respected friend, a politician, someone in a powerful government position, or someone prominent in popular culture such as music or film, then it is possible that people will be highly influenced by their opinions or tweets and believe them without question. This can lead to changes in public opinion, the way people view certain social or cultural groups or suspicion of government officialdom. It can potentially normalise what has previously been seen as inappropriate, for example, bad language, sexual references, making false statements without evidence, denigrating a person or group or bullying.

As businesses and leaders in political, social and cultural groups follow trends and viral topics and base their marketing upon them, there are other flow on effects as the marketing itself encourages or discourages not just the purchase of things, but the adoption of ideas and beliefs about what constitutes acceptable behaviour and attitudes. Therefore, it is important that users understand what is happening or what they are potentially doing, when they use the buttons that encourage them to retweet or follow. Similarly, they need to be thoughtful when hitting the 'like' button on Facebook, or similar 'buttons' in other social media.

Another aspect of the internet that occurs without users noticing is the tracking of the user's browsing habits. Users may notice that advertising for items or sites they have previously browsed suddenly appear on the screen when they are browsing in another site. This can occur because the sites previously visited used cookies to track the web browsing activity in order to place an advertisement for their site in another browsing session at the optimum time. This is called remarketing and businesses use it because it has been found that people rarely purchase or engage fully with a site the first time they visit, so they need to be encouraged to return, through advertising. More recently specific probabilistic matching software (for example Drawbridge) has been designed to identify trends across devices; thus a user may search for something online at work but when they bring the laptop home they find advertising for that site on their mobile and tablet. This is because often devices such as laptops, mobile phones and tablets share the same IP address (for example, through the use of a router at home) and this software has been designed to find a match across devices. Understanding this process and how it is designed to shape one's behaviour is an important aspect of using the internet in critical ways, being in control of one's life.

The concept of cross-marketing and how it targets children through movies and associated toys, games, apps and food, has been explored previously (Anstey and Bull 2006); however, it is worth briefly discussing the ways it is used to target adults. Product placement of particular brands of items, such as make-up, food, cars and computers, in films and television shows subliminally places a memory of those items and their brands used in particular contexts that may be attractive to viewers either as an aspiration or in terms of their membership of a social or cultural group. The repetitive sight of those brands being used or consumed makes them more easily remembered and desirable when the viewer is actually shopping for such an item.

Similarly, websites market trends in areas such as fashion, household items, home decorating or landscaping. Pages on the site display a 'look' and, advertising it as such, suggest consumers 'get the look' by purchasing the products displayed. For example, a furniture store might display an attractive lounge room and, below the image, list the items and their prices and a convenient link to them in the website; fashion websites might show a model with a combination of fashionable clothing, bags and jewellery with similar links. Once again the consumer needs to understand that they are being encouraged to buy more and engage in some critical reflection about the difference between their original intent when accessing the website and the behaviour being encouraged by the marketing strategy employed by the producers of the website.

Implications of changing technology and change in social, cultural and civic settings for multiliteracies and multiliterate pedagogies

Table 1.4 provides a summary of the relationships among the key characteristics of multiliteracies, changing technology and change in social, cultural and civic settings and the implications for pedagogy. Examination of the literacies and literate practices necessary to ensure a capacity to function in social, cultural and civic settings indicates that the concept of multiliteracies, as a way of preparing students for the future, is highly relevant. An ability to cope with change and evolve one's literacies and literate practices and use them in critical ways to take control of one's life and contribute to designing one's future is essential. The implications for pedagogy are also compelling, as traditional approaches to literacy education would not enable such knowledge, skills and processes to be developed.

The impact of the changes that technology and media have wrought globally is reflected in a recent development from the United Nations Educational, Scientific and Cultural Organisation (UNESCO). It has released Five Laws of Media and Information Literacy (MIL), explaining the reason this step has been taken:

> We are travelling towards the universality of books, the Internet and all forms of 'containers of knowledge'. Media and information literacy for all should be seen as a nexus of human rights. Therefore, UNESCO suggests the following Five Laws of Media and Information Literacy.
>
> UNESCO (2017)

Table 1.4 Relationships among multiliteracies, changing technology and change in social, cultural and civic settings, and pedagogy

Characteristics of multiliteracies	Changing technology, social, cultural and civic settings	Implications for pedagogy
• Multimodal rather than language dominant • Made up of multiple literacies and multiple literate practices • Will continuously evolve as local and global society, culture and technology, change the contexts in which literacy is practiced • Enables capacities to cope with change and effectively participate and contribute to all aspects of society: workplace, leisure, social, cultural and civic environments	• Increased use of multimodal texts in social, cultural and civic settings • Associated issues of equity and access • Individuals may have a preference for particular modes, which can inhibit comprehension and/or use of multimodal texts in these settings • Increased use of screens for reading and using texts in social, cultural and civic settings • Increase in range of social media available • Access to a wider range of social and cultural groups • Access to wider range of trends and events • Social media used by different groups for a variety of purposes • Access to social media may challenge shared community values and connections • Evolving etiquettes around use of social media • Spelling, grammar, punctuation and language: continuously changing with evolving technology, social media, purposes and contexts of use • Technology and social media have changed and will continue to change how social and cultural events are celebrated and shared • Rise in internet addiction • No text is neutral • Increase in need for critical literacy skills and practices • Increased need to understand how the internet works and how it can be manipulated to influence behaviour, beliefs, values and attitudes	Develop pedagogies that increase understanding and knowledge about: • how multimodal texts work • personal modal preferences and possible implications of them • consuming and producing multimodal texts for a variety of contexts and purposes, using a variety of devices • how screen and page work similarly and differently • how social media provides access to a wider range of social and cultural groups, trends and events, and how this might challenge and/or shape behaviour, beliefs, attitudes and values • how and why no text is neutral • critical literacy skills and practices • how and why etiquette and behaviours around technology evolve • how and why spelling, grammar, punctuation and language will continue to change • how the internet works • how and why individuals should monitor and reflect upon their intent and purposes when using the internet

The Five Laws assert the rights of everyone to access and create media information literacy, but they also acknowledge the fact that the information, knowledge and messages contained are not neutral. In addition they acknowledge the dynamic aspects of media and information literacy, stating that it cannot all be acquired at one time and that it will continue to evolve. QR Code 1.10 provides a link to the UNESCO website, the Five Laws and a written explanation and a graphic representation of them. The Five Laws encapsulate many of the concepts and ideas that have been discussed in relation to multiliteracies in this chapter.

QR Code 1.10 The Five Laws of Media and Information Literacy (MIL) (http://www.unesco.org/new/en/communication-and-information/media-development/media-literacy/five-laws-of-mil/)

Conclusion

The purpose of this chapter was to provide the historical, sociocultural and educational basis for using the term multiliteracies to describe literacy. It commenced by examining the reasons for continuously evolving definitions of the term *literacy* and the emergence of the term *multiliteracies*. The concept of change as the new constant of societies across the world, realised through increasing globalisation, social and cultural diversity, and developing technologies, was described. Finally, the impact of continuous change on the literacy and the literate practices of workplace, leisure, social, cultural and civic environments, together with the implications for literacy pedagogy, were discussed in detail.

Multiliteracies expands the definition of literacy, defining it as being multimodal rather than language dominant, being made up of multiple literacies and multiple literate practices that continuously evolve as local and global society, culture and technology change the contexts in which literacy is practiced. Tables 1.3 and 1.4 summarise how this is enacted in changing workplaces, social, cultural and civic settings and through changes in technology. The second part of the definition of multiliteracies asserts that multiliteracies enable capacities to cope with change and effectively participate and contribute to all aspects of society: workplace, leisure, social, cultural and civic environments. This part of the definition emphasises the need to examine the knowledge, skills, processes, attitudes and practices around literacy to ensure that individuals can achieve effective participation and contribution to society. The third columns of Tables 1.3 and 1.4 summarise the pedagogical implications of multiliteracies that are critical to the achievement of the second part of the definition of multiliteracies. The continuous change that students will encounter in their lives means that education cannot prepare them in terms of all the knowledge and skills that will be needed. However, literacy education can assist in the development of attitudes toward literacy and literate practices that equip them for the evolving nature of literacy. Literacy education can also develop students' thinking processes and the social emotional intelligence needed to enable them to develop and refine their literacies and literate practices as needed in the future. This is why multiliteracies and multiliterate pedagogy are essential foundations to literacy education.

REFLECTION STRATEGY 1.7

- The purpose of this Reflection Strategy is to conduct a final review, and, if necessary, revision, of the definitions you have been developing and refining since Reflection Strategy 1.1, and to consider the implications for pedagogy.
- Once the revisions and review have been completed, attempt to write an implication statement about pedagogy for each of the main points in each definition. For example, if you defined multiliteracies as being about multimodal text, what are the implications for that regarding how and what you will teach?

REFLECTION STRATEGY 1.8

- The purpose of this Reflection Strategy is to prepare you for the challenges that you may face as a teacher.
- Having read this chapter and refined your definitions about literacy, literacies and multiliteracies, together with consideration of their implications for pedagogy, how would you answer if you were asked to respond to, or comment upon, the following:
    o A politician who states that we need to return to 'the basics' to raise literacy levels, and consequently increase employment and 'mend' the economy.
    o A parent who challenges the content of your literacy program, suggesting there is not enough emphasis on language (for example, spelling, grammar, and punctuation) and too much time spent learning about and creating screen texts.
    o An editorial that suggests that, because of technology, we no longer need to teach about language, spelling, punctuation and grammar.

40 The rise of multiliteracies

REFLECTION STRATEGY 1.9

- The purpose of this Reflection Strategy is to consider how you, as a teacher of literacy, might respond to the situation portrayed in the following QR code link to YouTube of a documentary aired in Australia in 2017. In this chapter one of the issues raised was how changes to technology and global attitudes about and regulation of the environment, have impacted employment and sometimes whole communities. In Australia in 2017 a brown coal fuelled power station that had been the major source of income in the community for generations was closed. This documentary shows the impact on the community. It shows a variety of attitudes, values and beliefs of the people affected.
- Consider the various views about employment, social and cultural attitudes to community and family portrayed.
- Think about these views in relation to the evolving definitions of literacy and literate practice that have been discussed in this chapter.

QR Code 1.11 A community response to change (https://www.youtube.com/watch?v=VD6YC5KJVe8)

Bibliography

Anstey, M 2009, 'Multiliteracies: the conversation continues: What do we really mean by "multiliteracies" and why is it important?' *Reading Forum*, vol. 24, no. 1, pp. 5–15.

Anstey, M & Bull, G 2004, *The Literacy Labyrinth*, 2nd edn, Pearson Education, Sydney.

Anstey, M & Bull, G 2006, *Teaching and Learning Multiliteracies: Changing Times, Changing Literacies*, International Reading Association, Newark.

Applebee, A N 1981, *Writing in the Secondary School*, National Council for the Teaching of English, Urbana.

Australia's Future Workforce? 2015, Report from CEDA (Committee for Economic Development of Australia) viewed 22 February 2017, http://adminpanel.ceda.com.au/FOLDERS/Service/Files/Documents/26792~Futureworkforce_June2015.pdf.

Baker, E A (ed) 2010, *The New Literacies: Multiple Perspectives on Research and Practice*, The Guilford Press, New York.

Balanskat, A and Engelhart, S 2015, *Computing our Future: Computer programming and coding: priorities, school curricula and initiatives across Europe*, European Schoolnet, Belgium, viewed 28 February 2017, http://fcl.eun.org/documents/10180/14689/Computing+our+future_final.pdf/746e36b1-e1a6-4bf1-8105-ea27c0d2bbe0.

Bee, B 1990, 'Teaching to empower: Women and literacy', *Australian Journal of Reading*, vol. 13, no. 1, pp. 53–9.

Benedikt, C & Osborne, M 2013, *The Future of Employment: A working paper*, Oxford Martin Programme of Technology and Employment, Oxford Martin School University of Oxford, Oxford, viewed 22 February 2017, http://www.oxfordmartin.ox.ac.uk/downloads/academic/The_Future_of_Employment.pdf.

Bourdieu, P 1986, 'The struggle for symbolic order', (trans J. Bleicher), *Theory, Culture and Society*, vol. 3, no. 3, pp. 35–51.

Bull, G & Anstey, M 1997, *Investigating the Literacy Practices of School, Home and Community*, Commissioned monograph for Language Australia, Canberra.

Bull, G & Anstey, M 2009, *Finding the Gaps: Navigating Sustainable Futures for Indigenous Students: A Pilot Study*, report on research conducted for the Greater Toowoomba Regional Advisory Committee, Department of Education, Employment and Workplace Relations. Toowoomba, viewed 22 February 2017, http://www.ansteybull.com.au/media/2198/cwfinding-the-gaps-2009.pdf.

Carson, KP and Stewart, GL 1996, 'Job analysis and the sociotechnical approach to quality: A critical examination,' *Journal of Quality Management*, vol. 1, pp. 49–64.

Cazden, CB 1967, 'On individual differences in language competence and performance', *Journal of Special Education*, vol. 1, pp. 135–50.

Cazden, CB 1970, 'The situation: A neglected source of social class differences in language use', *Journal of Social Issues*, vol. 26, no. 2, pp. 35–60.

Cazden, CB 1972, *Child Language and Education*, Holt, Rinehart and Winston, New York.

Cole, DR and Pullen, DL 2010, *Multiliteracies in Motion*, Routledge, Abingdon.

Cope, B and Kalantzis, M (eds), 2000, *Multiliteracies: Literacy Learning and the Design of Social Futures*, Routledge, London.

Courts, PL 1991, *Literacy and Empowerment*, Bergin & Garvey, New York.

Davies, F and Greene, T 1984, *Reading for Learning in the Sciences*, Oliver and Boyd, Edinburgh.

Dawkins, J 1991, *Australia's Language: The Australian Language and Literacy Policy*, Department of Employment, Education and Training, Australian Government Publishing Service, Canberra.

Foundation for Young Australians 2017, *The New Work Smarts: Thriving in the New Work Order*, The Foundation for Young Australians, Sydney.

Frey, CB and Osborne, M 2013, *The Future of Employment: How susceptible are jobs to computerisation?* Oxford Martin Programme on Technology and Employment, Oxford viewed 2 March 2017, http://www.oxfordmartin.ox.ac.uk/downloads/academic/The_Future_of_Employment.pdf.

Gardner, P 2017, 'Worlds apart: A comparative analysis of discourses of English in the curricula of England and Australia', *English in Education* doi: 10.1111/eie.12138 http://onlinelibrary.wiley.com/journal/10.1111/(ISSN)1754-8845/issues.

Gee, JP 1992, *The Social Mind: Language, Ideology and Social Practice*, Bergin & Garvey, New York.

Gray, B 1980a, 'Concentrated encounters as a component of functional language literacy teaching', in T Le & M McCausland (eds), *Proceedings of the Conference, Child Language Development: Theory into Practice*, Launceston Teachers' Centre, Launceston.

Gray, B 1980b, *Developing Language and Literacy with Urban Aboriginal Children: A first report on the Traeger Park project*, Curriculum Development Centre, Canberra.

Halliday, MAK 1973, *Explorations in the Functions of Language*, Edward Arnold, London.

Heath, SB 1982, 'Questioning at home and at school: A comparative study', in G Spindler (ed), *Doing the Ethnography of Schooling*, Holt, Rinehart & Winston, New York, pp. 103–131.

Heath, SB 1983, *Ways with Words: Language, Life and Work in Communities and Classrooms*, Cambridge University Press, Cambridge.

Heath, SB 1986, 'The functions and uses of literacy', in S De Castell A Luke & K Egan (eds), *Literacy, Society and Schooling*, Cambridge University Press, Cambridge.

Hoh, A 2017, 'Kids now spending more time online than watching television, survey shows', viewed 16 February 2017, http://www.abc.net.au/news/2017-02-15/children-now-spend-more-time-online-than-watching-tv/8272708.

Holman, D, Wall, TD, Clegg, CW, Sparrow, P & Howard, A (eds) 2005, *The Essentials of the New Workplace: A Guide to the Human Impact of Modern Work Practices*, Wiley and Sons, Chichester.

Kalantzis, M, Cope, B, Chan, E & Dalley-Trim, L 2016, *Literacies*, 2nd edn, Cambridge University Press, Port Melbourne.

Landy, FJ, Shankster-Cawley, L & Moran, SK 1995, 'Advancing personnel selection and placement methods', in A Howard (ed), *Frontiers of Industrial and Organisational Psychology: The Changing Nature of Work*, Jossey-Bass, New York.

Lankshear, C & Lawler, M 1987, *Literacy Schooling and Revolution*, Falmer Press, London.

Lankshear, C with Gee, JP, Knobel, M & Searle, S 1997, *Changing Literacies*, Open University Press, Buckingham.

Lawton, D 1968, *Social Class, Language and Education*, Routledge and Kegan Paul, London.

Littleton, K & Mercer, N 2013, *Interthinking: Putting Talk to Work*, Routledge, London.

Luke, A 1993, 'The social construction of literacy in the primary school', in L Unsworth (ed), *Literacy, Learning and Teaching*, Macmillan, Melbourne.

Luke, A 1995, 'When basic skills and information processing just aren't enough: Rethinking reading in new times', *Teachers College Record*, vol. 97, no. 1, Fall, pp. 95–115.

Luke, A & Freebody, P 1997, 'Shaping the social practices of reading', in S Muspratt, A Luke & P Freebody (eds), *Constructing Critical Literacies: Teaching and Learning Textual Practices*, Allen & Unwin, St Leonards, pp. 185–225.

Martin, JR 1993, 'Literacy in science: Learning to handle text as technology', in MAK Halliday & JR Martin (eds), *Writing Science: Literacy and Discursive Power*, Falmer Press, London.

Martin, JR & Rothery, J 1993, 'Grammar: Making meaning in writing,' in B Cope & M Kalantzis (eds), *The Powers of Literacy*, Falmer Press, London.

McConnell, S 1992, 'Literacy and empowerment', *Australian Journal of Language and Literacy*, vol. 15, no. 2, pp. 123–38.

Mikulecky, L 2010, 'An examination of workplace literacy research from new literacies and sociocultural perspectives,' in EA Baker (ed), *The New Literacies: Multiple Perspectives on Research and Practice*, The Guilford Press, New York.

Mills, KA 2011, *The Multiliteracies Classroom*, Multilingual Matters, Bristol.

New London Group 1996, 'A pedagogy of multiliteracies: Designing social futures', *Harvard Educational Review*, vol. 66, no. 1, pp. 60–92.

Oxenham, J 1980, *Literacy: Writing, Reading and Social Organisation*, Routledge and Kegan Paul, London.

Rosenberg, T 2017, 'American Girl: How do you grow up healthy in an era of body shaming and anonymous bullying on social media? You fight back', *National Geographic*, vol. 231, no. 1, pp. 110-27.

Sanchez, JI 1994, 'From documentation to innovation: Reshaping job analysis to meet emerging business needs', *Human Resource Management Review*, vol. 4, no. 1, pp. 51-74.

Smith, F 1983, *Essays into Literacy*, Heinemann, Exeter.

Starcevic, V 2013, 'Is Internet addiction a useful concept?' *Australian and New Zealand Journal of Psychiatry*, vol. 47, no. 1, pp. 17-21.

Street, BV 1984, *Literacy in Theory and Practice*, Cambridge University Press, Cambridge.

Sutton, M 2017, 'Virtual Reality addiction threat prompts cautious approach as VR nears "smartphone-like" take-off', *ABC News*, 10 February, viewed 11 February, http://www.abc.net.au/news/2017-02-10/addiction-risks-as-vr-gets-set-to-take-the-market-by-storm/8252614.

UNESCO (United Nations Educational Scientific and Cultural Organisation) 1957, *World Illiteracy at Mid-Century*, UNESCO, Paris.

UNESCO, 2017 *Five Laws of Media and Information Literacy*, viewed 23 March 2017, http://www.unesco.org/new/en/communication-and-information/media-development/media-literacy/five-laws-of-mil/.

Unsworth, L 2001, *Teaching Multiliteracies Across the Curriculum: Changing Contexts of Text and Image and Practice*, Open University Press, Oxenham.

Varlander, S 2012, 'Individual flexibility in the workplace: A spatial perspective', *The Journal of Applied Behavioural Science*, vol. 48, no. 1, pp. 33-61.

Waber, B, Magnolfi, J & Lindsay, G 2014, 'Workspaces that move people', *Harvard Business Review*, October, viewed 14 March 2017, https://hbr.org/2014/10/workspaces-that-move-people.

Wallace, P 2014, 'Internet addiction disorder and youth', *EMBO Report*, vol. 15, no. 1, pp. 12-16, viewed 20 March 2017, https://www.ncbi.nlm.nih.gov/pmc/articles/PMC4303443/.

2 Being multiliterate: A repertoire of practices

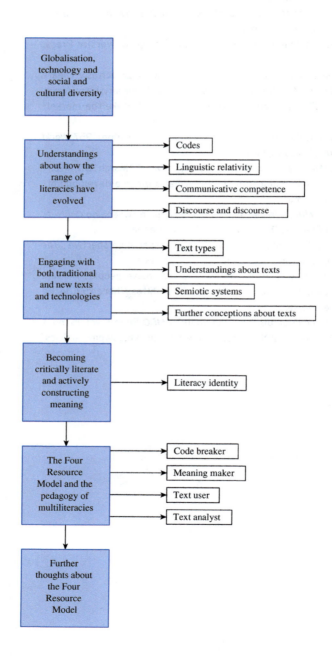

This chapter begins with a brief review of how globalisation, technology and diversity have influenced the development of new and evolving literacies. It will discuss how these literacies have led to new forms of texts that are produced and transmitted in differing ways in order to deal with continuous change. It will also explore how the ever-increasing pace of change has necessitated new understandings to be developed about what it is to be literate and multiliterate in the 21st century. This chapter also looks at the repertoire of skills and practices that are necessary to deal with these new understandings that will form part of everyday lifetimes in the 21st century. Finally, a model will be proposed that defines a pedagogy for the new literacies and multiliteracies.

Globalisation, technology and social and cultural diversity: Using new and evolving literacies in new contexts

One of the features of the 21st century (and to a lesser extent the late 20th century) has been the mass migrations and displacement of refugees reminiscent of those that took place after World War 2. Large population movements have produced diversities in both social and cultural contexts emerging from differing family patterns and social interactions and increasingly varied cultural practices. These sociocultural developments have influenced the evolving and new literacies and produced opposing tensions for change.

On the one hand, there is pressure to establish a 'universal' literacy where English becomes the official form of communication among varying social and cultural groups. While this has the potential to unify and empower across all groups it can also disempower particular groups through lack of access to the dominant literacies and loss of local literacies. Rymer (2012, p. 60) reported that 'one language dies every 14 days' and that it is likely that by the turn of the century 'nearly half of the roughly 7000 languages spoken on Earth will likely disappear', causing a fragmentation of social groupings and the loss of cultural practices. Rymer (2012, p. 62) reported further that 'In an increasingly globalised, connected, homogenized age, languages spoken in remote places are no longer protected by national borders or natural boundaries from the languages that dominate world communication and commerce'. The end result of the development of this tension is a **globalisation** of culture and of language practices.

On the other hand, when migrant groups in their adopted countries attempt to preserve their local languages and literacies, they are disempowered through lack of access to the dominant literacies and may become disaffected and unable to participate in the workplaces and other civic contexts. There is the potential to enrich their adopted country by increasing diversity but there is also the possibility that in order to preserve their local literacies they will isolate themselves from the mainstream. The impact of this choice on engagement with, and the learning of, the new language and adoption of the available new literacies is significant (see Lo Bianco 2000, particularly pp. 92-4, for further discussion).

Globalisation
Refers to economic and political trends that take place on the world (or global) stage rather than in one country, local area or within a particular social group. Globalisation can also refer to societal or cultural factors (cultural globalisation) that can impinge on language practices across, or within, societies.

The diversity created by the recent movements of populations has been augmented by a proliferation of new technologies incorporating systems and devices of instantaneous communication such as the internet, mobile phones and various forms of tablets, and reinforced by the development of globally integrated markets. The old notion of a single literacy that suited all purposes and contexts is no longer relevant. The diversity within the new mixes of multicultural populations demands a variety and growing number of literacies. The plethora of digital devices has led to the need for multiliteracies. As Jewitt (2006, p. 8) suggested, 'New technologies make available a whole range of multimodal possibilities'. Jewitt (2006, p. 24) stated further that individuals' use of computers and the like '...has the ability to transform and reorganise how they deal with intellectual and practical problems'. This technologically-mediated learning has produced a huge range of new texts and created a shift from page to screen that incorporates not only the word but also images, sounds and gestures. As Kress (2003, p. 140) suggested, the new forms of texts 'show the world rather than tell the world' and have consequences for writers (producers), readers (consumers) and designers of texts.

The issues relating to globalisation, technological change, increasing cultural diversity and social mobility have necessitated a reconsideration of concepts about literacy. As was discussed in Chapter One there has been a reconceptualisation of literacy towards literacies, multiliteracies and multimodality. The knowledge, skills and processes required to access literacies and multiliteracies and to design multimodal texts demand new literate practices. In order to engage with these new practices a multiliterate an individual needs to:

- be *flexible* and capable of actively responding to changing literacies and adopt, and sustain mastery over, new strategies
- have a *repertoire of practices* (knowledge, skills and strategies) that can be designed, redesigned and used appropriately for different purposes and audiences and in a range of different contexts
- understand and employ *traditional and new communication technologies* and understand that multimodal texts are delivered via combinations of paper, live (face-to-face) and digital technologies
- recognise how *social and cultural diversity* affect literate practices by the application of different knowledges, approaches, orientations, attitudes and values
- be *critically literate* by understanding that every literate practice requires reflective and analytical problem solvers who are strategic and creative thinkers and who are able to evaluate a variety of multimodal texts

These characteristics were developed earlier by Anstey and Bull (2006), Anstey (2009) and Bull and Anstey (2010) and identify what it is to be multiliterate and how individuals can engage with the new and evolving literacies.

Being multiliterate 47

REFLECTION STRATEGY 2.1

- The purpose of this Reflection Strategy is to reflect about your concepts concerning the characteristics of a multiliterate individual.
- Choose a contemporary picture book that you are unfamiliar with.
- Read/view the picture book and keep a record of your thoughts about the book as you read. It may be necessary to read/view the book more than once.
- Review the notes you have made and then compare them to the characteristics of a multiliterate individual.
- What range of strategies did you employ as you interpreted the book? Were the strategies flexible rather than using the same strategies throughout the book?
- Did you employ a range of literacy practices (knowledge, skills and strategies) that drew on different purposes, audiences and contexts?
- When reading the picture book did you draw on both word and image in order to make meaning?
- In what way did the picture book deal with social and cultural diversity? Did your written comments reflect this diversity?
- What aspects of critical literacy did your comments draw upon?

THEORY INTO PRACTICE 2.1

- The purpose of this Theory into Practice is to investigate how, or if, the literate practices that you employ are the same or different to those used by the students.
- If you are working with students, choose a book that is suitable for the age and ability level of the group or class. After you have previewed the book yourself it could be useful to get the students to read the book and then discuss with them how they went about making meaning as they read. This will give you some indication about whether they learnt what you thought you had taught them about reading/viewing a picture book in previous lessons.

If both Reflection Strategy 2.1 and Theory into Practice 2.1 are employed then it will be possible to assess student progress and the success, or otherwise, of a sequence of lessons. This can be achieved by utilising an auditing instrument.

Recent research into the impact of globalisation on the individual has led to a refocusing of attention on how literacies and literacy education might be utilised. Bean and Dunkerly-Bean (2015) argued that literacy education has often been described from a national, or western, perspective. They suggested that literacy education and literacies '…speaks to the possibilities of living

AUDITING INSTRUMENT 2.1

- The purpose of this Auditing Instrument is to engage in reflection about your concepts about literacy, the behaviours of a literate person and the literate practices that you employ in your planning of literacy lessons.
- Reflect on your definition of literacy or what you believe are the characteristics of a literate person.
- Alternatively, review the planning you devised for a literacy lesson or a sequence of lessons.
- While engaging with either or both of the tasks above, address the following questions as a way of guiding your deliberations:
    o How were you flexible in the selection and use of literate behaviours to complete the tasks?
    o Which of the range of your repertoire of practices (knowledge, skills, processes) did you employ?
    o How did you address both the new and traditional communication technologies (paper, live, digital)?
    o In what ways did you cater for social and cultural diversities?
    o How did your reflections about literacy or your planning for the teaching of literacy encompass considerations about critical literacy?

and learning at the intersection of the local and the global' (Bean and Dunkerly-Bean 2015, p. 46). They termed this view as *cosmopolitan theory* or *cosmopolitanism* based on the earlier work of Luke (2004), Hull and Stornaiulo (2010) and Hansen (2014), who stated that the interface between local and global was critical in developing the new approaches to literacies. This interface, in their view, no longer separated the local and global as separate entities but rather '... the local and the global are no longer separate spheres but interface through various processes with differing and at times contradictory effects' (Bean and Dunkerly-Bean 2015, p. 47). The distinction being made between the two processes is that globalisation is a more external process whereas cosmopolitanism is a more internal process from within an individual, and is therefore based on local experiences. The cosmopolitan theory can be seen as a bottom-up approach that originates from the local context acting on the individual, whereas globalisation is imposed from outside. Contemporary researchers envisage these two types of processes as occurring simultaneously. What this means for students, teachers and schools is that the new literacies need to account for 'a sustained readiness to learn from the new and different while being heedful of the known and familiar' (Hansen in Bean and Dunkerly-Bean 2015, p. 48). Such an understanding places emphasis on both the home and school, hence the focus on literacies and multiliteracies in current approaches to literacy teaching and learning.

Understanding about how the range of literacies has evolved from research about codes, linguistic relativity, communicative competence, discourse and Discourse

In the previous section of this chapter contemporary factors that have influenced the development of literacies and multiliteracies have been explored. In the following section the origins of theories about how different literacies developed will be investigated. Much has been written about the derivation of differing literacies, how they originated and the contexts from which they came.

Codes

Much of the research about these earlier concepts about literacies emanated from the work of Bernstein (1964, 1971, 1973, 1975, 1990), which focussed on the role that the home played and on the family-specific interactions that revolved around talk. Bernstein proposed that there was a relationship that linked literate practices around talk with social class membership and particular social and cultural practices in families. He developed the theory that different codes, which he described as elaborated and restricted codes, were associated with particular family types. He suggested (1964 and 1971, pp. 118-39 and pp. 170-89) that elaborate codes were predicated on different types of utterances that were peculiar to middle class families. These utterances tended to vary according to the use of pronouns, adjectives, adverbs and conjunctions as well as clauses, sequencing of ideas and repetition of phrases. Bernstein characterised elaborate code users as drawing their utterances from a broad range and variety of alternatives and therefore their language use was less predictable, more explicit and therefore more complex (elaborate). The literacy that that developed in such families was more flexible and creative. Conversely, restricted code was more predictable and implicit and less complex. It followed that the restricted code was therefore less flexible and less creative. Bernstein further suggested that working class families were more regulated and less open to change in family social structures whereas middle class families had more fluid roles in family structures and were therefore less regulated. Family members in a middle class context derived power within the home through personal competences and were therefore termed to be members of a person-oriented family. In contrast working class homes were seen as positional-oriented families where power was achieved through status within the family and where rigid roles were narrowly applied. In Bernstein's view, family structures produced characteristic ways of behaving and feeling that in turn created particular forms of language use and literate practice. This resulted in all individuals having access to the **restricted code** but only some having access to the **elaborate code**. Further

Restricted code
Originally described by Bernstein (1960, 1962a, 1962b, 1964) as having the following characteristics: short, simple and often unfinished sentences; limited use of adjectives, adverbs and subordinate clauses; infrequent use of personal pronouns; use of categorical statements; use of repetitive expressions; implicit meanings. These characteristics result in a narrow range of syntactical alternatives and a rigid approach to syntactic organisation.

Elaborate code
Proposed by Bernstein (1961) as almost the direct opposite of the restricted code and having the following characteristics: accurate and complex sentences; a discriminating selection of a range of conjunctions, adjectives, adverbs, prepositions; frequent use of the personal pronoun; use of subordinate clauses; use of generalised statements; complex and explicit meanings; language of possibilities. These characteristics result in a wide range of syntactical alternatives and a flexible approach to syntactic organisation.

discussions of these issues can be found in Anstey and Bull (2004, 2006) and Edwards-Groves, Anstey and Bull (2014).

The authors collected examples of what might be considered restricted and elaborate code while travelling to the airport by bus. These two examples presented in the vignettes below were contiguous with examples of what might be considered as differentiated child rearing practices possibly indicative of **positional** and **personal oriented** families.

The context was a bus travelling to the airport through heavy city traffic. There were many interesting things to observe, including many cars and trucks, a variety of tall buildings and occasional views of the river, on which there were ocean liners. A mother was sitting with her young boy, who was standing up in order to see as much as possible. The authors wrote down the following conversations, not wanting to interrupt to seek permission to record on their mobile phone.

Positional oriented family
A family where power and status is gained by an individual by virtue of their position in the family (father, mother, child). Child rearing is accompanied by and associated with threatening language and practices ('do as I tell you').

Personal oriented family
A family where power and status is gained by an individual by virtue of personal competence (a particular talent). Child rearing is accompanied by and associated with reasoning language and practices ('let's negotiate this').

Vignette 1
Mother: Sit down.
Child: No! (fairly forcefully)
Mother: I said sit down! (spoken emphatically)
Child: NO! (somewhat angrily in a stubborn tone)
Mother: Sit down or I'll belt you (losing patience)
Child: Reluctantly sits down.

Vignette 2
Mother: Sit down.
Child: I don't want to (in a tone that suggests that he does not want to miss anything)
Mother: I think you should sit down. (negotiating with child in a normal voice)
Child: Why? (makes no sense to me)
Mother: If you keep standing and the bus has to swerve or stop suddenly you might fall onto the bar of the seat in front and hurt your mouth (further negotiating with reasons given)
Child: Oh. OK.

The utterances in the two vignettes above are an accurate representation of the two conversations. The added descriptions in the brackets are interpretations based on tone and volume of voice, posture, gesture and gaze between mother and child and represent inferences that were drawn by the two authors at the time. While these inferences were drawn from the actions of the mothers and their sons, they could have been affected by the attitudes, values and experiences that the authors brought to the situations. However, what is not in doubt is that the two transcripts do illustrate some support for Bernstein's theory. The language in Vignette 1 is less complex than that in Vignette 2 in terms of both vocabulary and syntax. There is also a degree of negotiating and explaining evident in the latter that is not present in the former. There is also a significant degree of threat in Vignette 1 that is not present in Vignette 2.

It is important to realise that the definitions contained in the preceding glossary are based on Bernstein's early work. In later years Bernstein (1990) reviewed, revised and modified his position about codes and families as a result of further research and considerable challenges from other researchers in the field. However, his original theory gained immediate and wide acceptance in education systems in the U.K., U.S. and Australia and these ideas still predominate in some schools where there is a significant number of minority students (those who are migrant, coloured, poor, rural or isolated). This position is further complicated by varied interpretations and attributions of Bernstein's work, some of which have been overly simplified and are far from what he intended.

In recent times, researchers have begun to give some credence to Bernstein's theories, albeit in a more carefully argued way and in a more culturally appropriate manner. Gee (2004, p. 2) discussed '…academic and school-based forms of language and thinking that some people find alienating and others find liberating'. Further, Gee (2004, p. 3) suggested that 'Privileged children (children from well-off, educated homes) often get an important head start before school at home on the acquisition of such academic varieties of language; less privileged children (poor children or children from some minority groups) often do not'. For Gee the academic varieties of language of the school were those that featured highly specialised language that was related to content areas. Similarly, Littleton and Mercer (2013) stated that as school might be the only chance that some students get to learn that language it provides a mechanism for thinking and that such experiences can give access to the value of explicit, clear explanations. They suggested (2013, p. 95) that 'Reasoned discussion may be a genre that does not appear often in some children's out-of-school lives'. These researchers, while disagreeing with the reasoning behind the **Deficiency Hypothesis**, nevertheless do give some credence to the view that literacy practices learnt in the home may not prepare some students for those practices expected and used by the school. Unlike Bernstein, they are careful not to relate these differences between home and school to social class.

Deficiency Hypothesis
A belief that poor performance by students from a working class background can be attributed to factors operating within the home. This 'blame the victim' approach shifts responsibility for educational failure away from the school to families because of deficiencies that are believed to be present within the context of the home.

REFLECTION STRATEGY 2.2

- The purpose of this Reflection Strategy is to examine your approach to minority groups.
- Revisit your approach to the minority students in your classroom. If you are not in a classroom, then analyse your position about minority groups in your local area. Do you equate or explain the lack of educational progress of minority students with family background?

As a result of Bernstein's theoretical stance, an orthodoxy emerged that not only associated codes with social class, but also began to interpret access to particular codes as an explanation of success or failure at school. Students from working class families became marginalised because of the growing belief that failure at school could be attributed to family background. Certain students were seen by the schools to be 'culturally disadvantaged' or 'culturally deprived'. This belief neatly shifted the responsibility for failure away from the school and held the home accountable. Bernstein's position became widely accepted in educational circles and led some teachers to adopt the proposition that some children (from working class homes) were deficient in literacy. This led to the development of what became known as the Deficiency Hypothesis, although this was not a term that was used by Bernstein. Student performance could then be interpreted as a result of family background and child-rearing practices rather than the presence, or absence, of particular pedagogies. The effect of the Deficiency Hypothesis was to 'blame the victim', that is, the parent, and not the teacher. Bernstein's ideas gained wide acceptance in the 1960s and 1970s although they were the subject of much controversy and were strenuously challenged in the U.S., the U.K. and Australia. However, they continued to be widely accepted and researchers continued to find strong evidence of teacher beliefs and acceptance of the central ideas underlying the theory. Over 30 years after the publication of Bernstein's original article Freebody and Ludwig (1998), in their investigation of literacy practices in low socioeconomic communities, found the schools still attributed poor student achievement to membership of the working class. Parents from 'disadvantaged' or 'deficient' homes were still seen as the cause of poor performance rather than the practices or pedagogies of the school.

Linguistic relativity

While there has been some support of Bernstein's ideas in Australia (Poole 1972), the U.K. (Lawton 1968) and the U.S. (Williams and Naremore 1969), there have also been a number of critiques. One such criticism was that postulated by Labov (1966, 1969a, 1969b). He shared Bernstein's view that social and cultural factors influenced literacy practices but proposed a different explanation about the influences and outcomes of these factors. Labov carried out an intensive study of African American students living in New York. He found that there were differences in the way these students used language but rejected Bernstein's categories of restricted and elaborate code. Instead, he suggested that differences could be better accounted for through the concept of standard and non-standard English and termed this 'linguistic relativity'. This position, as well as offering an alternative explanation for differences in literacy practices, directly challenged the notion of the Deficiency Hypothesis. This interpretation became known as the Difference Hypothesis and proposed that the differences found could be attributed to differences in dialect. In Labov's terms, the non-standard English (NSE) spoken by the participants in his investigation was a different form of standard English (SE) and was just as elaborate as the standard form. He suggested that it should regarded by the school as an alternative form and not as an explanation for poor performance. As well as suggesting that non-standard English was an acceptable, but different, form of English, Labov's research also redirected the responsibility for dealing with difference back to the school. Labov concluded that speakers of non-standard English (NSE) possessed the same logic and the same capacity for conceptual learning as users of standard English (SE). Table 2.1, modified from Labov (1969b, p. 8), illustrates this point with the following comparisons between standard English and non-standard English.

Table 2.1 Comparing Standard English (SE) and Non-standard English (NSE)

Standard English (SE) form	Non-standard English (NSE) form
He doesn't know anything	He don't know nothing
Nobody likes him	Nobody don't like him
Hardly anybody goes there	Nobody hardly goes there
Nobody can do it	Can't nobody do it
He's tired	He tired

Labov proposed that 'He doesn't know anything' could be interpreted as a contraction of 'He does not know anything' in the same way that "He don't know nothing' could be seen as a contraction of 'He doesn't know anything'. The issue then becomes a problem of the teacher's expectations of what is appropriate language, compounded by the assumption that NSE is evidence of some form of cultural deprivation. The Deficiency Hypothesis would view these dialectic differences as a problem created by the home, whereas the **Difference Hypothesis** would interpret them as a problem generated by the school or teacher.

Communicative competence

Because Labov did not conclude that social class or family membership could explain differences in literacy practices, his position was more culturally appropriate than that of Bernstein. Another critic of Bernstein was Cazden (1967, 1970, 1972), who not only disagreed with the Deficiency Hypothesis, but also felt that Labov did not give an adequate explanation of difference. She proposed that both working class and middle class children had access to restricted and elaborate codes or standard and non-standard forms of English. Cazden felt that the problem lay not so much in knowing a particular code or dialect, but was rather a question of use. She suggested that middle class children were able to discriminate between contexts where it

Difference Hypothesis
Language and literacy practices present in the families of minority groups can be seen as alternative forms of standard English. The differences, termed linguistic relativity, can be interpreted as differences of dialect rather than as some form of penalty or explanation of poor performance at school. It then becomes the responsibility of the school to accommodate these differences rather than blaming the home.

was appropriate to use a code or dialect, whereas lower class children lacked this ability. She stated that middle class children were able to distinguish between more formal situations (school and workplace) and less formal situations (family and playground) and therefore able to judge when standard/non-standard English or elaborate/restricted codes were more appropriate. Cazden termed this ability as **communicative competence**, a theory that had been explored by Habermas (1970). As with Labov, Cazden's position was more culturally appropriate. However, neither Labov's concept of linguistic relativity nor Cazden's ideas of communicative competence gained the same degree of acceptance in schools or classrooms as those of Bernstein. The ideas of Bernstein still receive popular attention and are still commonly found in schools (see the previous discussion of Freebody and Ludwig, 1998) long after his initial theories were proposed. This may be partly due to the shifting of responsibility from school to home. For over three decades the literacy practices of students, both in school and in the home, have received close attention from researchers. Heath (1983), Hull and Schultz (2002), Dyson (2003) and D'warte (2014) have all investigated the various literate practices to be found in the home and other out-of-school sites. Other researchers, notably Lankshear and Knobel (2003) and Gee (2004), have noted that students' literate practices are rarely incorporated into school practices.

Discourse and discourse

So far the discussion about literacy practices in this chapter has concerned itself with what happens in homes and families relating to social class, and how this affects success or failure of students in school settings. In more contemporary times discussion has focused on those literacies that are made available in classrooms through consideration of **discourses** (Kress and van Leeuwen 2001). In addressing this point Gee (1990, 1992, 2004) suggested that what makes literacies available are **Discourses** (upper case 'D') and discourses (lower case 'd'). Gee (1990, pp. 139–45) postulated that discourses are strings of words that are joined together in some meaningful way in order to make some kind of sense and can be found in stories or conversations and in more formal school settings such as 'show and tell'. These discourses also show how sentences relate to one another throughout a text (Gee 2004, p. 18). On the other hand, Discourses are made up of values, attitudes, beliefs and gestures that describe how an individual should act and behave while involved in delivering a discourse. Discourses, as Gee suggested, are more to do with engaging in a social role while discourses are more to do with language and talk. Students therefore need to be literate but they also need to know how literacy is practiced in their classroom and school. They need to have access to the codes and conventions of both Discourses and discourses, otherwise they will become marginalised and disempowered.

Gee (1992, pp. 107–13) developed this idea further by proposing primary and secondary Discourses. **Primary Discourses** are acquired in the home

---

Communicative competence
Refers to the ability of middle class students to understand when it is appropriate to use standard or non-standard dialects (or elaborate and restricted codes) in formal or less formal contexts. While working class students know both the codes and dialects they are unable to judge when it is appropriate to use them. They are therefore not communicatively competent.

discourses
Refer to selections of language that connect together to make sense. They also refer to how sentences are related to one another in a text to make meaning.

Discourses
The social practices learnt in the home and community that produce characteristic ways of talking that are related to the attitudes, values, ideologies and behaviours that are adopted by individuals.

Primary Discourses
Those Discourses acquired in the home through oral interaction in natural settings with significant others.

and each individual acquires just one such Discourse through oral interaction in natural settings with significant others within the context of the home. According to Gee, once the individual leaves the context of the home and enters into settings such as school, church, workplaces and other civic situations then they will need to develop a range of secondary Discourses. These **secondary Discourses** will need to be learnt so that they can be applied in the appropriate settings, necessitating the learning of a number of literacies and literate practices. Secondary Discourses need to be consciously learned whereas primary Discourses will be automatically acquired. The school therefore needs to be aware of the primary Discourses that students will bring to the school and, at the same time, be aware of the range of secondary Discourses that need to be developed. Only then, according to Gee, will the students become literate. The balance between primary Discourses and secondary Discourses, and between Discourses and discourses, then becomes critical. In order to see how this might work, three vignettes are presented below that have been derived from those described by Anstey and Bull (2004, pp. 50-51).

Secondary Discourses
Those Discourses acquired in settings such as school, church, workplaces and other civic contexts.

Vignette 1 based on Gee (1990, pp. 117-27)

This vignette is taken from a transcript of a 'show and tell' session in a Year 2 class. The story is told by an African American girl from a low socioeconomic family. Using the discourse patterns and Discourses she has learnt and acquired from home, she offers a highly entertaining presentation that is relevant to her classmates using the oral discourse patterns of her culture. The talk is accompanied by rhythms and gestures that support her oral performance and encourages participation from her audience. While the students enjoy the presentation, it is judged unsuccessful because it does not follow the patterns of mainstream discourse and Discourses expected by her teacher and the school.

A second presentation in the same session is offered by a white, middle class student involving a factual recount. The class quietly listens. The story is not entertaining in the same way as the first and does not encourage participation by the audience. However, the second story is judged to be successful because it conforms to the expected discourses and Discourses of the school. One child succeeds and one does not, not because of ability but rather because of access to the required discourses.

Vignette 2 based on Lankshear and Lawler (1987, pp. 158-65)

This vignette is based on observations taken in two different classrooms in an Auckland school in New Zealand. One class was an academically streamed class of mainly white middle class students. The second was a lower streamed class made up mainly of Pacific Islanders and Maori students. The latter class expected that teachers were the font of all knowledge and their role was to write copious notes on the blackboard that they would then copy down. They did not relate learning to language, thinking, discussing or to expressing their own ideas through talk. Any variation from this approach by the teacher was met with strong resistance and problems with behaviour. The former group knew all about language and learning and constructed the teacher as a resource for confirming ideas and information and guiding discussion. As a result, the former group was largely successful in their attempts to enter university while the latter was rarely successful. The discourses and the Discourses that the Pacific Islanders and Maori students brought with them from their homes led to failure in the examination context. While ability played some part in their failure, as evidenced by their being placed in the lower streamed class, the lack of access to the appropriate discourses/Discourses also played a part.

Vignette 3 based on (Luke 1993)
Luke described a lesson involving a discussion in a Year 1 class about a story called 'The Princess and the Dragon'. The students were Torres Strait Islanders from North Queensland, Australia. In a discussion about what colour hair the princess could have, an Islander student suggested black (since most, if not all, Islanders have black hair). This suggestion was ignored by the teacher and greeted by hilarious laughter from the other students. This classroom event could have been used as an opening for a critical discussion and re-writing of the popular fairy story from a different social and cultural perspective. This would have provided a chance for a discussion about different discourses and Discourses and an opportunity to challenge the response from the class.

The inclusion of discourses and Discourses in everyday classroom practice becomes critical if the school is to confront the issues surrounding class and home/school differences in the same way that code, dialect and communicative competence need to be adequately addressed. If not, then there is the potential that one or more of these differences in literacy practices will become dominant to the detriment of the others. This is not just a questioning of different theories from a purely academic perspective but also a practical question of which students are advantaged and which are marginalised. Similarly, some Primary Discourses may be less valued by the school (such as those practised by working class, rural or minority students) than others seen to be possessed by middle class, urban and mainstream students. Alternatively, the selection of Secondary Discourses to be taught by the school may either reinforce what has been acquired in the home or be quite unfamiliar to some students. It must be remembered that it is not the discourse, code or dialect that is dominant but rather it is the way they are dealt with by the school that produces dominance and differentiates which students will succeed from those who will not.

REFLECTION STRATEGY 2.3

- The purpose of this Reflection Strategy is to see whether your classroom practice takes account of your beliefs about teaching and learning.
- To what extent does your theory, or your classroom practice, about the teaching and learning of literacies and multiliteracies take account of codes, linguistic relativity, communicative competence or discourses/Discourses?
- How do these beliefs affect how you plan your day-to-day lessons?
- If your theory, or classroom practice, does not take account of these beliefs, how might you change your planning and teaching?

Strategies, practices and repertoires for engagement in both traditional and new texts and technologies

Text types

As was pointed out in Chapter One, the concept of multiliteracies was derived from the development of ideas about the new and evolving literacies, about multiple literacies and multiple literate practices. It was argued that these new forms of literacies arose from changes in local and global societies and from ever-changing conditions in culture and technology. It would therefore seem appropriate to explore the strategies and practices that were generated by these vast changes. Part of these changes is the shift from page to screen as suggested by Kress (2003), that has given rise to a movement away from an emphasis on the written word. Yamada-Rice (2010) investigated this movement by exploring how the visual communication practices in the homes of young children had gone beyond an emphasis on words.

Concomitant with this move away from reliance on the written word only, there has been a dramatic increase in the variety of texts and literate practices. More recently, Bezemer and Kress (2016) critiqued research that took language as the foundation or starting point. They suggested that this position '...has been habitually justified by the claim, now profoundly challenged, that language, as speech and writing, provides the most developed and entirely comprehensive resource for all meaning making' (Bezemer and Kress 2016, p. 7).

The concept of multiliteracies has necessitated that, in order to be literate, individuals need to be familiar with, and to engage with, paper (the written word), live (face-to-face) and digital texts used across a range of contexts. Increasing rates of technological change has produced a vast array of digital texts that were not available in the early 20th century. Technology has also impacted on live texts that were once engaged in through face-to-face interactions conducted in real life contexts. In recent times, face-to-face or live texts, through the development of apps such as Skype, can permit real time interactions between individuals in different contexts. These developments necessitate a broadening of the concept of text that goes well beyond the emphasis only on the written word.

REFLECTION STRATEGY 2.4

- The purpose of this Reflection Strategy is to measure to what extent you have moved away from a reliance on paper text.
- Review your engagement with literate practices over a day.
- Classify the texts that you find embedded in your practices into paper, live or digital.
- If there is an imbalance across the three types caused by a preponderance of one text type, what does this say about your literate practices?
- How far have you moved away from a dependence on the paper to the exclusion of the other two text types?

AUDITING INSTRUMENT 2.2

- The purpose of this Auditing Instrument is to investigate whether you have a balance in the types of texts you include in your planning.
- Review your planning for literacy lessons.
- Is there an appropriate balance across all three text types?
- What changes do you have to make to redress the imbalance you found? (It may be that you will be satisfied with the balance you discover.)
- How did you decide what balance of text types to implement? If you are following school policy, are you aware of the reasons why the school chose to adopt this particular approach?

Understandings about texts

The term text is derived from the Latin *textus*, meaning 'tissue' and *texere* meaning 'weave'. The concept of text as weaving a tissue of meaning seems an appropriate metaphor since it suggests the weaving together of a combination of signs and symbols in order to convey various meanings. The consideration of text from this point of view explains how words, sentences, paragraphs, nouns, verbs and the like can be used to design texts from a linguistic perspective in order to convey a variety of meanings. However, with the advent of the new technologies, it is now necessary to consider the live and digital texts as well as the more traditional paper texts. In order to engage with live texts, individuals need to interpret meanings from such elements as music, art or drama. In the case of digital texts individuals need to interpret elements such as colour, movement or images (such as those used in film). Therefore, there is a need to develop a different method of 'reading' multimodal texts that can be shared by groups and rely on commonly held beliefs about making meaning.

Semiotic systems

The concept of **semiotic systems** is ideally suited to these sorts of interpretations of multimodal texts. A semiotic system is a system of signs and symbols that have agreed upon meanings within a particular group. It is therefore an inherently social process that depends upon interactions within groups of individuals. It is crucial to realise that these meanings may vary between, and within, varying cultural groups. Most classrooms are now multicultural because of the diversity created by the mass movements of populations. Multicultural classrooms are now the new norm in contrast to many classrooms pre-World War 2. Some cultures (Western) associate white with weddings while others (some Asian cultures) associate red with weddings. Similarly, white is associated with purity in Western cultures (perhaps a somewhat outmoded concept in contemporary society) but with death in Samoan culture.

> **Semiotic system**
> A system of signs and symbols that have agreed upon meanings within a particular group.

There are a number of semiotic systems that are required to deal with the diversity of texts that have now become an important part of everyday life. Each one of these semiotic systems has a method of systemically dealing with the organisation of meaning in a specific text using a grammar of elements and rules that is particular to that semiotic system. As Kress and van Leeuwen (2006, p. 1) suggested, 'Just as grammars of language describe how words combine in clauses, sentences and texts, so our visual "grammar" will describe the way in which depicted elements – people, places and things – combine in visual "statements" of greater or lesser complexity and extension.' They go on to suggest that what is expressed by choice of words or clauses in language can similarly be expressed by a visual grammar by choice of colour. As previously stated, this association of colour with a particular meaning can vary across, and within, a culture. Visual grammar, as with the traditional linguistic grammar, must be considered as culture-specific and not applied as some universal system of meaning making. Beyond the linguistic and visual grammars that have been discussed so far, there are other semiotic systems that are required to deal with the ever-increasing diversity of texts. These have recently been explored by Anstey and Bull (2004, 2006) and Bull and Anstey (2010, 2013), who proposed five semiotic systems. These are briefly outlined below (for a more in-depth discussion, see Chapter Three).

- Linguistic (written language, incorporating choice of nouns, verbs, adjectives and conjunctions)

- Visual (still and moving images, incorporating choice of colour, vectors and point of view)
- Audio (music, sound effects, incorporating volume, pitch and rhythm)
- Gestural (facial expression and body language, incorporating eyebrow position, movement of head, arms, hands and legs)
- Spatial (layout and organisation of objects and space, incorporating proximity, direction and position)

Each of the four 'new' semiotic systems has a grammar of its own that does the same work as the grammar of the linguistic semiotic system with which most individuals are familiar. Each semiotic system is governed by a grammar that serves to guide the user into using combinations of the individual terms to make meanings. These terms, or **codes,** provide a terminology that enables the reader, or viewer, to identify and describe how attention is captured and therefore how meaning is created, shaped or modified. As a case in point, the commentator of a tennis match may comment on a specific shot with emphasis or stress on particular vocabulary items (what a *spectacular* backhand cross-court volley). Similarly, the commentator of a football match may use escalating pitch, increasing pace of delivery and rising intonation to indicate that something exciting is about to take place. In this latter commentary, it may be that the audience attends less to the vocabulary being used and focuses more on pitch, pace and intonation. The codes are being differentially used by the tennis commentator when compared with the football commentator. The tennis commentator is most unlikely to ever use the commentary employed in the football broadcast. Codes are utilised in particular ways across various contexts and can therefore be said to have conventions for use. In summary, each semiotic system employs a number of codes that can be used conventionally (and sometimes unconventionally) in order to create meaning.

Conventions are the agreed upon, or accepted, ways of using the codes. Together the codes and conventions are the tools that come together to enable a reader/viewer to make meaning. There are codes and conventions that are associated with each semiotic system.

It is important to realise that the grammars of the Visual, Audio, Gestural and Spatial Semiotic Systems should be implemented differently from the traditional approach associated with the linguistic semiotic system. The rules governing the grammar of the linguistic semiotic system are frequently rigidly applied in order to achieve 'correct' usage within a system that is stable (not changing). The effect of such usage is sometimes the basis of judgement, not only about correct versus incorrect usage, but about who is properly educated and who is not. This can lead to the marginalisation of certain minority groups and an undervaluing of the literacies of the home. It can also, as Kress and van Leeuwen suggested, lead to students reading (or misreading) the dominant culture of the visual in the school context in terms of their home culture. With the case of the grammars of the Visual, Audio, Gestural and Spatial Semiotic

Codes
A terminology that can be used to create meaning in a particular semiotic system.

Systems, they are seen as a more dynamic and flexible set of rules for engaging in meaning making. As Kress and van Leeuwen (2006, p. 266) suggested with regard to the development of a visual grammar, such a grammar should be seen as '...a flexible set of resources that people use in ever new and ever different acts of visual sign-making'. The grammars concomitant with the Audio, Gestural and Spatial Semiotic Systems work in the same way as that of the visual. As Kress (2003, p. 142) pointed out, 'As the screen becomes the dominant site of communication... "reading" as the process of getting meaning from a textual entity, will need to deal with more than just writing and the image.'

The semiotic systems need to be seen as flexible, not just as operating within a single semiotic system, but rather across all the semiotic systems. As Kress and van Leeuwen (2001) pointed out earlier, the individual semiotic systems should not be interpreted as 'bounded and framed' as a single entity that produces meaning, but rather there as principles that act within, but also across, different systems. As a case in point both Jewitt, Bezemer and O'Halloran (2016, p. 62) and Bezemer and Kress (2016, p. 17) explore the concept of the production of intensity as realised across all semiotic systems. They suggest that intensity can be realised in the Audio Semiotic System as loudness of a sound, in the Gestural Semiotic System as speed or extent of a gesture, or in the Visual Semiotic System through colour as the degree of saturation of the colour. Similarly, intensity can also be realised in the Spatial Semiotic System through the degree of separation between two individuals and in the Linguistic Semiotic System through the addition of adjectives describing, or qualifying, nouns.

The result of considering these multimodal texts emerging from the new literacies and the new technologies is the development of a proliferation of available texts not limited to the written texts of the Linguistic Semiotic System. Going beyond the Linguistic Semiotic System to encompass the four other semiotic systems introduces a plethora of texts that promote a richness of communication possibilities.

REFLECTION STRATEGY 2.5

- The purpose of this Reflection Strategy is to review your classroom practice to see whether there is an appropriate balance in your engagement with the five semiotic systems.
- How often do you discuss the five semiotic systems with your class?
- If there is an imbalance, why has this occurred?
- In what ways can you change your classroom practice to redress this imbalance?
- How familiar are your students with the five semiotic systems?
- Do your students understand when it is appropriate to use each semiotic system?

AUDITING INSTRUMENT 2.3

- The purpose of this Auditing Instrument is to investigate how the five semiotic systems feature in the planning and implementation of your teaching.
- Do you include a range of semiotic systems in your teaching?
- Have you consciously achieved a particular balance of the semiotic systems in your day-to-day teaching? How successful have you been?
- In what ways does your teaching of the five semiotic systems agree with, or diverge from, the whole school approaches that have been implemented?

Further conceptions about texts

In addition to knowledge of the five semiotic systems, a multiliterate person must have some understanding about how texts are constructed, how they are consumed and what practices are necessary to engage with them. The term 'constructed' in reference to texts is used here to augment the term 'written', which has traditionally been used when dealing with the Linguistic Semiotic System. While it is pertinent to describe a paper text as being written or constructed, it does not follow that a visual text can be written. Visual texts, as with audio, gestural and spatial texts, can more appropriately be referred to as being constructed. Similarly, paper texts can be read, while visual, audio, gestural and spatial texts can be better described as being consumed. There are a number of understandings that an individual requires in order to understand the production and consumption of texts, and the practices around texts, across the five semiotic systems.

- All texts are consciously constructed and have particular social, cultural, political or economic purposes.
    o All producers of text have some conscious purpose in mind when constructing a text.
- Texts will continue to change as society and technology changes.
    o Texts are being constructed in more flexible and dynamic ways as producers attempt to deal with rapid societal and technological changes.
- All texts are multimodal.
    o All multimodal elements of a text need to be attended to, as both producers and consumers have realised that important meanings are not only contained in the written word.
- Texts can be interactive, linear or non-linear.
    o Consumers of text, particularly digital and live texts, can become actively involved in the construction of the text. Paper texts, because they are read page by page, are linear. Live and digital texts are produced idiosyncratically as there is often no predetermined way of constructing them.

- Texts may be intertextual.
  - Texts, whether they be paper, live or digital, may draw or make reference to other texts to make meaning.
- Texts are tending to become more screen-like as design and designing become more central to the production of texts.
  - The layout and organisation of written/paper texts are increasingly taking on some of the characteristics of screen-like texts.
- Texts can be created by the reader/viewer using the links in digital texts to produce hypertexts.
  - The consumer creates his or her own hypertext by navigating through the digital texts in a idiosyncratic manner.
- The social and cultural background of individuals influences the production of, and engagement with, text.
  - Individuals may bring their own notions about how texts are produced, dependent upon their social and cultural background and experiences. Therefore, individuals may respond quite differently to texts in school and in other contexts.
- A text may have several possible meanings.
  - There may be many possible meanings in a text, depending on the social, cultural, economic or political background of the reader/viewer and the context in which it is read. An individual's response to a text should be considered rather than the adoption of a single, authorised interpretation.
- The reader/viewer interacts with the text to actively construct the meaning of the text.
  - The author or producer of a text constructs it in a particular way in order to convey certain meanings. However, the reader/viewer of a text reconstructs the text in his or her individual way in order to gain meaning. The reader/viewer is an active participant in meaning making rather than a passive receiver. It is important that students realise that they have an important (active) role in the construction of meaning in any given text.
- The complexity of multimodal texts means that readers/viewers have to consciously differentiate the focus of their attention across the semiotic systems.
  - When a reader/viewer interacts with a text, they may focus on a particular semiotic system as part of their analysis. However, all the semiotic systems may play a part of the meaning making process while engaging with a text. It is important not to focus on the one semiotic system, or the same semiotic system, when interpreting a text. The reader/viewer needs to be conscious of this process and be capable of realising when to engage with the text in a particular way.
- No text is neutral.
  - Every producer of a text expects that the consumer will learn something from engaging with the text. Therefore, every text has a particular purpose that is designed to change the reader/viewer in some way. The reader/viewer should always be asking themselves, among other

things, 'What is this text trying to get me to do or believe?' Any text has a message or belief to convey and is, as a result, not neutral.

Each of these twelve characteristics above is essential to the understanding of the semiotic systems, and plays an important role in developing a multiliterate person. As a consequence, they are integral to teacher practice, pedagogy and planning.

REFLECTION STRATEGY 2.6

- The purpose of this Reflection Strategy is to review your classroom practice as it relates to the five semiotic systems and how you encourage your students to be multiliterate.
- Review a range of your recent lessons over the last two to three weeks and determine how often you explicitly teach about text production and consumption.
- Which of the twelve characteristics above did you address in your lessons? Was there a balance across the twelve characteristics?
- If you found that some of these characteristics did not feature in your classroom practice, what did that reveal about your approach to the teaching and learning of the characteristics?

THEORY INTO PRACTICE 2.2

- The purpose of this Theory into Practice is to use your findings from Reflection Strategy 2.6 to devise a sequence of lessons around one or more of the twelve characteristics.
- How different is this sequence of lessons from the way you normally teach?
- What does this tell you about how you are approaching the teaching of the semiotic systems and multiliteracies?
- Is there a need for you to modify your lesson planning? If so, how might this be achieved?

Becoming critically literate and actively constructing meaning

The focus on semiotic systems, multiliteracies and understandings about texts and rapid changes in technology have produced a proliferation of texts that have become available in schools and other social and cultural contexts. Students now have access to a variety of texts as never before and potentially can engage with these texts in new and interesting ways. This plethora of texts brings with it new possibilities. Simply accessing this variety of texts is only just the beginning. Students and teachers are now required, among other things, to analyse these multimodal texts, to engage in multiliterate practices, to uncover the purposes of texts, to decide which texts to attend to and to decide which are the most powerful and of most use to them. It is no accident that, with emphasis on multiliteracies and multimodality, there has also been a greater emphasis on what has become known as critical literacy. The concept of critical literacy, according to Kalantzis et al. (2016), has been around since the mid 1970s and has attracted the interest of a number of researchers such as Freebody and Luke (1990), Luke and Carrington (2004), Lankshear and Knobel (2006), Morrell (2008), Gutierrez (2008) Carrington and Robinson (2009) and Janks (2010). The interest from these researchers in the U.S., U.K., Australia and South Africa illustrates the importance accorded to the issues surrounding critical literacy.

With the number and variety of texts now readily available, it has become crucial that critical literacy becomes a central concern of literacy pedagogy. Students increasingly need to move beyond an initial understanding or comprehension of the meaning within the text. They need to address questions such as the possible bias or propaganda portrayed by the text and therefore what the text is trying to make them believe. In this approach, students need to interrogate the text by searching behind the meanings to uncover the interests and motives of those who produced the text and what gaps there are in the text. This requires an understanding of the multiple points-of-view expressed by the producers of text, who are themselves influenced by personal attitudes, values and beliefs. As Kalantzis et al. (2016, p. 180) suggested, '... a critically literate person identifies relevant and powerful topics, analyses and documents evidence, considers alternative points-of-view, formulates possible solutions to problems and perhaps also tries these solutions'. Further questions can be asked about whose interests the texts serve, who is being manipulated and why (Luke, Comber and Grant 2003) and who has been silenced. In short, all texts need to be examined for authenticity and authority. These questions reinforce the points that were made earlier in this chapter that 'no text is neutral' and that 'all texts are consciously constructed and have particular social, cultural, political or economic purposes'.

In the light of the discussion above, the concept of critical literacy goes beyond simply interrogating texts to include all literate practices. Implementing critical literacy in the classroom suggests that students (and teachers) will not only be involved in comprehending texts, but also looking beneath and behind the text to explore questions of authenticity and authority. It implies that interrogation of texts is followed by questions exploring possible action. If a text has influenced the reader/viewer, then it is reasonable to ask: 'What are you going to do about it – what is your next step?' If critical literacy is implemented in this way then students will be changed, not only by the text, but also by any action that they take in response to the text. In this way students are transformed by their participation in literate practices across a range of contexts as they use the knowledge, skills, strategies and ideas that are available to them. The following Reflection Strategy (2.7) is taken from Anstey and Bull (2006).

REFLECTION STRATEGY 2.7

- The purpose of this Reflection Strategy is to illustrate how students implemented critical literacy, took action and engaged in transformative activity.
- The background story: as part of a personal development health programme, one school's leaders decided to ask a well-known, local Olympic sportswoman to address the students about training, nutrition and motivation. The address was a great success and was also attended by representatives from the local newspaper, who had been invited by the school. The newspaper staff listened to the talk, took photographs and undertook to publish an article in the near future. Understandingly, the students were excited by this but were quite disappointed a few days later when the article appeared. Rather than focussing on the content of the Olympian's address, the article referred only to the looks of the sportswoman and her sporting and mothering achievements. The accompanying photograph depicted her in a seductive pose by incorporating a bottom-up point of view while she sat on the school fence. The students critically analysed both the article and the photo and then decided to take action. They wrote to the journalist and the photographer and pointed out how the sportswoman had been positioned and marginalised. The newspaper replied and acknowledged that the article had, in fact, covered the story in the manner the students had described. The newspaper further acknowledged that the article could have been written more accurately and from a different perspective. The staff from the paper returned to the school, held further discussions with the students and then published an additional article in a later edition of the paper. There were a number of positive outcomes to this story.
    - The students learnt what taking action meant and what could be achieved by it.
    - The students engaged in responding from a critical literacy perspective.
    - The students also began to develop a concept of what the process of transformation entailed and how engaging with texts could achieve this.
    - The teacher was able to successfully scaffold and support the students through a complex process of responding to a particular situation.

    (What is interesting about this story is why the sportswoman allowed herself to be portrayed this way, or whether she actually realised how she was being constructed.)
- Have you ever been in a similar situation, in which you found yourself being manipulated or constructed in a particular way? You may remember contexts such as marketing, conducting business in a bank, a medical situation or a workplace setting.
- What was it about the context that you were not expecting?
- How were you constructed? In what ways did you feel you were being manipulated?
- How, and why, did you allow yourself to be constructed or manipulated?

Literacy identity

The students described in Reflection Strategy 2.7 reacted to the situation they found themselves in firstly by virtue of the teaching and learning that had taken place in their classroom after careful guidance by an expert teacher. This context has been described by Cope and Kalantzis (2000) as the domain of a school-based world. However, the school-based world of the classroom is influenced by the various backgrounds of the students. Students bring to school a range of experiences from their social and cultural life or what Cope and Kalantzis refer to as their lifeworld, that is, everything that happens to them outside of school. Barton, Hamilton and Ivanic (2000) suggested that these life experiences provide a repertoire of resources about literacy and literate practices that contribute to an individual's identity. Students then draw on these experiences and this identity to make meaning and to engage in literate practices.

The combination of the school-based world and lifeworld assists in the development of what Anstey and Bull (2004) termed a **literacy identity**. What students know, understand and can do with texts relies on their being aware of the resources and the literate practices that are available to them. These practices and resources can then be used by students in different and new ways when seeking new information or reviewing existing knowledge. Literacy identity then becomes a strategy to be used in interpreting knowledge learnt both in school and out of school and encourages students, and teachers, to draw on both domains. A student's literacy identity includes social and cultural resources, technological experiences, all previous life experiences as well as specific literacy knowledge. It is therefore critical that teachers demonstrate to students how to know and use their literacy identities. Teachers also need to be aware of the value of incorporating both school-based and lifeworlds in their planning. One way of accomplishing this is to share with students exactly how literacy identity can be represented. Figure 2.1 below illustrates in a graphic representation how this might look. It is important to realise that the language in Figure 2.1 below will need to be adjusted to suit the age of the students with which it is being shared.

Access to Figure 2.1 demonstrates to students in visual form that school-based knowledge represents only part of what they know. There needs to be explicit discussions with students about literacy identities and how they are formed. Examples of knowledge that has been gained from both school-based and lifeworlds can be shared. This then illustrates to students how literacy identities can be used, and how everyone's resources and experiences are different.

The concept of literacy identity is inextricably linked to being multiliterate and being critically literate. Students need to engage with a variety of texts (print, live, digital) and be consciously aware of the resources available to them. At the same time, they need to select resources and make judgements about the appropriateness of these resources for engaging in

Literacy identity
Life experiences provide a repertoire of resources about literacy and literate practices that contribute to an individual's literacy identity. Students bring to school a range of experiences from their social and cultural life, which is their lifeworld, that is, everything that happens to them outside of school. Those experiences that take place in classrooms, after careful guidance by a teacher, form the student's school-based world.

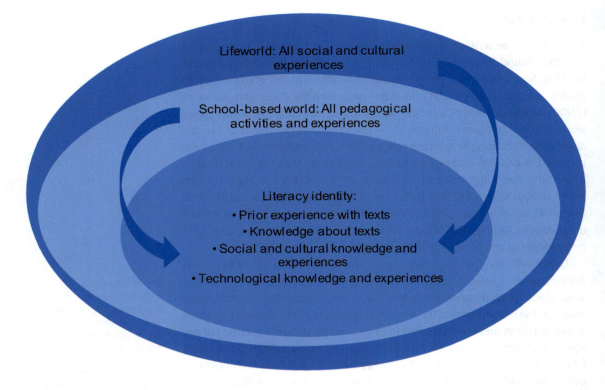

Figure 2.1 The concept of literacy identity

Adapted from Bull and Anstey (2010).

THEORY INTO PRACTICE 2.3

- The purpose of this Theory into Practice is to demonstrate how to use questioning and discussion to develop students' understandings about using their literacy identity as a resource for learning.
- Explain the concept of literacy identity to the students, using the graphic representation to illustrate the difference between school-based and life (out-of-school) worlds. A useful analogy to use with the students is the idea of literacy identity being a backpack or tool kit that is filled with experiences that are particular to each of them.
- Choose a text or task that is part of your current planning and discuss with the students what they already know about the text or task. Keep in mind that the text you choose can be paper, live or digital. Over a number of lessons there should be a balance of different types of texts. Identify similar tasks, texts or experiences that they have already undertaken. As they identify what they know, make a summary on the whiteboard and ask them to categorise each idea into either school-based or lifeworld experiences. Examine the list together and discuss the usefulness of each item and where it originated. Emphasise that all this information forms

part of their tool kit or backpack (literacy identity) and is a resource that they can draw upon. Referring to the graphic representation may assist students in this process.
- To guide the discussion, it may be helpful to use some of the following questions. These questions can be used by the teacher in discussion with the students or alternatively by the students themselves as they engage with a text.
    o   Where or when have you come across this topic or subject before? What did you do?
    o   What do you already know that might help?
    o   What else do you need to know or find out that might help you?
    o   Have you used a text like this before? How did you use it?
    o   What was your purpose for using the text?
    o   What prior experience from your tool kit (literacy identity) can help you here?
    o   Which semiotic systems were used in the construction of this text?
    o   Have you engaged with these semiotic systems in texts like this before? How does this help you?
    o   What is the purpose in using each semiotic system in the construction of the text?
    o   Have you used this technology or software, or something similar, before? How does that prior experience help you?

particular tasks. Students need to be constantly asking themselves, 'What do I know and what do I need to know?' This is a question that is also applicable to teachers. This raises further questions about which pedagogy is most suitable to implement and address multiliteracies, semiotic systems and critical literacy.

The Four Resource Model as a model for developing a pedagogy

One of the pedagogical approaches that has been used by teachers in many countries, particularly in the U.K., U.S. and Australia, has been what has become known as the Four Resource Model. The Four Resource Model became the major focus in a state-wide project, called *Literate Futures: Reading*, in the state of Queensland (Anstey 2002) and was later adopted throughout Australia. Originally Freebody and Luke (1990) and Freebody (1992) suggested four roles of the reader that were 'necessary but not sufficient' in a model of reading in a culture that was rich in texts. They posited that the four roles encapsulated a repertoire of capabilities that could address meaning making across a range of contexts. They developed the model in response to a prevailing idea at the time that literacy education could be defined as a unitary skill or model, essentially a psychological process, which could be applied in all contexts and to all individuals. Freebody and Luke disagreed with the idea that such a view of literacy could be judged as 'right' while alternative views could be considered 'wrong' – hence their use of the phrase 'necessary but not sufficient' when referring to the four roles of the reader.

Later Luke and Freebody (1999) and Freebody and Luke (2003) rejected the term 'role' because it suggested that it was something that an individual could play or adopt. This, coupled with their belief that literacy was a social process that was played out in a range of contexts, led them to adopt the term 'resources' rather than 'roles'. They also saw these resources being drawn from a range, or repertoire, of practices that could be accessed in the broader contexts of literacy events. Participants in these literacy events were then able 'to use or resource' (Freebody and Luke 2003, p. 56) the repertoire of resources. For this reason, the term *Four Resource Model* is used throughout this book instead of the *Four Resources Model* because it draws attention to the fact that students and teachers are using the model as a resource. The process of 'resourcing' has led to the popularisation of the expression, 'What is it that students need to know and be able to do', which was the original stimulus that led Freebody and Luke to develop the four roles of the reader.

The development of the Four Resource Model was based on the idea that effective literacy involved a repertoire of resources that could be drawn upon in order to engage in literate practices. Luke and Freebody (1999, 2000, 2003) proposed that these practices encompassed breaking the code of texts, participating in meaning making through texts, using texts functionally and critically analysing and transforming texts. These ideas led them to propose the four groups of practices that they called code breaker, meaning maker, text user and text analyst which could form the basis for developing literacy pedagogy, curriculum and assessment. Teachers could then extrapolate appropriate curriculum content and pedagogy that was flexible and could respond to change.

Code breaker

The practice of code breaking, put simply, means breaking the code of the text. Traditionally this practice focusses on the marks on the page and is referred to by a number of different terms, such as decoding, phonics, phonic analysis or phonic synthesis, knowledge of sounds and the alphabet and structural elements. Essentially it refers to transforming the written marks on a page into oral sounds when engaging with a print-based text. Given the discussions about multiliteracies and semiotic systems earlier in this chapter, it is necessary to go beyond considering only paper texts. Students and teachers are now required to 'decode' live and digital texts and be able to adapt, modify or recombine available resources to develop new practices. Since most, if not all, texts can be considered multimodal, students and teachers will need to decode live and digital texts, by accessing not just the Linguistic Semiotic System but also codes such as:

- facial expressions from the Gestural Semiotic System
- pitch, tone and volume from the Audio Semiotic System
- the positioning of participants from the Spatial Semiotic System
- colour from the Visual Semiotic System

Theory into Practice 2.4 provides a list of some generic questions (adapted from Bull and Anstey 2010) that could be used in supporting code breaker practices.

THEORY INTO PRACTICE 2.4

- This Theory into Practice aims to support the development of code breaker practices.
- Use a range of paper, live and digital texts over a series of lessons in discussing with students how to engage in code breaker practices. These discussions could involve asking the following questions as a way of scaffolding the discussion:
    o How do I crack this text?
    o How does the text work?
    o What do I know about texts like this one that might help me crack the code?
    o Is there more than one semiotic system operating here? If so, how do they relate to one another?
    o What are the codes and conventions employed in the text?
    o How do the different parts of the text relate to one another? (e.g. layout and organisation of the text)

Meaning maker

When engaging in meaning making practices, students (or teachers) employ their personal literacy identity. This enables participants to draw upon all the literate practices they have learnt as well as the social, cultural and technological resources they have at their disposal. These practices and resources enable individuals to detect literal and inferential meanings in the text. Meaning making practices are influenced by purpose and context. For example, one student may be reading a chapter about the Crimean War in order to uncover details about the conduct of the war, while another may be reading the same chapter to find out details about the life of Florence Nightingale. The specific details and inferences made by the two students will be quite different because of difference in purpose. The former student might be researching by him or herself, while the latter student might be investigating as part of a group. These two contexts will produce different results. Again, students will have to design or re-design new practices that will apply to the Gestural, Spatial, Audio and Visual Semiotic Systems as well as the traditional linguistic semiotic system. In order to successfully employ meaning making practices students will also need to engage in code breaking practices.

Theory into Practice 2.5 provides a list of some generic questions (adapted from Bull and Anstey 2010) that could be used in supporting meaning making practices.

THEORY INTO PRACTICE 2.5

- The purpose of this Theory into Practice is to support the development of meaning making practices.
- Use a range of paper, live and digital texts over a series of lessons in discussing with students how to engage in meaning making practices. These discussions could involve asking the following questions as a way of scaffolding the discussion. They will enable the reader to utilise his or her sociocultural background to identify the literal or inferred meaning of the text.
    o How will the purpose and context for my reading influence my meaning making?
    o What social, cultural, literate and technological resources do I have that might help me make meaning of this text?
    o How are the ideas in this text sequenced and connected and how does this affect the way I make meaning?
    o What are the other possible meanings and readings of this text?
- Here are two texts that can be used to lead discussions about meaning making.
    o Text One: Once upon a time, a long, long time ago there lived a king called Richard, whose lands ranged far and wide across the countryside…
    o Text Two: In the late 14th century, King Richard reigned over most of the lands that now form modern day England…
    o How do you predict each text will unfold?
    o What content do you expect to find in each text?
    o What is the purpose of each text?
    o In which context might each of the texts be used?

Text user

Text user practices are functional in that they are used in everyday situations to get something done. They involve negotiations around a text with others in service encounters in contexts such as shops, banks, post offices or hardware stores. These texts may also involve form-filling, application forms or booking tickets, which can be done online or face-to-face. They are often carried out in institutional settings such as schools, workplace, religious or medical situations. Participants need to draw on their literate, social, cultural and technological resources in order to engage in pragmatic practices in everyday interactions with service providers, friends, colleagues and family. In the school setting, text user practices often involve using literate practices in other discipline areas. Text user practices are dependent upon the use of meaning making and code breaking practices. Theory into Practice 2.6 provides a list of some generic questions (adapted from Bull and Anstey 2010) that could be used in supporting text user practices.

THEORY INTO PRACTICE 2.6

- The purpose of this Theory into Practice is to support the development of text user practices.
- Use a range of paper, live and digital texts over a series of lessons in discussing with students how to engage in text user practices. These discussions could involve asking the following questions as a way of scaffolding the discussion. They will enable the reader to utilise his or her sociocultural background to identify the functional aspect of the text. This enables the participant to identify the appropriate resources in order to use the text purposefully.
    o What is the purpose of this text and what is my purpose in using it?
    o How have the uses and purposes of this text shaped its production?
    o What should I do with this text in this context?
    o What could others do with this text?
- Have a number of blank forms that pairs of students will have to cooperate and negotiate with each other in order to fill in. After the forms have been filled in, ask the students to reflect on what resources and practices they employed.

Text analyst

Text analyst practices encompass the critical analysis of literate tasks and the texts that are the basis of those tasks. This analysis enables participants to make informed decisions about how to engage with texts and when, how and why to use them. An important feature of text analyst practices is understanding how texts construct and reconstruct perceptions of everyday life. Being a proficient text analyst allows individuals to have power over their lives and control over their futures. Text analyst practices incorporate the ability to critically analyse and transform texts and to decide what authority to accord particular texts and other participants. A text analyst understands the power that they have to create meanings from texts and the process of active, rather than passive, reading. With this type of reading comes the realisation that no text is neutral and that every text is shaped by the intensions, values, attitudes and beliefs of the author. Although the author produces the text, the consumer has the power to authorise it. As was suggested in the previous section on critical literacy, an important

THEORY INTO PRACTICE 2.7

- The purpose of this Theory into Practice is to support the development of text analyst practices.
- Collect a range of texts about a controversial issue, to be used in the classroom. Include digital as well as paper texts.
- Compare and contrast the different points of view expressed in each text.
- Discuss with the students how the different semiotic systems that have been incorporated into the texts have shaped the meaning.
- Discuss with the students what action they might take after engaging with the texts and how they have been transformed by the texts.
- These discussions could involve asking the following questions as a way of scaffolding the discussion:
    o How have you been shaped by this text?
    o What kind of person(s), with what interests, attitudes, values and beliefs, produced this text?
    o What are the origins of the text?
    o What is the producer of this text trying to make you believe or do?
    o What beliefs and positions are dominant in, or absent from, the text?
    o Who has been marginalised or silenced by the text?
    o What do you think about the way this text presents these ideas and what alternatives are there?
    o Having engaged with the text, what actions are you going to take?

AUDITING INSTRUMENT 2.3

- The purpose of this Auditing Instrument is to investigate how the four resources feature in your teaching.
- Do you include a range of the four resources in your teaching?
- Have you consciously planned for a particular balance of the four resources in your day-to-day teaching? How successful have you been?
- In what ways does your teaching of the four resources agree with, or diverge, from the whole school approaches that have been implemented?

feature of text analyst practices is taking action and engaging in transformation as a result of responding to texts. As with other practices, engagement in text analyst practices encompasses paper, live and digital texts and all five semiotic systems. The proliferation of multimodal texts and the central part that the internet and other social media plays in so many lives has substantially increased the importance of text analyst practices. Successful engagement in text analyst practices will only take place when code breaker, meaning maker and text user practices are conjointly used. Theory into Practice 2.7 provides a list of some generic questions (adapted from Bull and Anstey 2010) that could be used in supporting text analyst practices.

Further thoughts about the Four Resource Model

- The discussion in this chapter about the Four Resource Model has focussed on reading. It can also focus more broadly on literacy (Freebody and Luke 2003) and can be more specifically applied to listening, speaking, writing or viewing (Anstey and Bull 2004).
- When Freebody and Luke proposed the Four Resource Model they always thought of it as a possible model for literacy pedagogy, which is why they have continued to describe it as 'necessary but not sufficient'. Therefore, the model should not be seen as the 'correct' one, replacing all other approaches.
- The four practices of the Four Resource Model are not hierarchal. That is, code breaking is not easier than meaning making, nor is text user simpler than text analyst. Some have suggested that the code breaker and meaning maker practices should be taught in the primary/elementary school and the text user and text analyst practices should be taught at the secondary level. This is not the case. All four practices, with their associated resources, should be taught at all levels of schooling and across all disciplines.
- The four sets of practices should not be interpreted as separate entities. Ideally, they should be taught in relation to one another. This may not be possible when each set of practices is first introduced, but they should be taught in combination as soon as possible. This will ensure that there is a balance across all four sets of practices.
- The Four Resource Model is firmly situated in reading as a social process. This does not mean that knowledge, process and skills should be ignored but rather that they should be attended to when consideration is given to issues such as learner and community diversity and social, cultural and technological change. Literacy teaching and learning should therefore be embedded in real-life practices and should be taught explicitly.
- The Four Resource Model requires that emphasis be given to classroom talk and talk around text.
- The Four Resource Model can support both teachers and students in literacy teaching and learning. The generic questions that have been posed in this chapter for each of the four sets of practices can be equally supportive for both teacher and student learning.

Conclusion

The purpose of this chapter has been to explore the conditions that brought about changes in how literacy has come to be conceptualised. The chapter also explored how emerging conceptions of literacy increased understandings about what it is to be literate. These understandings led to the development of new literacies from which new forms of texts were created. The development of new text types led to a focus on multiliteracies and what it meant to be multiliterate. The focus on multiliteracies emphasised the crucial importance of critical literacy and the need to understand the concept of multimodality and the multimodal texts that evolved from these developments. Finally, the chapter addressed the question of a pedagogy of multiliteracies and the practices and resources that were associated with it.

Bibliography

Anstey, M 2002, *Literate Futures: Reading*, Department of Education, State of Queensland, Australia.

Anstey, M 2009, 'Multiliteracies: the conversation continues: What do we really mean by "multiliteracies" and why is it important?' *Reading Forum*, vol. 24, no. 1, pp. 5-15.

Anstey, M & Bull, G 2004, *The Literacy Labyrinth*, 2nd edn, Pearson, Sydney.

Anstey M & Bull, G 2006, *Teaching and Learning Multiliteracies: Changing Times, Changing Literacies*, International Reading Association, Newark.

Barton, D, Hamilton, M & Ivanic, R 2000, *Situated Literacies: Reading and Writing in Context*, Routledge, London.

Bean, TW & Dunkerly-Bean, J 2015, 'Expanding conceptions of adolescent literacy research and practice: Cosmopolitan theory in educational contexts', *Australian Journal of Language and Literacy*, vol. 38, no. 1, pp. 46-54.

Bernstein, B 1960, 'Language and social class' in *Class, Codes and Control, Vol. 1, Theoretical studies towards a sociology of language*, Routledge and Kegan Paul, London.

Bernstein, B 1961, 'Social structure, language and learning', *Educational Research*, vol. 3, pp. 163-76.

Bernstein, B 1962a, 'Linguistic codes, hesitation phenomena and intelligence', in *Class, Codes and Control, Vol. 1, Theoretical studies towards a sociology of language*, Routledge and Kegan Paul, London.

Bernstein, B 1962b, 'Social class, linguistic codes and grammatical elements', in *Class, Codes and Control, Vol. 1, Theoretical studies towards a sociology of language*, Routledge and Kegan Paul, London.

Bernstein, B 1964, 'Elaborated and restricted codes: Their origins and some consequences', in Ethnography and Speech, Monograph Issue of *American Anthropologist*, March.

Bernstein, B 1971, *Class, Codes and Control, Vol. 1, Theoretical studies towards a sociology of language*, Routledge, London.

Bernstein, B 1973, *Class, Codes and Control, Vol. 2, Applied studies towards a sociology of language*, Routledge, London.

Bernstein, B 1975, *Class, Codes and Control, Vol. 3, Towards a theory of educational transmission*, Routledge, London.

Bernstein, B 1990, *Class, Codes and Control, Vol. 4, The structuring of pedagogical discourse*, Routledge, London.

Bezemer, J & Kress, G 2016, *Multimodality, Learning and Communication: A Social Semiotic Frame*, Routledge, London.

Bull, G & Anstey, M 2010, *Evolving Pedagogies: Reading and Writing in a Multimodal World*, Education Services Australia, Carlton South.

Bull, G & Anstey, M 2013, *Uncovering History Using Multimodal Literacies: An Inquiry Process*, Education Services Australia, Carlton South.

Carrington, V & Robinson, M (eds) 2009, *Digital Literacies: Social Learning and Classroom Practices*, SAGE, London.

Cazden, CB 1967, 'On individual differences in language competence and performance', *Journal of Special Education*, vol. 1, pp. 135-150.

Cazden, CB 1970, 'The situation: a neglected source of social class differences in language use', *Journal of Social Issues*, vol. 26, no. 2, pp. 35-60.

Cazden, CB 1972, *Child Language and Education*, Holt, Rinehart and Winston, New York.

Cope, B & Kalantzis, M 2000 (eds), *Multiliteracies: Literacy Learning and the Design of Social Futures*, Routledge, London.

D'warte, J 2014, 'Exploring linguistic repertoires: Multiple language use and multimodal literacy activity in five classrooms', *Australian Journal of Language and Literacy*, vol. 37, no. 1, pp. 21-30.

Dyson, AH 2003, *The Brothers and Sisters Learn to Write: Popular Literacies in Childhood and School Cultures*, Teachers College Press, New York.

Edwards-Groves, C, Anstey, M & Bull, G 2014, *Classroom Talk: Understanding Dialogue, Pedagogy and Practice*, Primary English Teaching Association Australia (PETAA), Sydney.

Fisher, R, Brooks, G & Lewis, M (eds) 2002, *Raising Standards in Literacy*, Routledge, London.

Freebody, P 1992, 'A socio-cultural approach: Resourcing four roles as a literacy learner', in A Watson & A Badenhop (eds), *Prevention of Reading Failure*, Ashton-Scholastic, Sydney, pp. 48-60.

Freebody, P & Ludwig, C 1998, *Talk and Literacy in Schools and Homes*, Commonwealth of Australia, Canberra.

Freebody, P & Luke, A 1990, 'Literacies programs: Debates and demands in cultural contexts', *Prospect: Australian Journal of TESOL*, vol. 5, no. 7, pp. 7-16.

Freebody, P & Luke, A 2003, 'Literacy as engaging with new forms of life: The Four Roles Model' in G Bull & M Anstey (eds), *The Literacy Lexicon*, 2nd edn, Pearson, Frenchs Forest.

Gee, J P 1990, *Social Linguistics and Literacies: Ideology in Discourses*, Falmer Press, London.

Gee, J P 1992, *The Social Mind: Language, Ideology and Social Practice*, Bergin & Garvey, New York.

Gee, J P 2004, *Situated Language and Learning: A Critique of Traditional Schooling*, Routledge, New York.

Gutierrez, K D 2008, 'Developing a sociocritical literacy in the third space', *Reading Research Quarterly*, vol. 43, no. 2, pp. 148-64.

Habermas, J 1970, 'A theory of communicative competence', *Inquiry*, vol. 13, pp. 360-75.

Hansen, D T 2014, 'Theme issue: Cosmopolitanism as cultural creativity: New modes of educational practice in globalizing times', *Curriculum Inquiry*, vol. 44, no. 1, pp. 1-14.

Heath, SB 1983, *Ways with Words: Language, Life and Work in Communities and Classrooms*, Cambridge University Press, Cambridge.

Hull, G & Schultz, K (eds) 2002, *School's Out! Bridging Out-of-School Literacies with Classroom Practices*, Teachers College Press, New York.

Hull, GA & Stornaiulo, A 2010, 'Cosmopolitan literacies, social networks, and 'proper distance': Striving to understand in a global world', *Curriculum Inquiry*, vol. 44, no. 1, pp. 15–44.

Janks, H 2010, *Literacy and Power*, Routledge, London.

Jewitt, C 2006, *Technology, Literacy, Learning: A Multimodal Approach*, Routledge, London.

Jewitt, C, Bezemer, J & O'Halloran, K 2016, *Introducing Multimodality*, Routledge, London.

Kalantzis, M, Cope, B, Chan, E & Dalley-Trim, L 2016, *Literacies*, 2nd edn, Cambridge University Press, Cambridge.

Kress, G 2003, *Literacy in the New Media Age*, Routledge, London.

Kress, G & van Leeuwen, T 2001, *Multimodal Discourse: The Modes and Media of Contemporary Communication*, Arnold, London.

Kress, G & van Leeuwen, T 2006, *Reading Images: The Grammar of Visual Design*, 2nd edn, Routledge, London.

Labov, W 1966, *The Social Stratification of English in New York City*, Center for Applied Linguistics, Washington, DC.

Labov, W 1969a, 'The logic of nonstandard English', in N Keddie (ed.), *Tinker, Tailor: The Myth of Cultural Deprivation*, Penguin, Melbourne, pp. 21–66.

Labov, W 1969b, 'A Study of Non-Standard English', Center for Applied Linguistics, Washington, DC.

Lankshear, C & Knobel, M 2003, *New Literacies: Changing Knowledge and Classroom Practice*, Open University Press, Buckingham.

Lankshear, C & Knobel, M 2006, *New Literacies: Everyday Practices and Classroom Learning*, 2nd edn, McGraw Hill/Open University Press, Maidenhead.

Lankshear, C & Lawler, M 1987, *Literacy, Schooling and Revolution*, Falmer Press, London.

Lawton, D 1968, *Social Class, Language and Education*, Routledge and Kegan Paul, London.

Littleton, K & Mercer, N 2013, *Interthinking: Putting Talk to Work*, Routledge, London.

Lo Bianco, J 2000, 'Multiliteracies and multilingualism', in B Cope & M Kalantzis, *Multiliteracies: Literacy Learning and the Design of Social Futures*, Routledge, London, pp. 92–105.

Luke, A 1993, 'The social construction of literacy in the primary school', in L Unsworth (ed), *Literacy Learning and Teaching*, Macmillan, Melbourne.

Luke, A 2004, 'Teaching after the market: From commodity to cosmopolitanism', *Teachers College Record*, vol. 106, no. 7, pp. 1422–43.

Luke, A & Carrington, V 2004, 'Globalisation, literacy, curriculum practice' in T Grainger (ed), *The Routledge Falmer Reader in Language and Literacy*, Routledge Falmer, New York, pp. 52–66.

Luke, A & Freebody, P 1999, *Further Notes on the Four Resources Model*, viewed 21 March 2017, http://kingstonnetworknumandlitteam.wikispaces.com/file/view/Further+Notes+on+the+Four+Resources+Model-Allan+Luke.pdf.

Luke, A & Freebody, P 2000, *Literate Futures: Report of the Review for Queensland State Schools*, Education Queensland, Brisbane.

Luke, A, Comber, B & Grant, H 2003, 'Critical literacies and cultural studies', in G Bull & M Anstey, (eds) *The Literacy Lexicon*, 2nd edn, Pearson, Frenchs Forest, pp. 15–35.

Morrell, E 2008, *Critical Literacy and Urban Youth: Pedagogies of Access, Dissent and Liberation*, Routledge, London.

Poole, ME 1972, 'Social class differences in code elaboration: A study of written communication at the tertiary level', *Australian and New Zealand Journal of Sociology*, vol. 8, pp. 46–55.

Rymer, R 2012, 'Vanishing voices', *National Geographic*, July, vol. 222, no. 1, pp. 60–93.

Williams, F & Naremore, RC 1969, 'Social class differences in children's syntactic performance: A quantitative analysis of field study data', *Journal of Speech and Hearing Research*, vol. 12, pp. 777–93.

Yamada-Rice, D 2010, 'Beyond words: An enquiry into children's home visual communication practices', *Journal of Early Childhood Literacy*, vol. 10, no. 3, pp. 341–63.

3 Communicating through multimodal texts and semiotic systems

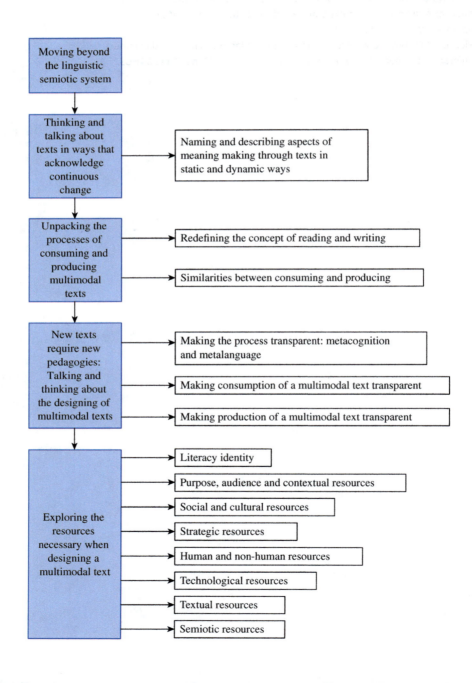

The evolving definitions of literacy and the reasons behind these changes in definition were explored in Chapters One and Two. It has been established that the social, cultural and technological influences on literacy mean that it will continue to change and that it is more appropriate to use the term *multiliteracies* in the educational context. This is because its definition acknowledges the multifaceted and multimodal nature of literacy, and includes the capacities to cope with change and participate in all aspects of society. The concept of multiliteracies supports the development of independent persons who are able to take control of and design their futures in response to change. These characteristics are often identified as the goals of education, hence the preference for the term *multiliteracies* in educational contexts.

In this chapter the focus is on unpacking the multimodal nature of text and how it changes the ways in which text might be thought about, how it is produced and consumed, and therefore how it compels a reconceptualisation of the processes of reading and writing. The knowledge, skills and processes necessary to communicating with multimodal texts now, and in the future, will be discussed in detail, together with the pedagogies to assist in their development. This will include further reference to the Four Resource Model, which was introduced in Chapter Two, together with specific information about the five semiotic systems.

Moving beyond the Linguistic Semiotic System

In Chapter Two the origins of the word *text* were described as being derived from the Latin *textus*, meaning 'tissue', and *texere*, meaning 'weave'. It was proposed that the concept of text as weaving a tissue of meaning was an appropriate metaphor since it suggests the weaving together of a combination of signs and symbols (semiotic systems) in order to convey meaning through a multimodal text. As Kress (2010, p. 6) determined, in the past three decades the ways in which meaning making is represented and disseminated has changed due to the range of technologies and semiotic systems available. Previously meaning making focussed more on consumption because the new technologies of production were not so widely available, and therefore the production of texts was limited to those who had access to those technologies. However, now, with greater availability, accessibility, connectivity and mobility, the focus has moved to production and design. As Kress (2010, p. 22) stated, 'much is produced for an unknown and potentially vast group.' For example, uploading on YouTube, creating wikis and blogs and using social media such as Twitter and Facebook enables the production and dissemination of a huge range of multimodal texts for meaning making. However, as Kress asserted, the audience of these posts is potentially far greater than the person who created and posted the text may have intended. There is also the possibility that the meaning making of these vast audiences may be different from that which was originally intended. There are several reasons for this, for example, as discussed previously, the cultural and social background and experiences of those viewing and reading these multimodal texts may predispose them to read and interpret the text in a particular way. However, it may also be that their knowledge and experience of interpreting the complexity of multimodal texts that employ several semiotic systems may be more or less than that of the person or persons who created the text. It is imperative that a multiliterate person now and in the future has knowledge of the semiotic systems and the ways in which meaning making is produced and consumed in multimodal texts to ensure that the plethora of available texts are able to communicate their intended meanings.

There is a tendency among those who did not grow up in the multimodal, technologically complex world of the 21st century to assume that because students use technology and social media to consume and produce texts they are already literate with multimodal texts. This is a dangerous assumption, which, if used to inform the teaching of literacy in schools (consciously or unconsciously), could mean that students of the future do not acquire the skills, knowledge and processes that they will need to remain literate in an increasingly complex and changing world. As Littleton and Mercer (2013, p. 63) point out, the computer, technology, app or software are the tools, and will not ensure clear communication; it is how they are used that does that. For example, when producing or consuming a multimodal text, students need a basic knowledge of the semiotic systems currently used, their codes and conventions, together with an understanding of what to consider when combining them in a multimodal text. They also need to know how to make informed selections regarding technology and dissemination of texts when consuming or producing them.

THEORY INTO PRACTICE 3.1

- The purpose of this Theory into Practice task is to find out to what extent the assertions made regarding students' multimodal literacy in the preceding paragraph apply to the students in your class. Of particular interest will be how well they can articulate their answers, that is, whether they have an adequate vocabulary to talk about multimodal texts and how explicit they can be when talking about how they produced or consumed a multimodal text.
- Use the following questions as the basis of a discussion with your students regarding their knowledge about producing multimodal texts. You may need to use the word *writing* if they are not used to the term *producing*.
    - Have you created and posted a multimodal text on the internet, e.g. YouTube, Twitter, Facebook?
    - How did you go about creating this text? (How much of their explanation is to do with the technological aspects of creating the text and how much is to do with actually creating the meaning?)
    - What semiotic systems did you use when you created the text, Visual, Linguistic, Audio, Gestural and Spatial? (Do students consider that, when posting an image of themselves or a group of friends doing something, both visual and gestural are used? Do they consider any linguistic additions such as comments, labelling, describing?)
    - Why did you use those semiotic systems and not others?

- o Why did you post this text – what was your purpose?
- o Who did you post this text for – who was your intended audience?
- o Will others have access to this text? Had you thought about this when posting it? How do you feel about this, having thought about it?
- Repeat the discussion, focussing on their consumption of multimodal texts by modifying the previous questions.
- Ask the students to reflect on the discussion in terms of how much they know about multimodal texts and how they consume and produce them. Discuss how this knowledge might help them make meaning when producing or consuming texts.

While it is generally the case that students these days spend a lot of time using technology as a form of communication and meaning making, it may be that they still perceive 'reading' as largely about paper text. Rennie and Patterson (2010, pp. 211–219) reported on research they conducted in an investigation of the range of students' reading habits in Australia. They concluded that students did not recognise reading on computers, mobile phones, magazines or newspapers as 'reading'. The students perceived reading as something done with thick books, novels and large amounts of paper text. Rennie and Patterson concluded that the students' perception of what counts as reading was shaped by what was happening at school; that is, reading at school was largely done with paper text and the actual teaching of reading practices and strategies was done with paper text. Given that much of the reading students do now, and will do in the future, involves multimodal texts delivered via both paper and digital technologies, this research indicates that it is imperative that teaching about multimodal texts and their semiotic systems, as well as the processes involved in producing and consuming them, is incorporated into the school literacy programme. A balance among texts delivered via paper, live and digital technologies should also be ensured. Furthermore, it is important that the programme is connected to students' lifeworld to ensure transfer of knowledge skills and processes between lifeworld and school world. (See the discussion of Literacy Identity in Chapter Two, particularly Figure 2.1.)

Thinking and talking about texts and literacy in ways that acknowledge continuous change

The research of Rennie and Patterson together with the discussion about Literacy Identity, lifeworld and school world in Chapter Two is a timely reminder regarding the need to think carefully about how literacy is planned, taught and practiced in classrooms. The ways in which literacy and texts are discussed in class, together with the texts used and the tasks engaged in with texts, shape students' perceptions about texts, what counts as literacy and the purposes for which literacy is used.

One of the issues that has been continuously addressed in the preceding chapters is the fact that literacy and texts will continue to change, and that an important aspect of developing multiliteracies is to enable students to cope with change. Therefore, it is important that the ways in which the characteristics and components of texts are named, engaged with and talked about in the classroom acknowledges change as normal. As Jewitt and Kress (2008 pp. 9-10) stated, the semiotic systems in multimodal texts are a social and cultural construct. That is, their codes and conventions have their origins in the agreed upon ways people have used them and these ways may vary among social and cultural groups. For example, within the Visual Semiotic System the cultural associations of red and white are good examples. While red might be associated with danger in some cultures, it is associated with wedding celebrations in others. In other cultures, wedding celebrations focus on white, and in some Pacific cultures white is used as a mark of respect when a death occurs in a community and during funeral services. Drawing on the ideas of Jewitt and Kress (2008) and Jewitt (2009), it follows that if the codes and conventions are regarded as 'rules' (as they were in traditional approaches to teaching the grammar of the linguistic semiotic system), then the social and cultural basis or agency of people in the design of texts becomes lost and a static or a 'frozen in time' concept of literacy is promulgated. This approach discourages students from understanding and embracing change and realising their agency and role in designing texts as a consumer (reader) and producer (writer), both now and in the future.

Naming and describing aspects of meaning making through texts in static and dynamic ways

Kress (2010) suggested that there are static and dynamic ways of understanding, naming and describing text. He discussed these contrasting ideas about text in a series of metaphors that examined the concepts associated with the processes of creating and making meaning of a text. He concluded that the most appropriate and forward looking way of describing the processes of representing and communicating ideas through text (meaning making) was to think of it as design. The idea of design being at the centre of meaning making was also shared by Cope and Kalantzis (2000) and Kalantzis et al. (2016). Kress's discussion of metaphors around text arose from a concern that the terms used for describing and talking about text may create particular ways of viewing text, for example, a view of text being static, unchanging and governed by an entrenched set of rules. The implication is that, if particular terms are used without discussion and reflection when teaching about text, it can encourage ways of understanding text that are not useful to students who are, and will continue to be, producing and consuming texts in a changing world. That is, similar to the students who thought that reading was only associated with engagement with large amounts of paper text at school, these ways of talking about text could engender a static, rule-based idea about texts.

Drawing upon Kress's metaphors, Figure 3.1 has been created to encourage reflection about ways of talking about the processes and decision-making during text production and consumption. A commentary is provided at the right and should be read in conjunction with reading and viewing the figure.

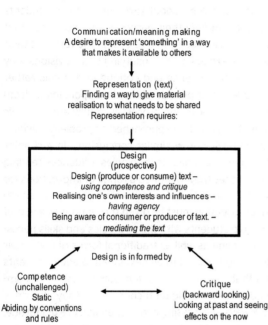

Commentary: to be read in conjunction with viewing Figure 3.1

- The use of the term Design is central to the figure. It is a term that denotes *active processing, problem-solving and invention* in order to achieve *a purpose or outcome*. Therefore, it constructs the production and consumption of text as *dynamic*, that is, a forward looking, (prospective), inventive process. Design also means the consumer/producer must have *agency* and realise the need to *mediate* the text in order to achieve the desired purpose.
- Communication/meaning Making indicates this figure refers to both the *production and consumption of text*. It also reinforces the *purpose* of producing and consuming texts.
- Representation indicates the *use of all available resources* to produce or consume the text in order *to achieve* a communicative or meaning making *purpose*, for example, consideration of semiotic systems, cultural and social influences, available technologies, lifeworld and school world knowledge and experiences.
- The producer's or consumer's competence and critique are processes that inform designing. The multiple double headed arrows indicate this process can be *cyclic* – that is, it may need to be *reviewed, combined and recombined in multiple ways and multiple times* to inform a design that will *achieve the desired purpose*.
- Competence refers to existing knowledge about texts, technology, semiotic systems, their codes and conventions. In a changing world, this knowledge may or may not be useful in its current state. If it is talked about and thought about only *as competence, and is not challenged*, then it encourages a *static* view of knowledge: that it cannot evolve, be modified or used in different ways when designing. *Competence is necessary, but not sufficient; it must be thought about and used in dynamic ways.*
- Critique refers to *examining* previous designs, ways of designing, and use of resources. It involves *reviewing* how previous designs, ways of designing and use of resources, have succeeded in achieving particular purposes *in particular contexts* and how they would succeed in achieving *the current purpose now*. It involves *looking backward, critically, in order to be able to look forward* and design.

Figure 3.1 Text and design: Encouraging talk about texts as dynamic rather than static

The purpose of Figure 3.1 is to emphasise the dynamic nature of producing and consuming text. If students are to be multiliterate, able to cope with change and have agency in their futures, then all aspects of text and designing text must be thought about and talked about as dynamic. Having knowledge, skills, processes and strategies that are useful now, means students are competent in today's world with its associated ways of being literate. For example, they may be able to use their knowledge of the linguistic grammar and combine it with other semiotic systems to create a multimodal text that can be viewed by others on a particular piece of software and disseminated via the internet. Similarly, they may be able to use research skills online to find and view a film clip and use the five semiotic systems to critically analyse the text and find information about a topic they are researching. Students may have what is necessary now, but it may not be sufficient for the future. In the future, that software may be obsolete, the internet may have morphed into some other form of communication and the linguistic grammar and other semiotic systems may have new conventions and codes. There may even be other semiotic systems. This is not to say the students' current knowledge, skills and processes are not important – *they are necessary, but not sufficient*. They need to be taught and talked about as resources that are dynamic and that may change. These resources may need to be modified or used in new ways, in order to produce or consume a text to achieve a particular purpose in the future. The process of critique, that is, the review and consideration of these resources and their capabilities for particular purposes in particular contexts, must be part of talking about text. For example, students may examine texts that work well and fulfil their purposes and also those that don't, and consider why this is the case. They could re-design the text that their critique reveals does not work well, explaining and justifying their revisions. Any teaching about text must balance competence and critique in dynamic rather than static ways. Learning episodes must provide authentic opportunities from students' lifeworlds to use knowledge, skills and processes in new and dynamic ways. Producing and consuming texts must be approached as problem-solving.

Hartman, Morsink and Zheng (2010) drew similar conclusions. In a chapter examining how the move from paper to digital technologies influences reading and reading comprehension processes they identified a range of implications for education. They suggested that the ways in which lessons are planned needs to be reviewed and that continuous attention must be given throughout all levels of schooling to the best ways to equip students with the strategies and skills necessary to access and comprehend online as well as traditional forms of text. Their concern was that effective pedagogy needed to be developed to equip students with self-regulation strategies that support the problem-solving nature of comprehending multimodal texts delivered via digital technologies. They also drew attention to the need to rethink ways of assessing comprehension in a digital age. Hartman, Morsink and Zheng (2010 pp. 153–4) were concerned that comprehension assessment, particularly that associated with state, national and worldwide testing, such as NAPLAN in Australia and the international PISA testing, must assess reading comprehension of text delivered by both traditional and digital technologies and that it must assess beyond a narrow set of skills or tools used in particular technologies such as email. Their concern was that the more complex skills and processes associated with reading multimodal texts and on-line texts, that involve higher level thinking skills (for example, breaking down a problem, synthesising and communicating results) were not being addressed. They noted that in 2009, PISA assessments for 15-year-olds in 22 of the 67 countries included a section on reading electronic texts. Fortunately, there has been some further development in assessment since then; however, developing assessment of processes and the strategic use of skills and processes with multimodal and digital text are challenging in large scale testing.

The concerns of Kress together with those of Hartman et al., have implications for planning and assessment at the classroom level. It is important to consider how not only lesson planning and pedagogy, but also assessment, can influence students' perceptions about what constitutes being literate and whether 'being literate' is a static or dynamic state. If our discussions about consuming and producing texts focus on the dynamic, but assess it in static ways, then there is pedagogical dissonance, resulting in mixed and potentially confusing messages to students. Just as there needs to be balance in teaching, so there needs to be balance in assessment. For example, it is necessary to assess whether students understand and can identify particular codes and conventions in a text (that is, their competence with a particular semiotic system). This would be static assessment. However, it is also necessary to assess whether they can provide an explanation of the appropriateness of a code and how that code contributes to achieving the purpose of the text (assessing their ability to use knowledge to critique, specifically, what they know about the links between representation and purpose as part of producing and consuming text). This assessment focusses on the dynamic aspects of text and design. Both types of assessment are necessary to a dynamic view of text and design.

REFLECTION STRATEGY 3.1

- The purpose of this Reflection Strategy is to review your current teaching and assessment around text in terms of whether it focusses more toward a static or dynamic view of text and design.
- Examine your planning and assessment items regarding reading comprehension and consider the following questions:
   - What is the balance of skills and processes among the learning focus/goals of your learning episodes? That is, does your planning emphasise the process of comprehension (meaning making) with multimodal texts, as well as the necessary skills? For example, do you teach the linguistic grammar and the structure of different texts, such as reports or narrative, but fail to discuss how this knowledge is useful and is applied when reading a text?
   - How do you assess reading comprehension? Do you use assessment tasks and strategies that enable you to assess how students go about comprehending a text – that is, that show you their thinking processes, the resources they draw upon?
   - Do you plan for, and talk, about the process of comprehension and meaning making as problem-solving and model this process?
   - Replan one of your recent lessons with a view to emphasising both skills and process.
   - Try to identify ways of assessing students' thinking processes as well as their skills.

Unpacking the processes of consuming and producing multimodal texts

Redefining the concept of reading and writing

Teaching and learning about multimodal texts and the semiotic systems within them in dynamic ways necessitates an understanding of how texts are produced and consumed. The terms *producing* and *consuming* have been adopted rather than *writing* and reading because they better describe the ways in which meaning making and communicating is represented with multimodal texts. Describing a multimodal text as 'written' predisposes thinking to a linguistic text conveyed by paper, because of the historical associations of the word 'writing'. The reality of multimodal texts is that they are produced for particular purposes, audiences and contexts, through the combination of at least two semiotic systems, often by a group of people, each contributing particular expertise. They are disseminated by a range of technologies, sometimes several, simultaneously. For example, an advertisement may be prepared for a new car and the text to be produced and released simultaneously may include print (for magazine and newspaper), film (for television and online) and audio (for radio). The same core text may be used, but parts of it modified, re-combined and used for different audiences and contexts, and the different technologies by which it will be disseminated. Stills may be taken from the film and combined with written language for print and magazine. The same written text (language) and music may be taken from the film and remixed as audio and sound for radio. A team would be involved in the production of these texts, each having different expertise. The team may include a combination of people from both the car manufacturer and an advertising agency, possibly including marketing experts, graphic designers, film-makers and copywriters. At a simpler level, in the area of journalism two journalists may combine research to co-write an article and then work with a photographer or graphic artist to identify and source appropriate visual material. The finished piece may be disseminated on-line and by paper. For example, in Australia the ABC News website will often have written versions of the news and other documentary style programmes presented on television at other times, complete with stills of the visual material to be presented. This is common practice across the world.

Teaching and learning about the production of a text as something that is written, complete and finite, never to be **redesigned** and disseminated in different ways, is simply not appropriate or reflective of current practices of communication. Yet often this is how 'writing' is presented to students in the classroom. In order to reflect current and possible futures in the production of text, students must have opportunities to learn and practice how to produce texts independently, in groups and for different audiences and technologies. The problem-solving and collaborative nature of **producing** multimodal texts for authentic purposes and contexts must be foregrounded. Excellent examples of how real contexts can be found to provide these opportunities for student to talk around, consume and produce text for authentic purposes and audiences can be found in the work of Silvers and Shorey (2012). In their book *Many Texts, Many Voices*, they detailed how linking literacy and social justice can provide real contexts for students to talk around text and work together collaboratively to achieve a real goal.

Similar to producing, consuming is used to describe the reading process because once again the term *reading* has historical associations with the written word and paper technology. Consuming a multimodal text requires meaning making for a particular purpose in a particular context, for example, searching for information on the internet, using instructions to assemble a bookcase or reading a novel for pleasure. It requires attending to multiple semiotic systems, their codes and conventions, and working out what meaning each conveys and contributes to the meaning making. In addition, decisions must be made related

Redesign/Redesigning
The combining, recombining and reworking of the selected resources to consume or produce a unique multimodal text.

Producing
Engagement in the design and creation of a multimodal text, together with the selection of an appropriate means of dissemination, that will fulfil a particular communicative purpose, for a specific audience and context. May involve collaboration with others to access specific, needed expertise.

to the reading purpose and context, about how to engage with the text and what parts to focus upon. It is also necessary to understand how to process different technologies; for example, searching online for information will require different skills and ways of processing information to reading a novel for pleasure (whether the novel is paper or an eBook). While traditionally, consuming a text may be seen as an activity that is done in isolation and is often taught that way, in reality multimodal texts are often consumed during interaction with others. At the simplest level people are often seen sharing websites, Facebook posts, images and accompanying text on mobile phones during a conversation over coffee in a café. At a more complex level conversations around text may occur over contracts in a bank or real estate transaction. In workplaces people may work together to solve a computer glitch by Googling it online, discussing which sites to access from the search results, viewing them and then conversing about whether that helps or not and how they might refine the search. In leisure activities people who belong to book clubs come together to discuss a novel they are reading. **Consuming** text is an active and interactive process that involves problem-solving, planning, revising strategies, sharing, listening and responding. Even when reading in isolation, readers have a conversation with themselves as they redesign what they are consuming in ways that suit their purpose in making meaning of the text.

Consuming
Making meaning with multimodal text in order to fulfil a particular purpose, in a particular context. It may involve interaction with others to achieve the purpose. The text may be disseminated via a range of technologies.

Similarities between consuming and producing

While producing and consuming are different acts, they involve many of the same processes. Both are dynamic and involve continuous interpretation, shaping and reshaping, as representations of meaning are processed, designed and redesigned. Both potentially involve interaction with others as resources in the process of production or consumption. Both require drawing upon and using multiple resources in order to fulfil a specific purpose in, or for, a specific context. The notion that producing and consuming (or writing and reading) involve similar processes is not new. In the 1980s, when a focus on the writing process informed the teaching of writing (sometimes referred to as 'process writing') a cycle of stages and thinking for this process was identified. Anstey and Bull (2004) examined the similarities between the writing process and the reading process using figures similar to those presented in Figure 3.2. While these figures nominally addressed the advent of digital literacies and multimodal texts, they did not adequately reflect the dynamic nature of producing and consuming multimodal texts, the multiple technologies for dissemination of texts and the interactive nature of the production and consumption processes, in a changing world.

Although these representations of the reading and writing processes are no longer satisfactory, they do focus on understandings about the processes involved in reading and writing, emphasising that reading and writing as processes involve higher order thinking skills and problem-solving. They also draw attention to the range of knowledge, skills and thinking processes necessary to engage successfully in reading and writing. Comparison of the

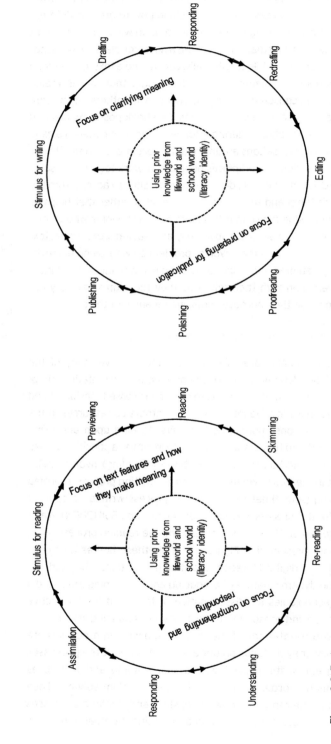

Figure 3.2 Early comparisons of the writing and reading processes

two processes reinforces the fact that many of the higher order thinking skills used in the different stages of each cycle are the same. For example, both re-reading and editing require critical reflection and evaluation, while previewing and drafting both require analysis and **synthesising** that aids in refining the purpose of the reading and writing task. The recursive nature of the processes also indicates that the producer and consumer of multimodal texts will need to engage in self-regulation, monitoring progress and rethinking, modifying or recombining strategies as necessary.

Synthesising
The ability to engage in the processes necessary to move back and forth among a repertoire of resources, including semiotic systems, to make or represent meaning.

Other investigations of the consumption and production of multimodal texts in the context of multiliteracies by Anstey (2002), Anstey and Bull (2004) Kress and van Leeuwen (2001, 2006), Kress (2003, 2010), Bearne and Wolstencroft (2007) and Kalantzis et al. (2016) focus on the concept of design as the major influence on the process. Figure 3.3, and the discussion following, combine and interpret these ideas in a way that emphasises the

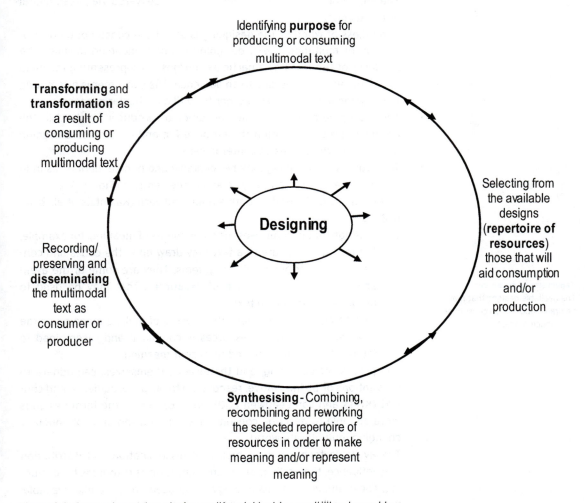

Figure 3.3 Consuming and producing multimodal text in a multiliterate world

dynamic nature of the process of consuming or producing text in a multiliterate world. It also acknowledges how the consumers' or producers' unique literacy identities influence both the process and the communicative outcome.

The following points elaborate the concepts underpinning Figure 3.3 and should be read while viewing and processing it:

- The consumer or producer of the multimodal text has a purpose for engaging in the design process. Their designing will be influenced by:
  o the audience, which will be themselves if they are consuming the text, but if producing the text the audience will be others
  o the context in which the designing takes place
  o the literacy identity of the audience, that is, the consumer or producer of the text.
- The multimodal text being designed may be delivered via paper, digital or live technologies.
- Regardless of whether the designing is about the consumption or production of multimodal text, designing is about meaning making. The producer of the text has a particular purpose in representing meaning to communicate a message to an audience. The consumer is attempting to make meaning of a text in order to fulfil a particular purpose.
- There may be more than one consumer or producer involved in the designing process as often the purpose for, and process of, designing necessitates the process, be interactive.
- The process of designing may be recursive and non-sequential, as indicated by the arrows on the cycle and in the centre of Figure 3.3.
- The term *design* is used as both a noun and verb (Kalantzis et al. 2016, p. 221):
  o A design (noun) comprises the components of meaning, for example, the form or structure of a text may draw upon the codes and conventions of various semiotic systems. They are some of the available designs, or **repertoire of resources**, that may be used to produce or consume a text.
  o 'Designing' (verb) describes the process of making meaning as the selected repertoire of resources is combined and recombined to interpret, communicate and represent meaning.
- The process of designing, and the designs themselves, can adhere to conventions or be innovative, responding to purpose, audience and context (Kress and van Leeuwen 2001, pp. 5–6). Hence the term *design* is more suitable to describe consuming and producing in a continuously changing multiliterate world.
- The available technology or means of dissemination and distribution may influence, that is, limit or expand, selection of resources for designing. For example, if the technology to be used has no audio available, then other semiotic systems will have to be used to make meaning.

Repertoire of resources
The available designs that may be drawn upon when consuming or producing a text.

- Dissemination of a text may include technical preservation (as in a work of art) or recording (as in a live performance) leaving a trace that becomes an archive of available designs and resources for the future (Kress and van Leeuwen 2001, pp. 86–93).
- Resources have particular representational and communicational affordances. There will be particular ways in which they might aid or limit meaning making and this will influence selection of them. For example, the use of full colour as a resource in an image, rather than black and white, may enable important aspects of the image to be highlighted, shaping the meaning making in a way that better meets the purpose of the multimodal text.
- **Transformation** is the result of the process of design. As designers (consumers and producers) use a repertoire of resources to design, they redesign an aspect of the world. Designers (consumers and producers) have a literacy identity which makes them unique and therefore they will make meaning in unique ways. No two redesigns the producers or consumers design will ever be the same. The redesigns will become part of the available repertoire of resources to be used in the future.
- The process of design involves synthesising, that is, moving back and forth among different semiotic systems and other resources to make meaning.
- An important aspect of the design process is knowing how to represent and communicate in multiple semiotic systems, for example, knowing how to represent or interpret the idea of excitement through the semiotic systems chosen for use, such as Linguistic, Gestural and Visual.

Transformation
The result of the process of design. The consumer will have been transformed by engaging with the available resources and multimodal texts in new ways in order to make meaning. Conversely the production and dissemination of a multimodal text will have transformed those who engage with it.

New texts require new pedagogies: talking and thinking about the designing of multimodal texts

Making the process transparent: metacognition and metalanguage

Discussion of the processes of **designing**, consuming and producing texts, describes a process that, because it involves problem-solving, gathering and analysing, combining, recombining and reworking available resources, largely goes on in the head. Therefore, it is invisible. In order to engage in pedagogy and practices that will help students to explore and think about these processes, they have to be made transparent. A body of research that examined strategies for teaching comprehension of text in the area of cognitive psychology in the 1970s provided a way of making these processes more transparent to students. It also generated strategies that would assist them in monitoring their thinking processes. In the preceding section there has been reference to the fact that designing requires the producer or consumer to engage in self-monitoring and self-regulation, as they strategise,

Design (noun)
Refers to the components of meaning, for example, the form or structure of a text.

Designing (verb)
The process of making meaning as the selected repertoire of resources is combined and recombined to interpret, communicate and represent meaning through a text.

rethink, modify or recombine strategies in order to achieve their purpose. The consumer or producer must be an active rather than passive participant in the process. Consequently, the ways in which the consumption and production of multimodal texts are discussed in the classroom must facilitate understandings about these dynamic processes in order to engage in self-monitoring and self-regulation. In a review of the research examining the classroom application of self-regulated learning (SLR), Paris and Paris (2001, p. 89) defined it as follows:

> SLR...emphasises autonomy and control by the individual who monitors, directs and regulates actions toward goals of information acquisition expanding expertise and self-improvement.

Another researcher in the area, Zimmerman (2000, p. 14), described self-regulation in the following way:

> [SLR] refers to self-generated thought, feelings and actions that are planned and cyclically adapted to the attainment of personal goals.

These two definitions clearly relate to the preceding definitions and descriptions of the processes of consuming and producing text. They also emphasise many of the concepts underpinning the definitions of multiliteracies and being multiliterate discussed in Chapters One and Two, for example, agency and the ability to adapt and change as necessary in order to have control over one's life.

Self-regulated learning is a term often used interchangeably with the term **metacognition**. The concept of metacognition was first developed by cognitive psychologists, who used the term to describe awareness and control of the cognitive processes. One of the earliest researchers in the area, Brown (1978), described it as thinking efficiently, and her research investigated its application to problem-solving, particularly predicting, checking and monitoring, which she suggested needed to be controlled and co-ordinated in order to learn and solve problems. During the 1980s and 1990s the research expanded to classroom application and strategies that would facilitate the development of metacognition. Paris, Cross and Lipson (1984) suggested that three kinds of metacognitive knowledge needed to be taught. Anstey and Bull (2010) added a fourth. They can be summarised as:

- Knowing that: knowing a range of metacognitive strategies
- Knowing how: knowing how to use the strategies
- Knowing when: knowing the best strategy to use to achieve one's purpose in a particular situation and at a particular time
- Knowing why: knowing why the strategy selected is the best one to use.

Metacognition
Knowledge, monitoring and control of one's thinking processes in order to employ the most appropriate strategies to achieve a goal.

REFLECTION STRATEGY 3.2

- The purpose of this Reflection Strategy is to investigate the level of awareness you have about how you go about a simple everyday literacy task and what is involved in completing it. In other words, how aware are you of your metacognitive processes and what are the implications of this for your teaching?
- Find a very simple recipe (online or in a book) that you want to make. Either make it or pretend to make it. It would be preferable to make it as this will help you make more accurate notes about the task.
- As you engage with the text and go through making the recipe, write down what you do, what you think about and the strategies you use. Most importantly, every time you write something down, write down why you did it.
- Read your notes and assess whether you noted down:
   o The strategies you used and any others you considered
   o How you used those strategies
   o Why you used those particular strategies at that point
- An example of the types of notes that might be made before commencing the cooking is provided. These notes pertain to previewing the recipe. The 'why' notes explain why previewing is important. This is important information when teaching strategies such as previewing to students, as it helps students understand the utility of the strategy and then they are more likely to transfer its use to another situation.

What I did and what I thought about	Why
Before I started I read through the ingredients and thought about whether I had them and if I had enough of each one. For some ingredients I went and checked.	If I did not have the ingredients I could not go any further, so it was important to check this first.
I also read through the method, but just focussed on the utensils and bowls and kitchen aids I would need and got them out ready. I also noted anything I had to do before I started, like putting the oven on to heat.	If I had everything ready I would not waste time, or maybe mess something up, because I had to stop and get things out. It's important to do anything that needs to be done beforehand, otherwise it can stop you doing things that need to be done in a particular time and sequence.
I looked at the coloured photograph of the finished cake.	I focussed on how the cake was presented to give me ideas. I looked at the colour and texture of the cake where it was cut in order to help me with gauging the colour it needed to be when I took it out of the oven and how it should look when I cut it. The picture gave me clues about how to assess my success in following the recipe.

- When you have completed your notes, read through them and think about how much detail there is.
  - Have you described all your thinking processes and decision-making and why you thought about these things?
  - If you handed these notes to someone who had not used a recipe before would it help them through the process? Do you need to revise, add detail?
  - How difficult was it for you to think about your thinking?
- Much of what adults do as proficient readers is automatic, but in order to articulate and describe the complexities of reading/consuming or using a text to novice readers, it is essential to be able to describe and model thinking processes and decision-making.

THEORY INTO PRACTICE 3.2

- The purpose of this Theory into Practice task is to plan a lesson in which you model the use of an instructional text such as a recipe or instructions.
- Using your reflection task analyses as a guide, analyse the text and task you will model and identify:
  - the specific things about the text that you would identify and talk about
  - the terminology you would use
  - the strategies that would be useful and that should be modelled and discussed
  - the thinking processes and decision-making processes you would model
- How would you sequence the lesson?
- What resources would you use to facilitate the modelling?

AUDITING INSTRUMENT 3.1

- The purpose of this Auditing Instrument is to monitor your modelling of metacognitive skills in terms of whether you modelled:
  - knowing that
  - knowing how
  - knowing when
  - knowing why
- If you have the opportunity, implement the lesson you planned in Theory Into Practice 3.1, or another lesson where you are modelling a strategy. Tape it, listen to and/or watch it and evaluate your modelling.
- Use a table with the headings 'knowing that', 'knowing how', and 'knowing when and why'. Each time you hear yourself specifically provide that type of information, place a tick. At the

- end of the lesson total up the ticks in each column and reflect upon the amount of metacognitive knowledge you provided and the balance among the types of metacognitive knowledge.
- Consider any changes you feel you need to make. Introductory information about audio-taping and evaluating lessons as a way of improving pedagogy and practice is provided in Chapter Four and addressed in detail as part of an Action Learning Cycle for teachers in the complementary volume to this book, *Elaborating Multiliteracies through Multimodal Texts: Changing Classroom Practices and Developing Teacher Pedagogies.*

Other researchers in metacognition identified that it was not only important to teach specific strategies, but that if students are informed about the importance and utility of the strategy they are more likely to employ it strategically (Paris, Newman and McVey 1981). Brown and Palincsar (1982) found that reciprocal teaching and peer tutoring, in which students were taught monitoring strategies and actively discussed their reading using these strategies as they read, facilitated the transfer of these strategies to other situations and discipline areas. The specific monitoring strategies taught in the reciprocal teaching research were paraphrasing the main idea in a paragraph, discussing how they would summarise the information in the paragraph, hypothesising about what else might follow in the text and commenting upon any confusion that was encountered.

While all this research about metacognition was conducted with paper texts that did not feature images, nevertheless it is possible to extrapolate its significance for consuming and producing multimodal text. Developing a repertoire of resources that aid in using metacognitive skills during consumption and production of multimodal texts is essential, but these resources must aid metacognitive practices with all aspects of a multimodal text and the processes of consuming and producing them. Therefore, a major resource for students is having an appropriate **metalanguage** to talk about all aspects of multimodal texts. In its original form, the term *metalanguage* traditionally referred to a language for talking about language, that is, the Linguistic Semiotic System. In the Linguistic Semiotic System this terminology would be used to name and describe phrases and clauses and parts of speech such as nouns and adjectives. It enables a producer or consumer to describe or analyse a text using a shared vocabulary with others. If students are discussing the written description of a dog in a piece of literature they might comment upon how well the adjectives enable them to visualise the dog. Similarly, if sharing writing, or collaboratively writing, metalanguage enables students to comment meaningfully on each other's work and articulate their thoughts. A student might comment to another that

Metalanguage

In the context of a multiliterate classroom, *metalanguage* refers to terminology that enables producers and consumers of multimodal text to clearly articulate and describe all features of a multimodal text, including the codes and conventions of the semiotic systems and technologies used in its construction, together with the processes of consuming and producing the multimodal text.

98 Multimodal texts and semiotic systems

they liked the use of the adjective 'black' in the description of the dog, but a few more adjectives might help them visualise whether it was a big dog, or a hairy dog. Alternatively, they might suggest the addition of another sentence that adds to the description of the dog. A shared language about language facilitates meaningful learning and discussion about the production or consumption of text.

However, in the context of multimodal texts, limiting the definition of metalanguage to simply being a language for talking about language is insufficient. Students need a language to talk about the whole process and everything within it. This would include a metalanguage for identifying, developing understandings and talking about:

Conventions
The agreed upon, or accepted, ways of using the codes. Together the codes and conventions are the tools that come together to enable a reader/viewer to make meaning. There are codes and conventions that are associated with each semiotic system.

- The codes and **conventions** of the semiotic systems
- The thinking processes involved in the consumption and production of text
- The structure of text
- Describing and navigating online text
- The technologies associated with producing and consuming text

In terms of a multiliterate approach to literacy the term *metalanguage* is expanded to encompass all of these.

Making consumption of a multimodal text transparent

In order to explain the concepts of metacognition and metalanguage further, and how they assist both teachers and students in understanding the processes of designing text, Table 3.1 presents a detailed application of these concepts to the consumption of a text. To contextualise Table 3.1 and make it a more authentic depiction of the process of consuming a multimodal text, an illustration from a picture book called *The Lost Thing* by Shaun Tan (2000) has been used to create the table. The illustration can be accessed on Shaun Tan's website via QR Code 3.1 (or it can be accessed from the picture book section of Tan's website at http://www.shauntan.net/books.html). Once the picture book section of the website has been accessed, click on the thumbnail of the cover of the book 'The Lost Thing' and scroll down to the first illustration, captioned 'saying hello'). This book has been selected because it was also produced as an animated film and both are discussed further in Chapter Five, comparing and contrasting the picture book and film.

Three stages are identified during the process of consuming a multimodal task: before, during and after. In the centre column are questions the consumer might ask themselves and things they might monitor as they consume the text, in other words, metacognitive prompts that might be used. Because it represents the actual questions and thoughts of the person, it is written in the first person. In the final column, the knowledge and metalanguage that might be necessary to investigate and talk about these questions and prompts is provided. It includes reference to how the Four Resource Model might be applied. The questions and metalanguage are not exhaustive; they are simply provided to aid understanding of the concepts of metacognition and metalanguage as they apply to the consumption of multimodal texts. In reality the consumer of the text would move back and forth between and among the before, during and after stages of the process. Therefore, the table should not be read as simply a three stage, lock step process. Possible answers have been provided in the Before stage, but only prompts, types of knowledge and possible metalanguage are provided in the During and After stage. Questions, answers and metalanguage are written as an adult and proficient consumer of a multimodal text in order to provide maximum information to the reader. Readers should extrapolate as to what they might expect of students in the age and ability level they teach, but keep expectations of students high – if the appropriate scaffolding is provided, then these levels can be achieved. Teachers participating in long term projects investigating change in their pedagogy and practices with multiliteracies and multimodal texts, which were run by Bull and Anstey (2010) and based on an Action Learning Cycle, have consistently reported this. (See the complementary volume, *Elaborating Multiliteracies through Multimodal Texts: Changing Classroom Practices and Developing Teacher Pedagogies*, for detailed information about Action Learning Cycles and their implementation.)

QR Code 3.1 Shaun Tan's website (http://www.shauntan.net/books.html)

Making production of a multimodal text transparent

In order to explain the concepts of metacognition and metalanguage as they apply to producing a text, Table 3.2 applies the process to a real production task. As in Table 3.1 three stages are identified during the process: before, during and after. The centre column provides sample metacognitive prompts the producer might generate and in the final column, the knowledge and metalanguage that might be necessary to investigate and talk about these questions and prompts is provided. As for Table 3.1 the questions and metalanguage are not exhaustive, they are simply provided to aid understanding of the concepts of metacognition and metalanguage as they apply to the production of multimodal texts. It is important to remember the producer of the text would move back and forth between and among the before, during and after stages of the process.

Table 3.1 A metacognitive view of the process of consuming a multimodal text

Contextualising information about the story so far: A boy is retelling a story (in the first person) about something that happened to him a few years ago. He recalls that he was working on his bottle-top collection on the beach and came across 'a thing' that was just sitting on the beach doing nothing. No-one else was taking any notice of it. The boy was intrigued. He decided to investigate. The page being viewed at this point is the next one, on which the 'Investigation' begins.

Stage	Metacognitive prompts	Knowledge needed and Associated Metalanguage
Before (Turning to the next page)	*What am I thinking about at this stage of the story?* What will happen next? Will the thing be friendly, antagonistic or shy? *What reading practices from the Four Resource Model do I need to use?* I need to be a code breaker and crack the codes of the semiotic resources available and think about their possible meanings. I need to be a meaning maker and link the information from previous pages, previous picture books and previous books by this author to what is on the page and predict what might come next. I need to be a text analyst because I need to look at all the evidence from my code breaking and meaning making and draw conclusions from it about what might happen next. I also need to see if there is any conflicting evidence from the resources, and whether there are other possible conclusions and predictions. *What are all the resources available to aid my predictions?* Knowledge about picture books, the semiotic resources present and their codes and conventions, what I know about story structure, what I know about the story so far, what I know about the characters so far, what I know from reading other books by Shaun Tan. *What do I know about picture books from my Literacy Identity that might help my predictions?* This page is a double page spread and I know that the use of a double page spread often means there is lots of information here or something important is happening that will influence the next part of the story. So, I need to look and think carefully about all that is available on this double page spread, how it relates to what came before, what is there, and what it might suggest about happens next. *What semiotic resources can I draw upon to help me?* *What has the boy observed and said in the linguistic part of the pages so far that might help my predictions?* The boy has said that 'The Thing' has not hurt anyone; no-one is taking any notice of it. It is just sitting, not interacting or attempting to interact with anyone. *What have the Visual Resources told me about 'the thing's' character so far?* The boy is shown looking at its different parts, and it has not moved or hurt him. The colour of 'the thing' is warm, which can be associated with something friendly rather than frightening. *What do the Gestural resources tell me so far?* The boy does not have a scared facial expression depicted in his eyes or mouth. His face has an inquisitive expression. His body position is rounded, which makes him look calm and inquisitive. The posture of 'the thing' is passive because it is not moving, it is just sitting. *What do the Spatial resources tell me so far?* They show the boy in close proximity to 'the thing'. If the boy felt afraid he would not move so close, so it must not be doing anything to frighten him. *What do I know about the structure of stories that might help with my predictions?* The story is being told in the first person, so the boy lived to tell the tale, so he probably won't be hurt.	*About processing text* • Predicting, prediction • Evidence/justifying • Drawing conclusions • Characteristics of picture books • Page layout *About practices of the Four Resource Model* • Code-breaker • Meaning maker • Text analyst *About Literacy Identity* *About Semiotic Resources* • Linguistic • Visual • Gestural • Spatial *About the codes and conventions of the semiotic systems* • Facial expression • Body position • Posture • Colour • Warm colours • Proximity *About text structure* • Story structure • Character • First person • Retelling

	Is the information from the semiotic resources and the story structure all providing similar evidence that leads to just one conclusion and prediction, or are there pieces of evidence that suggest alternative conclusions and if so, what are they? It is all suggesting the same conclusion. What are my conclusions from the information/evidence available in the semiotic resources and the story structure before I turn the page? It will be a friendly encounter.	
During (Perusal of the page that has one framed illustration and the linguistic text, 'It was quite friendly though, once I started talking to it.')	Are my predictions confirmed or not, and how will I know? What resources can I draw upon to gather evidence to confirm or refute my predictions? What is the first thing that I notice when I turn the page? Is there anything new or different about this page to the previous one/ones? Are there any new resources available that were not available before? What reading practices from the Four Resource Model do I need to use to confirm or refute my predictions? What am I thinking about as I read on and how should I go about doing that? Do I need to gather more information?	About processing text • Predicting, prediction • Infer, inference-making • Evidence • Drawing conclusions • Characteristics of picture books • Page layout About practices of the Four Resource Model • Code-breaker • Meaning maker • Text analyst About Semiotic Resources • Linguistic • Visual • Gestural • Spatial About the codes and conventions of the semiotic systems • Facial Expression • Body position • Posture • Colour • Warm colours • Proximity About text structure • Story structure • Character • First person • Retelling
After (Perusal of the page before turning to the next page)	What was my reading purpose when I started reading? Am I still focussed upon that? How am I going about that? Are the strategies I am using working or do I need to add some or change the ones I am using? What am I thinking about as I read on? How do I go about doing that? Do I need to gather more information?	

N.B. For introductory details of the codes and conventions of the Five Semiotic Systems, see later in this chapter. For full definitions and explanation, together with a recommended sequencing across school levels, see Chapter Three in the complementary volume to this book, *Elaborating Multiliteracies through Multimodal Texts: Changing Classroom Practices and Developing Teacher Pedagogies*

REFLECTION STRATEGY 3.3

- The purpose of this Reflection Strategy is to practice the process of consuming a multimodal text while consciously using and monitoring metacognition and associated knowledge and metalanguage.
- As previously explained, in Table 3.1 columns two and three for the before, during and after stages are not complete. Using the QR code provided, which links to the page of *The Lost Thing* (or the web address link, or the book, if you have access to it), view the page, monitor and record your thoughts, answer the questions provided and add any metacognitive prompts and associated knowledge and metalanguage of your own.
- Once completed, try to make a list of the general types of resources, knowledge and metalanguage that might be used when consuming any multimodal text, for example, semiotic resources (visual, linguistic, gestural, audio and spatial), knowledge about different text types and their typical structure. This list could provide a starting point for discussing the consumption process in a dynamic way, focussing on its problem-solving nature and the necessity for active rather than passive consumption. It could also be a useful beginning as a checklist when planning for teaching, particularly modelling.
- Examine your current planning for teaching about the consumption of multimodal texts. Consider whether you need to revise the current structure or outlining and the level of detail you use in order to regularly and specifically incorporate metacognition and metalanguage in your teaching repertoire. If so, how might you do this?

Exploring the resources necessary when designing a multimodal text

Much has been discussed in terms of the resources a person draws upon when designing and redesigning a multimodal text. Figure 3.4 provides a visual summary of the range of resources that might be drawn upon when consuming or producing (designing/redesigning) a multimodal text. Many of these resources have been discussed in relation to the concepts of multiliteracies and multiliterate practice in Chapters One and Two and in the discussion of multimodal texts in this chapter. However, it is now appropriate to discuss each of these resources explicitly, together with the implications for pedagogy and practice around multimodal texts. While reading the following section, it might be tempting to dismiss the level of detail and thinking that is explored as 'over the top'. However, this is because the reader is competent and no longer thinks at this level of detail, having reached a level of automaticity with many of these

AUDITING INSTRUMENT 3.2

- The purpose of this Auditing Instrument is to gauge your students' current metacognitive awareness. You can use this information together with the information you gathered about your own metacognitive awareness in Reflection Strategy 3.2 to inform your planning and practice.
- Use the following questions to stimulate a discussion about what students do and think about before, during, and after consuming or producing a multimodal text. You can modify the language to suit the age group of your students and you can also conduct it as an individual written self-report or interview if you prefer. If your students currently use only the terms *reading* or *writing* when discussing the consumption or production of multimodal text, then substitute those words.
- It may help to have an actual text to discuss in terms of consumption or a real writing /production task to discuss. If you are running a discussion be careful not to guide the discussion too tightly in case, you influence the students' answers.
- Questions regarding consuming a multimodal text:
  o What do you think makes someone good at consuming a text?
  o When you are going to consume a text, are there particular things you do before you start?
  o What do you look at before you start to consume a text?
  o What do you think about before you start to consume a text?
  o Which parts of the text do you engage with, for example, the images, diagrams, words, sound track? What do you think about when you engage with those parts of the text?
  o What do you do or think about when you come to something you have not seen before or do not know, for example, a word you don't know?
  o What do you do or think about if you cannot make sense of a part of the text?
  o When you have finished consuming the text what do you do or think about?
- Questions regarding producing a multimodal text:
  o What do you think makes someone good at producing a text?
  o What do you do before you start to produce a text?
  o What do you think about before you start to produce a text?
  o How do you go about producing the text, are there particular things you do or think about?
  o Do you use anything to help you produce a text? How do those things help and what helps you decide when to use them?
  o What do you do or think about if you are having trouble with producing your text?
  o When you have finished producing the text, what do you do or think about before you disseminate it?

strategies, possibly now unaware that they are being done. But students are not competent readers; they are novices, and while some may have lifeworlds that have provided much of this knowledge and the ability to transfer it to different situations, there are many that do not. Therefore,

Table 3.2 A metacognitive view of the process of producing a multimodal text

Contextualising information: The producer of this text has been asked to talk to a class of inner city 10-year-old students who have started an edible garden in the school grounds. It is part of their science studies about how scientific knowledge is used to solve problems and inform personal and community decisions. The students have been studying how plants grow and reproduce and also environmental issues associated with growing plants. Recently they have begun to focus on the role of bees in their garden. They are aware bees play a role in reproduction of their plants and they would like to know more about these things. They have not seen a lot of bees in their garden and they are wondering why this might be so and if it's a problem. The students have asked the producer of this text, a well-known local figure in the gardening world and local nursery owner, to come and talk with them about these issues. The teacher has indicated that an inquiry approach is used in science and the students' questions are part of this. The teacher wants the talk to provide information specific to the topic but also generate reflection that might open up further avenues of inquiry for the students.

Stage	Metacognitive prompts	Knowledge needed and Associated Metalanguage
Before (Identifying and clarifying purpose and planning)	*What is the purpose of this text?* To provide information about bees in terms of their role in the garden, as a source of food, and if a lack of bees in a garden might be a problem and why there might be few bees. *Who is my audience?* 10-year-old students who are growing a garden at school but live in the inner city so may not have a garden themselves if they live in apartments. They are novice gardeners. *What do I know about my audience and the purpose of the text that will influence my choice and selection of technologies, semiotic systems and the text type/s I use?* They live in apartments so I may need to explain more about bees and gardens and environment because of their lifeworld experiences. I will need to have a variety of semiotic systems such as picture or film or another expert to keep them interested. I could use a hyperlink in my PowerPoint from a website about bees, for images. I have some photos of bees from my garden, too. I could ring my friend Don, who keeps bees, and record a Skype video interview with him and play that for them, which would vary the information and give them an expert opinion. *What is the context in which this text will be disseminated?* The classroom has Wi-Fi available for linking to internet. *What technologies are available to disseminate this text?* I have a laptop that will connect to their data projector and Wi-Fi to display images. *What resources will I need to produce this text?* I will need to use linguistic and visual semiotic resources in the PowerPoint and audio in my oral presentation and Don's interview and I'll have to use spatial when designing the layout of my PowerPoint. I will use Don as an expert resource as well as internet websites. I need to use some of my research skills and strategies to gather the information. I need to refresh my memory on constructing a PowerPoint. I'll need to practice presenting so I will have to draw on my knowledge of the gestural semiotic system too.	*About the production process. Role of:* • Purpose • Audience • Lifeworld (producer and audience) • Context *About text* • Interview *About technology* • Skype • Recording and replaying a Skype video interview • Inserting and using hyperlinks in a PowerPoint presentation • Using PowerPoint as part of an oral presentation • Connecting and using laptop, data projector and Wi-Fi in a presentation *About semiotic systems* • Linguistic • Visual • Audio • Spatial • Gestural

During Production – (Gathering resources and synthesising).	*How can I organise myself and get this started?* I need to brainstorm what I might include under headings for the three pieces of information they want and identify where I might find it. *What resources will I access to find information the students and teacher have requested?* *How will I sequence the information?* *How will I decide what to include?* I need to keep going back to their questions and be conscious the teacher wanted me to leave things they might want to explore further. I need to think about how much time I have. *How do I set up my PowerPoint?* I need to select a layout design and colour scheme for the PowerPoint that is appropriate for the topic. I need to keep it simple so it does not detract from the images and what I am saying.	*Using the internet* • Using search engines • Checking authenticity of sources *Text types* • Report structure • Sequencing information *Research and writing strategies* • Brainstorm • Sequence • Headings *About the codes and conventions of the semiotic systems* • Design • Layout • Colour scheme
After (Completing final draft before dissemination)	*Have I answered the questions but left space for inquiry?* *Have I used the appropriate vocabulary for the audience?* *How do the different semiotic systems work together?* *Have I used the best semiotic system to convey the different pieces of information?* *Have I rehearsed and checked timing for actually doing the presentation?* *Have I rehearsed my posture, eye contact, pitch, tone, pacing, modulation and phrasing for the oral part of my presentation?*	*About the codes and conventions of the semiotic systems* • Vocabulary • Posture • Eye contact • Pitch • Tone • Pacing • Modulation • Phrasing

it is necessary as a teacher to be aware of these complexities and reflect upon them in order to help every student in the class. The following two statements were sighted on a school staffroom noticeboard. Their origin is unknown but they encapsulate why the following discussion about resources is necessary:

Those who use literacy take it for granted but those who cannot use it are excluded.

The act of teaching is to take that which is intuitively known to that which is explicitly shown.

When discussing resources from a pedagogical perspective it is useful to keep in mind Tables 3.1 and 3.2 that explore the designing process in terms of before, during and after stages. It is important to remind students that resources will be drawn upon at all stages, possibly several times and in different ways, which is why designing requires active rather than passive participation by the consumer/producer. Another point that is important to remember is that the resources have to be considered in relation to one another, as often a decision about one set of resources will influence decisions about other resources. An obvious example is the relationship between decisions about technological resources and those about semiotic resources, as typically choices about technology will influence which semiotic resources are available for use in the multimodal text. A decision to use paper technologies will mean moving images or film as part of the Visual Semiotic System, together with Audio, are not going to be available for use. However, there are other, more subtle relationships, for example, those between audience resources and semiotic resources, where knowing that the audience comes from a social or cultural group that prefers images would suggest that the suggest that the Visual Semiotic System should be foregrounded in the text. Exploring the possible relationships by posing particular scenarios for students to explore in groups, making decisions about the most important aspects of the resources to be considered and drawing conclusions about the relationships among them, are useful strategies for developing this understanding.

Many of the strategies that students will engage in and use when exploring the concepts around resources will require discussion, group work, good listening and speaking skills and an ability to work collaboratively and negotiate. These skills require the application of dialogic talk in the classroom. Chapter Four has introductory information about classroom talk and dialogic talk, and Chapter Four in the complementary volume to this book, *Elaborating Multiliteracies through Multimodal Texts: Changing Classroom Practices and Developing Teacher Pedagogies*, has more detailed information.

The preceding section focussed on the role of self-regulated learning and metacognition in designing texts. Paris and Paris (2001, p. 93) identified

Multimodal texts and semiotic systems 107

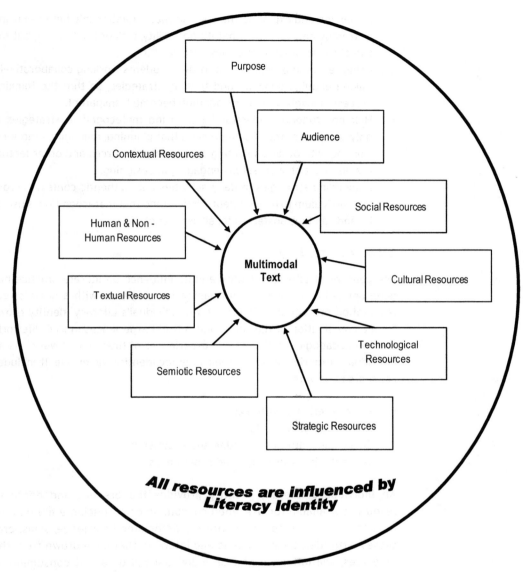

Figure 3.4 Resources that may be drawn upon when producing or consuming (designing) a multimodal text

key aspects of pedagogy that help with the development of metacognition. These aspects have been adapted for multimodal texts and inform the following discussion of the use of resources. They are:

- Modelling and explicitly teaching the types of strategies available across all semiotic systems and technologies.
- Exploring how, when and why they might be used.

- Explaining and exploring the specific causal relationship between using a strategy and success – that it's not ability, luck or the teacher, but the use of the strategy that brings success.
- Using teaching practices that involve students working collaboratively, talking about, explaining and trialling strategies, so that the thinking processes involved in metacognition become transparent.
- Helping students understand that using metacognitive strategies is only one part of the design process; that planning, managing emotions, working with others, selecting appropriate resources and other factors are also part of successfully engaging in designing.
- Embedding strategies in daily activities and authentic contexts across the curriculum to help students understand that metacognition is useful in, and can be transferred to, all aspects of life.

Literacy Identity

The concept of Literacy Identity and its influence on literate practice has been defined and discussed in Chapter Two, together with a graphic representation presented in Figure 2.1. An individual's Literacy Identity grows from a combination of the social and cultural experiences in their lifeworld and the pedagogical activities and experiences of their school-world. As an individual's experiences grow, their Literacy Identity will evolve. It includes concepts to do with:

- Prior experience with texts
- Knowledge about texts
- Social and cultural knowledge and experiences
- Technological knowledge and experiences

An individual's Literacy Identity provides the breadth and depth of resources available for use when consuming or producing a multimodal text. The resources, together with the associated knowledge, skills, processes, attitudes, beliefs, values and interests that have grown from the resources, will influence how an individual will go about consuming or producing a multimodal text. This is why in Figure 3.4 it is stated that all resources will be influenced by Literacy Identity.

Awareness of one's Literacy Identity as a set of available resources is key to being able to consume and produce multimodal texts. Applying metacognitive strategies such as self-questioning about one's Literacy Identity will help identify the resources to draw upon, and those that are not available and will therefore need to be sought, and assist in developing an overall strategy to complete the design process.

THEORY INTO PRACTICE 3.3

- The purpose of this Theory into Practice is to take the ideas about the concept of Literacy Identity that were developed in Theory into Practice 2.3 in Chapter Two and develop a specific set of metacognitive prompts students could use when encountering any text in any context. These prompts would become part of their strategic resources, ready for use.
- In Theory into Practice 2.3 the following questions were used to explore what students already knew from their Literacy Identity that might help them with reading a text.
    o Where or when have you come across this topic or subject before? What did you do?
    o What do you already know that might help?
    o What else do you need to know or find out that might help you?
    o Have you used a text like this before? How did you use it?
    o What was your purpose for using the text?
    o What prior experience from your tool kit (Literacy Identity) can help you here?
    o Which semiotic systems were used in the construction of this text?
    o Have you engaged with these semiotic systems in texts like this before? How does this help you?
    o What is the purpose in using each semiotic system in the construction of the text?
    o Have you used this technology or software, or something similar, before? How does that prior experience help you?
- Ask the students to think about how these questions might be useful before producing a text. Ask for suggestions about how they might be modified and develop a list for activating Literacy Identity before producing a text.

Purpose, audience and contextual resources

Whether consuming or producing, it is important to consider purpose as a resource, rather than simply a statement about the outcome or goal. One of the problems, when completing a complex task that comprises many steps and often includes working with others, is that it is easy to lose sight of the original purpose and focus. Therefore, it is important firstly to clearly understand the purpose, and secondly to identify points at which it would be appropriate to check that, at that point, the purpose is still being worked towards and/or fulfilled. Once again these are metacognitive prompts, but it is important to ensure that students actually have strategies to assist them with these prompts and that they understand why they are important. So, a 'purpose resource strategy' might simply be that before starting the task students can explain the task in their own words. Ask students to practice this in pairs and to give each other feedback on how clearly they have articulated the task. Eventually they should simply be able to do this in their heads, but it is important to start with a concrete strategy or task to help develop the concept. For complex 'purposes' and tasks it might be necessary to break down the purpose into a series of smaller purposes or steps in order to achieve the overall purpose. Similarly, it is important students understand why this is an important strategy – because it helps them work out whether they understand what they have to do and if not, what they need help with to understand it.

A strategy for monitoring whether the purpose is still being fulfilled could be taught as part of planning. Students could be taught to list in note form how they think they might go about the task, in other words, develop a plan for the before, during and after stages. This is particularly useful when students are engaging in the inquiry processes in all disciplines, researching for information on the internet, working in a group where different people have different tasks, or when producing a text in any of the aforementioned situations. As part of planning they could build in checkpoints where they monitor how the plan is going, whether it needs modifying or revising and whether the purpose is still clear and being met by the plan and actions so far.

Audience is a concept mostly associated with producing a multimodal text, where the person or persons producing the text consider the Literacy Identity of their audience in order to make the text appropriate for them. However, when consuming a text where the audience is oneself, it is also important to consider one's own Literacy Identity and how that might shape or influence consumption of the text. Therefore, students should be thinking about their Literacy Identity, how it helps or hinders their purpose, attitudes toward and ability to consume the text and then formulate a plan that will help the consumption process. Using the questions and metacognitive prompts that were developed in Theory into Practice 2.3 and 3.2 would assist students with this process.

Contextual resources refer to the context in which the designing (consumption or production) of multimodal text takes place. Contextual resources will need to be considered in relation to other resources, for example, technological resources, social and cultural resources and semiotic resources. Considering the physical location in which the text is to be engaged with and used, together with the technologies available in that location (context), will influence many aspects of the process. If consuming a text, it may be that particular technology and software needs to be available where the text is to be consumed. Should the consumption of the text involve other people and require particular behaviours and actions, the dimensions of the space (context) and what it contains, become relevant. Are chairs and tables needed and available, are methods for recording interaction and actions to be taken necessary and how should any or all of these things be arranged to facilitate interaction?

Similarly, when producing a multimodal text, it may be necessary to consider the physical setting (context) if the multimodal text will be a live performance. The availability of technological resources (hardware and software) would need to be considered when preparing multimodal texts for specific audiences and specific contexts. The availability of technology in the context where the multimodal text is to be produced and consumed can also influence the inclusion or exclusion of particular semiotic systems in a multimodal text. A colleague helping teachers prepare books in the local language in the Philippines found that the local photocopier only reproduced in black and white. Coloured printers were not available and if teachers wanted to use colour when producing these multimodal texts, it required the use of a packet of colouring in pencils or coloured markers. Similarly, when preparing multimodal texts for Australia's isolated community contexts, consideration needs to be given to electricity supply being reliable (if it is run by diesel it is notoriously unreliable). The capacity of the local computers and software available on them must also be considered, or the text may not even be able to be downloaded. This is why resources cannot be considered in isolation. Developing a checklist to help examine the features of the context that might influence consumption or production of text and including cross references to other resources that might influence the designing of texts would be a useful strategy.

Social and cultural resources

In Chapters One and Two the influence of social and cultural background on literacy and literate practices was discussed in detail. Social and cultural experiences contribute knowledge, experience, attitudes and values toward literacy and literate practices and shape an individual's literacy identity. Therefore, it is important to consider one's own social and cultural experiences when consuming a text and also those of the author or authors (if known). These social and cultural resources enable the consumer to predict what might be familiar or unfamiliar in the text and any existing attitudes, values or beliefs they might bring to their consumption of the text (about its content or text type). The consumer may also be able to predict how the content will be structured and any values, attitudes or beliefs that may have informed it. These predictions enable the consumer to adjust the strategies they will use when approaching the text and employ critical literacy strategies that will assist when reading it. Similarly, when planning for the production of a text for a particular audience, knowledge of the social and cultural background of the audience can inform decision-making about other resources to be used when producing the text. It may be necessary to produce a paper multimodal text for some contexts even when other technology is available, because the audience has a preference for paper texts. In this situation consideration of contextual resources would need to be cross referenced with audience and possibly social and cultural resources that provide understandings of the characteristics of the audience. Consideration should also be given to social and cultural aspects of the Literacy Identity of those involved in the production of the text that may create difficulties in producing a text that meets the purpose and audience of the text.

Strategic resources

The term *strategic resources* is often associated with strategies learned in the school world because that is the context in which strategies are often explicitly taught. However, sometimes strategies are learned implicitly, for example, from friends when playing a computer game and a strategy for avoiding being eliminated is shared, or the football coach when working out a game plan using different colours, symbols and arrows to map it out on a diagram of the field. Some of these strategies can be transferred to designing texts. Therefore, it is important when discussing strategic resources to once again remind students to consider both their school world and their lifeworld as a source of these resources. Strategic resources will be used at all stages of the design process, before, during and after, and the selection of the resources to be used will be guided during consideration of all the other resources.

There is a plethora of strategies that students are taught and use as they move through school, such as PMIs, hot potato, graphic organisers, brainstorming, storyboarding and cloze. Similarly, there are many books and resources in schools which provide lists and descriptions of these strategies for teachers to use. However, often students are using these strategies but not thinking about, or knowing, why they are using them. Sometimes they view them as simply something the teacher wants them to do, a time filler, or an 'activity'. This can occur when the purpose of using the activity and the contexts in which it might be useful were not explored when the strategy was introduced, or revised from time to time when the strategy was being used again.

The authors have observed a tendency for teachers to provide the strategies when students are engaging in consuming or producing a text, rather than asking students to consider the strategies they know and select those they think might be appropriate. Students need authentic contexts in which to make these decisions and part of the authenticity is allowing them to make mistakes, that is, allowing students to select and use a strategy that won't really help or work, consider why it's not working and select another based on what they have learned. It is only through these authentic situations that students develop resilience and learn that mistakes are part of learning and should sometimes be celebrated for the learning that comes from them.

The Four Resource Model, introduced in Chapter Two, is an important set of resources and practices that students can draw upon, particularly from a metacognitive perspective. The overarching question a designer can ask themselves when approaching the consumption or production of the text, 'What is it that I need to know and be able to do...in order to design/consume this text?' is particularly important as a metacognitive prompt when considering purpose. Identifying how and when the four literate practices (code breaker, meaning maker, text user and text analyst) would be engaged in at each stage of the process (before, during and after), is another metacognitive strategy that can be used to remain focussed on purpose and select appropriate strategies to aid those practices. Theory into Practice 2.4, 2.5, 2.6 and 2.7 in Chapter Two provide questions that could be used as metacognitive prompts when identifying and using the practices to be engaged in.

As has been discussed in Chapter One, designing (consuming or producing texts) in lifeworlds such as the workplace, is seldom a solitary action. Frequently the design task itself requires a team effort, or at various points others might be brought in to provide expertise. Strategic resources must therefore include strategies to promote effective listening and speaking when working in groups and strategies for productive oral interaction when problem-solving or creating as part of a team. Strategies to assist understanding and tolerance when working with a range of personalities, cultural and social groups and communicative styles are also necessary. In many classrooms part of establishing a classroom culture is establishing protocols for working together productively and developing strategies such as those just described. They are part of a dialogic approach to teaching literacy (see Chapter Four). Part of planning for the consumption and production of texts would be identifying which of these strategies will need to be accessed during the process and considering whether all participants in the process would be aware of them, and, if not, how this could be achieved.

Human and non-human resources

When commencing the design process, particularly at the stage of identifying and scoping 'purpose' in order to plan, the need for human and non-human resources becomes apparent. The knowledge necessary from these resources may be anything from knowing about a text type or knowing content about the topic, to knowing how to use a particular piece of software. The source of this knowledge might be human, for example, a friend, teacher, expert in the field; or non-human, for example, a book, pamphlet, website or blog. The critical decisions for the designer when accessing human and non-human resources are:

- Which sources are the best ones to use, (issues of purpose, audience, authenticity, reliability and availability)
- What information is needed and how and where it is best to access it
- When to access these resources during the design process
- How to ensure that the purpose of the design is being fulfilled when accessing them, (issues of remaining focussed on task)

Technological resources

Technological resources can be considered from a number of perspectives, including the hardware and software necessary to fulfil the design process and the use of technology to access information necessary to fulfil the design process. Each one of these will require facility with technology and a metalanguage for understanding and talking about technology and the web. QR Code 3.2 provides a link to the section of an ICT website developed in the U.K. for teachers and students. It introduces the parts of a web page and the metalanguage for describing them. There are many similar resources available, but this one is particularly useful for developing a metalanguage that students and teachers can use to talk about the process of consuming and producing when using websites as a resource.

QR Code 3.2 A website that provides metalanguage for talking about the web (http://www.teach-ict.com/gcse_new/software/web_design/miniweb/pg5.htm)

For some the ability to write code (or access expertise in this area) to use animation, gaming and moviemaking software, such as Tynker, Hopscotch, Beebots, Daisy the Dinosaur and Tickle, is necessary. Students will also need to develop skills that are specific to reading and accessing information on-line. Coscarelli and Coiro (2014) assert that while reading on the internet uses many of the traditional reading skills, it actually makes their use more complex. This is because online readers need to deal with hypertextuality and multimodality at the same time as navigating across multiple sources of information. As they are doing this they are engaging in multiple tasks such as navigation, location, selection and evaluation. Once again it must be remembered that just because students use the internet does not mean they are using it well. An in-depth examination of these issues as they apply to the consumption (reading) and production (writing) process, is discussed in Chapters Five and Six of the complementary volume to this book, *Elaborating*

Multiliteracies through Multimodal Texts: Changing Classroom Practices and Developing Teacher Pedagogies.

Textual resources

For some years researchers have advocated the need for students to know more about the generic structure of texts (see reference to this in Chapter One), but this information has largely been related to the linguistic aspects of the text. Generally, the structure of six text types has been taught: recounts, instructions, narratives, information reports, explanations and arguments. In Australia, a widely-used resource on the structure of text by teachers has been the work of Bev Derewianka (1990, 2015), who has written extensively on functional grammar and exploring the structure of texts. Students are encouraged to explore the textual features of different text types (sometimes referred to as genres) in order to develop a repertoire of resources they can use when producing or consuming text. Typically, this exploration includes the purpose of the text type, the variations within that text type (for example, within recount there can be personal recount and factual recount), text organisation and language features (grammar).

There is no doubt that this information develops a very comprehensive and useful repertoire of textual resources for students, provided it is taught in ways that acknowledge the dynamic nature of text and the role of the other semiotic systems present in a multimodal text. If text structure is taught as a rigid set of rules to be adhered to, then once again literacy is being taught as a static rather than dynamic concept. The reality is that many texts are not 'pure' examples of one genre or text type. Many have multiple genres within them in order to fulfil the purpose of the text. Many texts will combine text structures and textual features in order to meet a particular purpose and audience, and/or employ specific technology and combinations of semiotic systems. Recently Derewianka and Jones (2016), Coffin and Derewianka (2009) and Derewianka and Coffin (2008) have acknowledged the overlaps and mixing of features across genres and also explored the role of the Visual Semiotic System in text types associated with the history and science curriculums.

Knowledge about texts and their structure that is restricted to linguistic features and taught as static and finite knowledge is not appropriate or sufficient in a changing multiliterate world. Unfortunately, despite the fact that curricula around the world acknowledge the existence of multimodal texts and advocate their teaching, many education systems still only assess the linguistic features when conducting high stakes testing of students' writing skills. Nevertheless, it is essential that teachers address all aspects of the teaching of writing multimodal text with their students. In Australia this is still the case for the National Assessment Plan – Literacy and Numeracy (NAPLAN). QR code 3.3 links to advice for teachers regarding the writing test for NAPLAN in 2017 and includes a typical statement about the generic structure of narrative and persuasive texts.

QR Code 3.3 Advice to teachers regarding the writing test for NAPLAN (https://www.nap.edu.au/naplan/writing)

Primary colours
These are red, yellow and blue, and have a pure pigment, that is, no other colour has been mixed with them and they cannot be made by mixing any other colours together. They are the basis of all other colours.

Secondary colours
These are the next level of colours and result from mixing the primary colours. They are orange (red plus yellow) green (blue plus yellow) and purple (red plus blue).

Tertiary colours
These result from one primary colour being mixed with one of its nearest secondary colours, yellow plus orange results in yellow/orange, red plus orange results in red/orange, red plus purple gives a red/purple, blue plus purple results in blue/purple, blue plus green results in blue/green, yellow plus green results in yellow/green. Consult a colour wheel to see a visual rendition of this.

Semiotic resources

Previous discussion of the semiotic systems has acknowledged that their social and cultural derivation means that they will change and interpretation of meaning may vary among social and cultural groups. Nevertheless, students need to learn the generally accepted codes and conventions of the semiotic systems in order to engage in combining, recombining, designing and redesigning them as they consume and produce texts. As Kress (2000 p. 160) stated: 'Design takes for granted full competence in the use of resources…but beyond that it requires the orchestration and remaking of these resources.' When teaching the codes and conventions of the semiotic systems it is important to provide a combination of focussed learning episodes, together with opportunities to practice and explore the application of learning about the codes and conventions in group work and individually. There should also be opportunities to transfer and link learning to previous and new learning situations across all curriculum areas, using a variety of authentic texts that are delivered by paper, live and digital technologies (Anstey and Bull 2016).

In Tables 3.3 to 3.7 an introductory set of codes and conventions for the five semiotic systems, together with a Theory into Practice activity for four of them, has been provided as a starting point for exploration. The Linguistic Semiotic System does not have a Theory into Practice activity, as it is the most familiar semiotic system to the reader. Most of the semiotic systems draw upon information and theory from the arts and it is useful to consult with colleagues who are specialists in art, music and the performing arts and consult the curricula for these areas to broaden knowledge. For a full explanation and discussion of each code together with a suggested sequence for introduction throughout the school curriculum, see the complementary volume to this book, *Elaborating Multiliteracies through Multimodal Texts: Changing Classroom Practices and Developing Teacher Pedagogies*, particularly Chapters Three, Five and Six.

THEORY INTO PRACTICE 3.4

- The purpose of this Theory into Practice is to investigate a multimodal text and its structure in terms of all semiotic systems present.
- Gather a range of texts that all have the same purpose, for example, a range of informative texts on the same topic or sets of instructions (they can be on any topic). Ensure they are delivered by a range of technologies – digital and paper.
- Using a whole class discussion and focussing on one set of texts, examine one of the texts from the collection. Focus on the following questions:
    o   What is the purpose of this text? Why would you use it?
    o   Who would be the audience for this text?
    o   What semiotic systems are present?
    o   What does each semiotic system contribute to the meaning of the text and how does it achieve its purpose? (For example, in instructions the Visual Semiotic System is often used to provide photos of the finished product or equipment being used or diagrams.)
    o   How effective would the text be if any of the semiotic systems was removed? (If a digital text is used that has sound or a voice over, try playing it without the sound to help students reflect on this questions.)
        - What information would no longer be provided?
        - Would this be a problem for the prospective audience and if so, how?
    o   How is the text structured? Does it have distinctive parts that contribute particular information toward the purpose of the text? (An instructional text may have a list of materials at the beginning and the steps will be sequenced and numbered to ensure they are completed in the correct order to achieve the purpose.)
    o   Once students have the idea of how to analyse a text ask them to work in groups and examine the other texts you have collected. Provide them with a checklist of questions or develop a retrieval chart they can use to summarise their findings.
    o   When completed, ask the groups to share their findings and as they share construct a comparison – contrast table on which the common features are listed , as well as and those that are different.
    o   Discuss the differences and why they were different. Discuss whether the differences enhanced or detracted from the usability of the text for achieving its purpose. Point out that variations may not be a problem, but that sometimes they can make the text less effective. Emphasise the need to consider purpose and audience when selecting and using semiotic and textual resources.
    o   Make a summary of the features of the text type, its structure and how it employs the semiotic systems for future reference when consuming or producing these types of texts. It might include statements like:
        - When consuming an instructional text I should:
            • check to see if it tells me what I need at the beginning

- use the diagrams and photos to help me understand the written steps and the outcome I'm trying to achieve
- take notice of the sequence to ensure I do the steps in the right order
- use any numbering of the steps to help do the steps in the right order

o Discuss how these texts can be metacognitive prompts when consuming a text.

Table 3.3 Introductory list for the codes and conventions of the Visual Semiotic System

Colour: • Placement   • Saturation   • Tone   • Media/opacity/transparency
Texture
Line   • Quality   • Type   • Actual or implied
Shape
Point of View   • Top down   • Bottom up   • Eye level
Framing   • Cropping   • Close up, medium or long shot
Focus
Lighting
Editing   • Parallel cutting   • Speed   • Inserts   • Pacing   • Transitions

THEORY INTO PRACTICE 3.5

- The purpose of this Theory into Practice activity is to explore colour as a starting point to the Visual Semiotic System. Understanding colour theory and how the colour wheel works will inform many of the other concepts in the Visual Semiotic System. Use your favourite search engine to find images of the colour wheel and select one that has **primary, secondary and tertiary colours** (see the Running Glossary for definitions). Download a colour wheel (check copyright) and reproduce one for each student. Collect a range of texts, such as magazines, newspapers, nonfiction and picture books, and bookmark some websites that have contrasting colour schemes on iPads or tablets. Put these on tables arranged for group work later in the lesson.
- Hand out the colour wheels and have a large one to discuss as a whole class. Talk to students about the colour wheel and the location of colours on it. Distinguish between warm and cool colours and discuss when you might choose to use them (for example, to show the temperature or season in an illustration or to depict mood).
- Talk to students about selecting colour schemes for websites or non-fiction books and brochures and ask them why particular colour schemes might be used and if they can think of any they have noticed. Have some examples to look at and discuss as a whole class.
- Tell the students that they are going to conduct an investigation. Each group has some texts on their table and they are to examine these texts and think about how colour has been used. They are to identify examples where they feel particular colours have been selected and to theorise possible reasons for the selection of those colours.
- Ask students to share their findings and summarise them for all to see. Ask the students to come up with some generalisations from their investigation. For example, 'Warm colours were used to show happy occasions.' 'Cool colours were often used to show sad occasions.' 'Colour was sometimes selected to emphasise beliefs; for example, websites about environmental issues used greens, which made users think of a healthy environment.'
- Another exploration with the colour wheel could focus on colours being on opposite sides of the colour wheel being discordant while those close to one another are harmonious. Students could investigate the use of harmonious and discordant colours.
- Other lessons might use art time when students mix colours to help them understand primary, secondary and tertiary colours or tone.

Table 3.4 Introductory list for the codes and conventions of the Audio Semiotic System

Volume and audibility Aspects of volume and audibility related to voice • Modulation • Projection • Articulation • Timbre • Intonation and stress
Pitch
Pace • Phrasing • Pause • Silence

THEORY INTO PRACTICE 3.6

- The purpose of this Theory into Practice is to introduce students to the ways in which audio codes add meaning to the linguistic codes.
- Ask students to identify their favourite sports that they watch, on television as well as live. Ask them if they listen to the audio commentary when they watch. Ask them what information it provides.
- Explain to the students that you are going to play a segment of a sport replay that has visuals and audio commentary and that you want them to think about where they focus their attention while watching and why (ensure the segment has something exciting happening where the commentary varies pitch, tone and pace). Once finished ask them where their focus was at different times and why. Ask them if there is anything they can recall about the audio commentary – whether it changed at all or was all the same.
- If the students have difficulty, play the segment again with only the audio and ask them to tell you if there was any variation and why (usually when something exciting happens the pace of the commentary speeds up, the voice of the commentator rises in pitch and their volume increases). Talk to the students about how these aspects affect their engagement with the game and what is happening and how important these changes in the audio commentary are if you cannot see what is happening.
- Ask the students if they can think of other situations where changes to pace, pitch and volume might be important (for example, giving instruction during an emergency).

Table 3.5 Introductory list for the codes and conventions of the Linguistic Semiotic System

Vocabulary Parts of speech • Noun/pronoun • Verb • Adjective • Conjunction • Tense
Punctuation • Quotation marks • Commas • Contractions • Apostrophes
Phrases
Clauses
Sentences • Simple • Compound
Cohesive devices • Paragraph

Table 3.6 Introductory list for the codes and conventions of the Gestural Semiotic System

Bodily contact
Proximity
Orientation or body position
Appearance • Hair style • Make-up • Costume • Props
Head nods
Facial expression • Eyes • Eye brows • Mouth • Nose
Kinesics
Posture
Gaze and eye movement

THEORY INTO PRACTICE 3.7

- The purpose of this Theory into Practice activity is to introduce students to the codes of appearance and facial expression in the Gestural Semiotic System. Gather a range of photos of individual people who are essentially the same in every aspect (age, gender, ethnicity), except for their facial expression and appearance (hairstyle, make-up, costume and props, such as a walking stick or headphones, etc.). Ensure the photos can be displayed in a size that is sufficient for students to see all details of appearance and facial expression (use an electronic whiteboard).
- Introduce the appearance and facial expression codes and metalanguage by showing one of the photos and identifying and describing them. Discuss what appearance and facial expression might tell the consumer of a text or how they might be used by a producer to provide information in a text. Ask students to think of occasions when they have made assumptions about someone based on appearance or facial expression. Discuss whether they have been accurate assumptions or not and discuss why this was the case and how they determined the accuracy of their assumptions.
- Ask the students to view each photo and consider any theories they have about the person's character, beliefs, values and interests based on their appearance and facial expression. Explain that they must justify their answer and use the metalanguage of the Gestural Semiotic System. You may wish to model this by looking at one of the photos yourself and identifying a characteristic and then justifying your theory. For example, 'I think this person is generally a happy person because their facial expression shows them smiling and they have wrinkles around their eyes and mouth that show this is an expression they use often.' This could be a whole class or group activity.
- Annotate the students' observations on the photos (or if working in groups ask the students to do so) as the discussion continues. If students disagree with an observation, ask them to justify their disagreement and discuss. If a conclusion cannot be reached put both observations down. Ask students how they might investigate further to gather evidence to make a final decision about this characteristic. If it is a person in a story, newspaper article, documentary, etc., they could examine the linguistic information for clues, or the actions of the person previously or later in the text. This is a good opportunity for students to learn the need to examine information provided through all semiotic systems in order to gain meaning.
- Once the whole class discussion has finished or group work has been shared ask students to make some general statements about the use of appearance and facial expression when consuming or producing a text that can be recorded for future reference (these statements could be added to a learning wall that is being built, where students summarise their learning about the semiotic systems).

Table 3.7 Introductory list for the codes and conventions of the Spatial Semiotic System

Position on page or screen • Left-right • Top-bottom • Centre-margin • Foreground-background
Distance • Degree • Angle
Framing • Real • Implied

THEORY INTO PRACTICE 3.8

- The purpose of this Theory into Practice is to develop introductory concepts about distance in images and live performances. Collect still and moving images that depict groups of people interacting in different settings. Include images of live performances such as plays.
- Using one of the images, introduce students to the concept of distance as a way of portraying relationships. That is, how close or distant the people are is an indicator of how engaged or comfortable the people are with one another. Explain that the angle at which people are facing one another can also provide further information about relationships. If people are facing one another directly, then it is most likely there is a strong interest or relationship, but if they are facing one another at an angle or turning away, then it may indicate the person is being sidelined or detached from the situation.
- In groups, examine the different still and moving images and ask students to theorise about the relationships between those present, based firstly on distance and angle. Once they have done this, if they have previously engaged with the Gestural Semiotic System ask students to see if there are any gestural codes or conventions that reinforce or weaken their theory. Once again have students explain and justify their answers using the appropriate metalanguage.
- Finally, after sharing, ask students to add what they have learned about the Spatial Semiotic System to their learning wall. Ask them to select some annotated images that they feel best illustrate their learning about these codes to add to their statements.

Conclusion

The purpose of this chapter was to examine the nature of multimodal text and the concept of design, that is, producing and consuming text. There has been a focus on the dynamic and changing nature of multimodal texts and the necessity to focus on the processes of designing them as complex, involving active problem-solving rather than passive consumption and reproduction. The social and cultural influences on the process of designing multimodal texts, and the fact that they will continue to change, has been emphasised.

The following have been identified as essential to teaching about designing multimodal texts in a multiliterate world:

- higher order thinking skills and metacognition
- the ability to work collaboratively and interact in productive ways around the consumption and production of text
- the ability to select and use available resources strategically to fulfil the desired purpose and context
- understanding the codes and conventions of the semiotic systems and their role in representing meaning in multimodal texts
- the role of planning, in terms of before, during and after, when designing text
- the use of pedagogy and learning episodes that present literacy and the repertoire of resources for literacy as dynamic rather than static
- the role of modelling, metacognition and the use of metalanguage
- the use of authentic texts and contexts for designing texts
- the need for focussed learning episodes, opportunities to practice and opportunities to transfer, adapt and apply knowledge about multimodal text in new contexts

Bibliography

Anstey, M 2002, *Literate Futures: Reading*, AccessEd, Department of Education, State of Queensland, Coorparoo.

Anstey, M & Bull, G 2004, *The Literacy Labyrinth*, 2nd edn, Pearson Education, Sydney.

Anstey, M & Bull, G 2016, 'Pedagogies for developing literacies of the visual', *Practical Literacy: The Early and Primary Years*, vol. 21, no. 1, pp. 22–4.

Bearne, E & Wolstencroft, H 2007, *Visual Approaches to Teaching Writing: Multimodal Literacy 5–11*, Paul Chapman Publishing, London.

Bull, G & Anstey, M 2010, 'Using the principles of multiliteracies to inform pedagogical change', in DR Cole, and DL Pullen (eds), *Multiliteracies in Motion*, Routledge, Abingdon, pp. 141–59.

Brown, AL 1978, 'Knowing when, where and how to remember: A problem of metacognition', in R Glaser (ed) *Advances in Instructional Psychology, Vol. 1*, Lawrence Erlbaum, Hillsdale.

Brown, AL & Palincsar, AS 1982, 'Inducing strategic learning from texts by means of informed, self-control training', *Topics in Learning and Learning Disabilities*, April, pp. 1–17.

Coffin, C and Derewianka, BM 2009, 'Multimodal layout in school history books: The texturing of historical interpretation', in G Forey & G Thompson (eds), *Text Type and Texture: In Honour of Flo Davies*, Equinox Publishing, London, pp. 191–215.

Cope, B & Kalantzis, M (eds) 2000, *Multiliteracies: Literacy Learning and the Design of Social Futures*, Routledge, London.

Coscarelli, CV & Coiro, J 2014, 'Reading multiple sources online', in *Linguagem & Ensino, Pelotas*, vol. 17, no. 3, pp. 751–76.

Derewianka, BM 1990, *Exploring How Texts Work*, Primary English Teaching Association, Rozelle.

Derewianka, BM 2015, 'The contribution of genre theory to literacy education in Australia', in J Turbill, G Barton & C Brock (eds), *Teaching Writing in Today's Classrooms: Looking Back to Looking Forward*, Australian Literary Educators' Association, Norwood, pp. 69–86.

Derewianka, BM & Coffin, C 2008, 'Time visuals in history textbooks: Some pedagogic issues', in L Unsworth (ed), *Multimodal Semiotics: Functional Analysis in Contexts of Education*, Continuum, London, pp. 187–200.

Derewianka, BM & Jones, P 2016, *Teaching Language in Context*, 2nd edn, Oxford University Press, South Melbourne.

Griffith, RL & Ruan, J 2005, 'What is metacognition and what should be its role in literacy instruction', in SE Israel, CC Block, KI Bauserman & K Kinnucan-Welsch (eds), *Metacognition in Literacy Learning: Theory, Assessment, Instruction and Professional Development*, Lawrence Erlbaum, New Jersey, pp. 3–18.

Hartman, DK, Morsink, PM & Zheng, J 2010, 'From print to pixels: The evolution of cognitive conceptions of reading comprehension', in EA Baker, (ed), *The New Literacies, Multiple Perspectives on Research and Practice*, The Guilford Press, New York, pp. 131–64.

Jewitt, C 2008, *Technology, Literacy and Learning: A Multimodal Approach*, Routledge, Abingdon.

Jewitt, C & Kress, G 2008, *Multimodal Literacy*, Peter Lang, New York.

Kalantzis, M, Cope, B, Chan, E & Dalley-Trim, L 2016, *Literacies*, 2nd edn, Cambridge University Press, Port Melbourne.

Kress, G 2000, 'Design and transformation: New theories of meaning', in B Cope & M Kalantzis (eds), *Multiliteracies: Literacy Learning and the Design of Social Futures*, Routledge, London.

Kress, G 2003, *Literacy in the New Media Age*, Routledge, London.

Kress, G 2010, *Multimodality: A Social Semiotic Approach to Contemporary Communication*, Routledge, Abingdon.

Kress, G & van Leeuwen, T 2001, *Multimodal Discourse: The Modes and Media of Contemporary Communication*, Arnold, London.

Kress, G & van Leeuwen, T 2006, *Reading Images: The Grammar of Visual Design*, 2nd edn, Routledge, London.

Littleton, K & Mercer, N 2013, *Interthinking: Putting Talk to Work*, Routledge, London.

Paris, SG Newman, RS & McVey, KA 1981, 'From tricks to strategies: Learning the functional significance of mnemonic actions', unpublished manuscript, University of Michigan, Ann Arbor.

Paris, SG, Cross, DR & Lipson, MY 1984, 'Informed strategies for learning: A program to improve children's reading awareness and comprehension', *Journal of Educational Psychology*, vol. 76, no. 6, pp. 1239–52.

Paris, S & Newman, R 1990, 'Developmental aspects of self-regulated learning', *Educational Psychologist*, vol. 25, pp. 87–102.

Paris, SG & Paris, AH 2001, 'Classroom applications of research on self-regulated learning', *Educational Psychologist*, vol. 36, no. 2, pp. 89–101.

Rennie, J & Patterson, A 2010, 'Young Australians reading in a digital world', in DR Cole, & DL Pullen, *Multiliteracies in Motion*, Routledge, Abingdon, pp. 207–23.

Silvers, P and Shorey, M 2012, *Many Texts, Many Voices: Teaching Literacy and Social Justice to Young Learners in the Digital Age*, Stenhouse, Portland.

Tan, S 2000, *The Lost Thing*, Lothian, Port Melbourne.

Zimmerman, BJ 2000, 'Attaining self-regulation: A social cognitive perspective', in M Boekarts, P Pintrich, & M Zeidner (eds), *Self-Regulation: Theory, Research, and Applications*, Academic, Orlando, pp. 13–39.

4 Teaching and learning multiliteracies: Examining classroom pedagogy and practices through a focus on teacher talk and dialogic talk

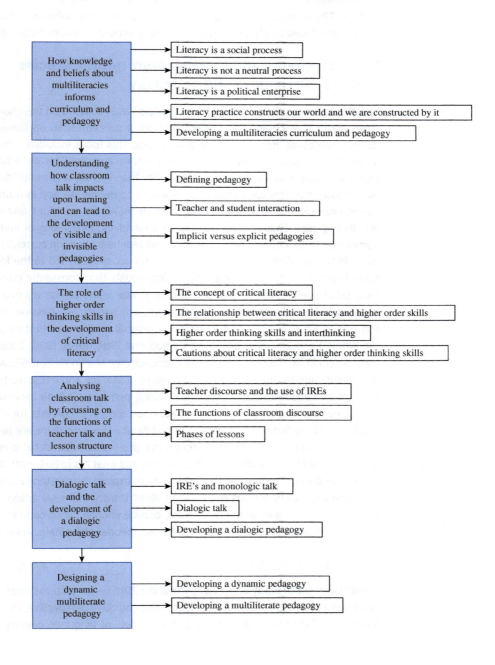

This chapter begins by translating the knowledge, skills and understandings about literacies and multiliteracies presented in the previous two chapters into classroom practices. It will be proposed that simply understanding the concepts of literacies and multiliteracies will not necessarily change classroom practices. Classrooms as social and cultural sites will be explored and the relationships among literacy learning, higher order thinking skills, classroom talk and pedagogy will be investigated. Tools will be presented that will enable the examination of different functions of teacher talk and the structures of lessons. The concepts of dialogic talk and a dynamic multiliterate pedagogy will be introduced as effective vehicles for developing multiliterate practices.

How knowledge and beliefs about multiliteracies informs curriculum and pedagogy

The discussions in the previous three chapters have focussed on the changing views about literacy and the movement from a concentration on literacy to the exploration of literacies and multiliteracies. This focus included consideration of the practices involved in becoming literate and multiliterate. A careful case was made to investigate literacies rather than literacy and multiliteracies rather than multiliteracy. In the past, attempts to define literacy as a unitary concept have led to fierce debates about which definitions are 'right' and which are 'wrong' (see Chapter One, discussion on evolving definitions of literacy). Sometimes these debates recommended that teachers abandon currently held views in favour of more 'appropriate' ones and occasionally led to the formation of groups or camps of like-minded individuals that constantly criticised each other over preferences about how particular views of literacy might be adopted. In Australia one such debate that became particularly passionate, and sometimes led to vehement criticisms of personal beliefs, was that involving the Whole Language Approach (see Cambourne 1986, 1988, 1994; Goodman 1986; Smith 1978, 1982) and the Genre Approach (see Martin 1985, 1992). At the time the debate did little to clarify the concept of literacy and left some teachers confused about how to implement a literacy pedagogy in their classroom.

The idea that a single definition of literacy could apply in all contexts, for all individuals, all of the time, seems fraught with difficulty. However, there are general statements that can be made about literacy that provide sufficient detail to enable the development of ideas about literate practices and what it is to be literate. These statements provide, on the one hand, a platform to explore the substantial changes in knowledge, understandings and opinions about literacy that have arisen in the last three decades, and on the other hand, provide enough background to assist individual teachers in the construction of personal theories about literacy pedagogy.

Literacy is a social process

Traditionally, particularly in the early to middle 20th century, literacy was characterised as skill-based from a psychological or cognitive perspective. This view arose from the prevailing psycholinguistic models of language development at the time from theoreticians such as Vygotsky (1962), Chomsky (1965) and Lenneberg (1967). These theorists interpreted the study of language and literacy through a focus on the mind and thinking. In the 1970s an alternative view of literacy began to be developed that interpreted literacy as a social process drawing on the foundational work of researchers such as Bernstein, Labov and Cazden (previously discussed in Chapter Two). In contrast to **psycholinguistic** theory, this perspective was based on a **sociolinguistic** viewpoint that examined roles and relationships in social contexts and acknowledged the social, cultural, political, ideological and economic nature of literacy.

From a sociolinguistic perspective, literacy is practised in many different ways, in many different contexts, for many different purposes. Conversely, the psycholinguistic perspective involves engaging in literacy through an invariant sequence of developmental steps or stages and is sometimes described as the psychologising of literacy. The movement towards viewing literacy as a social process required a dramatic paradigm shift proposed by researchers such as Luke (1995), Freebody and Luke (1990), Green and Weade (1990) and Street (1993). This theory of literacy as a social process was founded on observations of everyday social practices, in particular, cultural contexts in the home, school and other social institutions and the community. These practices can be as disparate as reading maps or road signs, texting on a mobile (cell) phone or talking, writing or reading about a text in a school setting. Social practices influence how children learn and what they understand by literacy, how teachers construct literacy in their classrooms and how teachers respond towards different students. These practices therefore take account of the life world/school world proposed by Cope and Kalantzis and of the D/discourses suggested by Gee, as previously discussed in Chapter Two.

As in the earlier discussion about the whole language and genre approaches, the psycholinguistic and sociolinguistic theories were sometimes presented to teachers as a choice between conflicting ideas. The value of the sociolinguistic theory was that it described what parents, teachers and literacy learners did and why they did it. As Freebody and Freiberg (2001) pointed out, this was something that psycholinguistic theory was unable to do. This does not lead to the proposition that psycholinguistic theory should be abandoned because there are situations in which students can profit from explicit instruction about the knowledge and thinking skills involved in literacy learning, as discussed in the section on metacognition in Chapter Three. The important question to ask is how sociolinguistic theory can support and augment psycholinguistic theory rather than how it can replace it. A balanced approach that incorporates both theories is a more relevant proposition since neither theory is appropriate for all contexts.

Psycholinguistics
A theory of language and literacy learning and teaching that draws on the fields of psychology and linguistics. As such, it integrates the study of cognition (psychology) and language (linguistics) and focusses on the structure of skills and thinking processes that take place in the mind. It is, therefore, largely internal, invisible and highly individualistic. According to some theorists, it can sometimes involve a series of developmental stages.

Sociolinguistics
A theory of language and literacy learning and teaching that draws on the fields of sociology and linguistics. It focusses on social interaction and inter-personal communication in social settings. It is based on the study of language in use and is therefore able to be observed externally in groups and other social situations.

Literacy is not a neutral process

Each text that a parent, teacher or another community member selects for students to consume carries with it ideas about how the world is constructed. Every text, whether paper, live or digital, is based upon a collection

AUDITING INSTRUMENT 4.1

- The purpose of this Auditing Instrument is to investigate your classroom practices to determine whether you have a balanced approach in your pedagogy.
- Review your lesson planning to establish whether you rely on a single definition of literacy in your everyday teaching, or whether you are implementing a balanced approach that attempts to vary your approach to suit a particular context or student.
- Tape a lesson, or part of a lesson, and listen to how you are engaging students in literacy learning. Are you favouring a psychological or a sociological theory or are you attempting to achieve some balance between the two?
- If you are dissatisfied with your planning or your practice, how might you go about changing your approach?

of attitudes, values, ideologies and beliefs that support particular meanings contained in that text. The author of the text has authored (produced) a text that authorises (ascribes importance to) a set of attitudes, values, ideologies or beliefs. The author may have intentionally selected particular attitudes, values, ideologies and beliefs or may not be aware that certain perspectives have been represented. As a case in point, Anstey (1993c) was giving a presentation at a conference that involved the analysis of the attitudes, values and beliefs portrayed in a book by a particular author/illustrator. After the presentation, a very excited individual, who turned out to be the author/illustrator of the book, came to the front of the room and began a discussion that revolved around the fact that he had not realised that he had portrayed those attitudes, values, ideologies and beliefs but that the analysis that had been presented added important weight and meaning to the book.

Every author (producer) of a text, whether intentionally or not, constructs certain meanings in a text which in turn constructs the consumer of the text. No text is neutral just as no literacy practice is neutral. The talk around the text, whether by the teacher or the student, can have the effect of empowering or disempowering participants in a learning episode. Some students will bring from home particular ways of talking that are those valued by the school. If home and school talk are analogous then students will be empowered and able to take an active part in classroom conversations. The effect that the difference between home and school talk has on student performance at school received early attention by researchers such as Tough (1976), Taylor (1983) and Heath (1983) and later by Gee (1990, 1992), who analysed the differences between home and school talk by investigating D/discourses. The concept of D/discourses has previously been discussed in Chapter Two but it is interesting to note that Gee (1992, pp. 111-13) suggested that Discourses were inherently value and ideologically laden and therefore had the power to marginalise viewpoints.

It is important that teachers are aware, not only of what Discourses they valourise in their classrooms, but also what Discourses their students bring to school. Students also need to be encouraged to engage with the texts they encounter by asking themselves questions such as 'What are the attitudes, values, ideologies or beliefs being portrayed in this text?', 'What is this text trying to make me believe?' and 'What should I do with this text?'.

REFLECTION STRATEGY 4.1

- The purpose of this Reflection Strategy is to review the literacy practices involved in your talk around text.
- When you are analysing texts with your class, to what extent do you discuss the attitudes, values, ideologies or beliefs that are represented in the text?
- What investigations have you undertaken in order to determine the types of talk that the students bring to your classroom?
- How are your students able to engage in talking around text, both independently and with direct support from you?
- Are there students in your class who have been marginalised because the Discourses they have brought from home are different from the ones that you value? How will you identify these students and what will you do to support them?

Literacy is a political enterprise

In any classroom, particular literacy practices are foregrounded and valued by the teacher over others. This is the result of teachers continually making decisions about which strategies to utilise, which method of instruction to employ, which text or other resource to select and which lesson needs to be taught and when, or how, the lesson should be introduced. Once a particular literacy practice is preferred over another, some students will be empowered and others constrained because of experiences that they have, or have not, been exposed to. By virtue of membership of a certain social or cultural group, some students will benefit by having their existing literacy practices reinforced while others will have their practices devalued or challenged. This process of ongoing choice by the teacher or the school results in literacy practice being inherently political. Every teacher has learnt and values certain D/discourses (to use Gee's terminology) over others because of their own experiences. These D/discourses maybe be overt and especially selected because the teacher judges them to be appropriate for a particular class, situation or context. Conversely, they may be covert and employed automatically as a default position because this is the way it has always been done. This default position may be employed for a number of reasons, including the pressure to cover content, challenging behaviour by the students, unfamiliarity with the content or some other stressful situation or a lack of knowledge about the background of the students.

In the Australian context Bull and Anstey (1995) were researching in a very isolated and remote area adjacent to the Gulf of Carpentaria in far north-western Queensland. A lesson in English for Year 10 students was observed, where Greek myths and legends were being studied. Most of the students in the class were Aboriginal and were, not surprisingly, uninterested in the topic of the lesson. They did not enjoy the lesson, they learnt little from it and it did not relate in any way to their life experiences. The majority of the students were not going to progress past Year 10 and few were willing to leave the district. There did not seem to be any reason why the lesson was being taught and when the teacher was later questioned about the reasons for embarking on such a series of lessons they remarked that the study of myths and legends was in the curriculum and this was the way they had taught it the year before (in a large capital city). The irony of this situation was that the school had a vibrant Aboriginal centre managed by an Aboriginal woman who was currently engaged in collecting Aboriginal stories from the local elders. Some of these stories were traditional narratives, some were songs and some were dances that were carefully scripted performances of stories, all of which had been handed down through generations and were highly valued because they had recorded important social and cultural events. Starting with the students' culture and moving to other cultures may have engaged students more successfully. Because the teacher had selected certain literacy practices, the students were being shaped in ways that constrained them as individuals, disempowered their culture and devalued their existing literacy, social and cultural practices. Comparable observations resulting in similar cases of disempowerment were found by Bull and Anstey (1996, 1997).

The lesson that has been described above contained a number of choices that had been made by the teacher that caused it to be highly political. These choices may have been covertly made as a result of the teacher adopting a default position because of some stressful situation. Whether the choices were made covertly or overtly does not change the outcome of the lesson. What this lesson does indicate is that in any focussed literacy activity teachers need to be cognisant of the political choices that have been made. It is not just a matter of getting the lesson done, but how and why it is done.

AUDITING INSTRUMENT 4.2

- The purpose of this Auditing Instrument is to examine the choices that you have made in selecting which strategies, lessons, texts and methods to employ in your day-to-day teaching.
- What sort of balance is there in the strategies you have selected to introduce to your class?
- Review the lessons you have taught over the last couple of weeks to determine whether they are often focussed only on covering content.

- What steps have you taken to investigate the literacy identities of your students to establish whether the lessons you are teaching are meeting the needs of the students?
- What methodologies are you using when engaging in literacy teaching? Do you tend to use just one approach, and if so, how is this influencing student performance?

Literacy practice constructs our world and we are constructed by it

As has been argued previously, literacy is a political enterprise. There are, however, other social and cultural forces at work related to expectations about what literacy practices schools should employ and even how literacy can be defined and operationalised. Tensions can arise in schools and classrooms when parental or societal expectations about content and methodology do not match those of the school. As Levett and Lankshear (1990) reported in the New Zealand context, parents and students were concerned about the balance of theory and practice in the curriculum content and also the purposes of particular content. Earlier Lankshear and Lawler (1989) had explored the impact of different expectations between the home and school about how literacy should be constructed and taught through consideration of what they termed 'proper' and 'improper' literacy. These differences in expectations can lead to certain groups of students being marginalised or silenced, leading to failure to successfully progress through the education system. Similar results were found by Louden and Rivalland (1995) in Western Australia, where students had learnt particular cultural and religious literate practices with text that relied only on remembering and repeating word for word what they had read.

Lankshear and Lawler reported on research by Jones (1986), who studied two groups of secondary classrooms, one predominantly white, middle class, and the other made up of Pacific island students. The middle class students expected their teacher to be a facilitator who supported them through discussion and inquiry. The Pacific island students expected their teacher to be the font of all knowledge whose role was to deliver material for them to memorise. For them education was best conducted through note-taking exercises taken from blackboard summaries provided by the teacher (proper teaching). If their teachers attempted to facilitate learning through discussion, then this was interpreted as bad teaching (improper teaching). Student expectations about methodology, and about literacy learning, led to educational success for the white, middle-class students and to failure for the Pacific island students. In Cazden's (1967, 1970, 1972) terms, as was discussed in Chapter Two, the white, middle class students were communicatively competent because they adopted particular literacy practices that supported success in that classroom context. Conversely, the Pacific island students continued to adopt practices, which other Pacific island students had adopted before them, that led to failure. As Jones' (1986) study had indicated, the holding of particular expectations led to social reproduction.

In a similar situation to the New Zealand context, Bull and Anstey (2009) conducted a study in an Australian setting aimed at investigating sustainable learning futures for Indigenous students. They found that a significant proportion of Aboriginal parents expected that learning at school, especially literacy learning, would be centred around modelling and demonstrations by teachers as supporting mentors. This expectation was founded on well-established strategies developed by the local Aboriginal people (and by other Aboriginal groups across Australia) over a considerable period of time. These strategies grew out of social and cultural norms that regarded direct question and answer sequences as inappropriate and impolite. Since question and answer sequences are a dominant form of instruction in the majority of Australian classrooms, a 'gap' between Aboriginal and non-Aboriginal student achievement has resulted.

AUDITING INSTRUMENT 4.3

- The purpose of this Auditing Instrument is to ascertain whether the literacy practices that you are employing are appropriate for your students.
- What type of **environmental scan** have you completed to find out what expectations the parents have about your literacy practices?
- In what way do your literacy practices meet the expectations of the parents?
- How have you involved parents in determining which methodologies to employ?

Environmental scan
An environmental scan is conducted to identify factors that may inform the educational philosophy and pedagogical practices of a school. Data would be collected regarding the physical and geographical environment and characteristics of the community regarding, work, income, social and cultural activities, education levels, attitudes toward, and expectations of education. Questionnaires, interviews, surveys and government information sources can be used to gather data.

Developing a multiliteracies curriculum and pedagogy

The four statements about literacy that have been previously discussed, together with (a) the implications for pedagogy presented in Chapter One, (b) the characteristics of a multiliterate person that were developed in Chapter Two and (c) the discussion of multimodal texts and semiotic systems in Chapter Three, generate a set of principles that can be used to guide the development of a curriculum and pedagogy for multiliteracies. These principles can assist teachers and support students by providing opportunities to engage with multiliterate practices. A multiliterate curriculum and pedagogy encompasses:

- Investigating how literacy and literate practices operate in a variety of contexts
- Understanding that multimodal texts are designed using combinations of semiotic systems (Linguistic, Visual, Audio, Spatial, Gestural)
- Developing understandings about, and application of, critical literacy
- Consuming, producing and transforming multimodal texts in a variety of contexts and purposes

- Understanding that multimodal texts are delivered via combinations of paper, live and digital technologies
- Involving students in working collaboratively on authentic tasks,
- Promoting students' ability to problem-solve and create meanings through talk
- Developing understandings about how literate practices relate to social, cultural, political and economic and ideological aspects of society
- Understanding that multiliteracies and multiliterate practices are dynamic

AUDITING INSTRUMENT 4.4

- The purpose of this Auditing Instrument is to investigate the pedagogy that you are implementing in your classroom.
- Review the lessons that you have been teaching over the last 2–3 weeks. Are there clear statements in your planning about how and why you are teaching particular lessons?
- Are you relying on one pedagogical approach to the neglect of others?
- If there is not a definite pedagogical approach in your lessons, what impact is this having on student learning?

It is important to realise that implementing the nine principles suggested here will not lead to the successful teaching and learning of multiliteracies if they are used only for the selection of content. While the principles are useful in developing a curriculum that will support learning about multiliteracies, the realisation of the full potential for learning will only be achieved through the design of a pedagogy that underlies the curriculum. It is also important, given the preceding discussions about such issues as D/discourses, literacy identity, diversity and expectations, that such a pedagogy should be appropriate and inclusive.

REFLECTION STRATEGY 4.2

- The purpose of this Reflection Strategy is to make judgements about the quality of your approach to pedagogy.
- Given the literacy identities of the students in your class, how appropriate is your pedagogy?
- Are you using a range of pedagogical approaches to cater for the range of abilities in your class?
- Is your pedagogical approach inclusive by catering for different social and cultural backgrounds?

Understanding how classroom talk impacts upon learning and can lead to the development of visible and invisible pedagogies

Defining pedagogy

The concept of pedagogy has attracted the attention of many researchers, curriculum planners, boards of education, schools and teachers. In 1998 and in 2017 the National Board for Professional Teaching Standards in the U.S. stated that the term *pedagogy* referred to the skills that teachers employed to impart the knowledge or content related to their discipline. Later, MacNeill, Cavanagh and Silcox (2003, p. 3) suggested that 'Pedagogy is a planned action, designed by human agency … which directly results in the acquisition of new knowledge, beliefs or skills for the learner.' What these two definitions share, along with many others in the same period, is the idea that pedagogy focusses on the teacher and the act of teaching and is therefore concerned with what teacher practices are required for an effective pedagogy. Neither of these definitions acknowledges that student learning should be considered as an important facet of pedagogy. More recent views of pedagogy take into account both the teacher and learner. Jewitt (2006, p. 141) suggested that pedagogy was '… realised through the practices of the teacher in their interpersonal interaction with students' while Burn and Parker (2008, p. 58) stated that pedagogy '… represents a set of beliefs about what is to be learnt and how the learning might best be organised'. These latter two definitions, because they regard the roles of both teacher and student as necessary in engaging in learning, construct a deeper understanding of pedagogy. Further to these considerations, Kress (2010, p. 144) proposed that conceptions of **pedagogy** were inherently political and would need to attend to questions of power and the agency of learners.

Pedagogy
The concept of pedagogy explains the relationship between teaching and learning. It defines the conditions necessary for students to fully participate in learning while also describing the teaching practices necessary to support such learning. Literacy pedagogy needs to take account of developments in contemporary society such as cultural and linguistic diversity and also the range of new texts produced by the semiotic systems and the new technologies, the advent of new literacies and consideration of literacy identity.

REFLECTION STRATEGY 4.3

- The purpose of this Reflection Strategy is to look at the focus of your pedagogy.
- Read the definition of pedagogy in the Running Glossary.
- Have you concerned yourself with thinking about your pedagogy in these ways? If not, what effect do you think this has had on your teaching?
- What approach to pedagogy have you employed?

Teacher and student interaction

One of the significant impacts on classroom pedagogy is the characteristics of the interactions between teachers and students. The classroom is a distinct social context that has particular routines and ways of interacting that are not typically found outside of it. The ubiquitous question and answer sequence followed by an evaluative comment does not occur outside of the classroom. Teachers often ask questions that they know the answers to and students are well aware of this 'game'. Imagine what the reaction might be if the following conversation were to take place in a suburban street.

TRANSCRIPT 4.1

Driver: I seem to be lost. Could you give me directions to Hopeville?
Pedestrian: Certainly. If you go down that way and take the third street on your left, you will be on the right road.
Driver: That's the correct answer. Well done!

Routinised behaviour has an impact on pedagogy but it is not the only influence. If the pedagogy is learner focussed, the teacher-student interactions will influence the types of knowledge conveyed and the way that knowledge is constructed in the classroom. In employing a learner focussed pedagogy, the teacher might utilise self-directed or discovery learning. Conversely, if they employed a teacher focussed pedagogy, they might use explicit, teacher directed instruction. Pedagogies are driven by student-teacher interactions, and these interactions are realised through talk, whether it be teacher talk, student talk or some combination of the two. A considerable body of research has been conducted since the 1990s around aspects of the pedagogy of literacy lessons. Baker (1991a, 1991b), Baker and Freebody (1989a, 1989b), Freebody, Ludwig and Gunn, (1995), Edwards-Groves (1998, 2003a) Freebody and Freiberg (2001), Anstey (1991, 1993a, 1993b, 1998) and Edwards-Groves, Anstey and Bull (2014) all reported that teacher talk, and the resultant student talk, around the routines and interactions of the classroom had a powerful effect on the success, or otherwise, of the students' literacy learning. The transcript below is taken from the research of Anstey (1993a) and is similar to many of the transcripts in Edwards-Groves, Anstey and Bull (2014). It illustrates how confusion can arise in students' minds when teacher talk is not precise. The transcript was taken from a lesson on the research/inquiry process in a Year 5 classroom where the average age was 10 years.

TRANSCRIPT 4.2

T: You people over here, turn the books in front of you to the article entitled 'Titles and subtitles' on page 24 and 25. Have you got that in front of you? OK. What is the general title of the story?
S: 'Games'?

> T: Games is the first heading. Right, what are the three sub-headings, or the, yes, there are three, sorry there are three sub-headings to the word, to 'Games' in the title? What are they? (nods to student)
> S: 'Games played by…'?
> T: No. No. The three sub-headings, the title is 'Games', what is the first sub-heading? (nods to student with hand up)
> S: 'Party Games'?
> T: 'Party Games'. Good girl. OK. What is the next sub-heading? (nods to student with hand up)
> S: (reading) 'Racing Games'.
> T: 'Racing Games'. OK, and the third one? (nods to student with hand up)
> S: (reading) 'Team Games'?
> T: Now underneath the sub-heading 'Party Games' there are three statements made there, things the article might be about: 'Games you Might Play by Yourself, Games that Show How to Live, Games that are Fun for All'. Now if you were reading part of an article just on 'Party Games', which one of those would you expect to be reading about, before you even start to read? Write out. I'm sorry, get out your comprehension books in front of you. Just set it up, 'Titles and Sub-titles' please. (pause while students get books out) Just set it up, 'Titles and Sub-titles' please. (pause while students continue writing) If you've finished writing those questions down that you might find, now which of those first ones would you expect to find under 'Party Games'? Quickly write it down. (pause while students write, T walks around looking over students' shoulders) Write it down quickly; I think there is only the one there. Party games we would expect. What do you call party games? … Which of the three would you expect to read about under party games?
> S: 'Games that are Fun for All'?
> T: 'Games that are Fun for All' Who wrote that? (glances around room at hands up) Who had anything else? (no hands up)

At first glance, what is striking in this excerpt of the lesson is that the transcript contains a preponderance of teacher talk. There is nothing inherently wrong with a teacher giving detailed instructions, especially when new work is being introduced (as is the case in this lesson). However, in this excerpt the students have little opportunity to talk except when they answer questions posed by the teacher. The students do not get any chance to initiate discussion or to ask questions for clarification. Had they been allowed such chances, they may have been able to achieve a greater understanding of what it was they were supposed to be learning and also provide more feedback to the teacher about the quality of their learning. The question marks at the end of most student responses have been placed there to indicate rising intonations, which illustrate that the students were unsure of their answers and were, in fact, guessing. The students' confusion was exacerbated by the teacher, who also appeared unsure about the metalanguage that was being introduced. Terms such as 'titles', 'headings' and 'sub-headings' were used interchangeably with no clear definitions given, and no information given about how they had different purposes in the passage under discussion. This gave the students little opportunity to engage in metacognitive behaviour in order to understand the purpose of the lesson, or what meanings they were supposed to be making, by thinking about questions such as:

- What am I supposed to be learning here?
- What is this lesson about?
- How are headings different from sub-headings?
- When, and how, do I use headings and sub-headings?
- How do I participate in this lesson?
- What information has been provided that I need to learn?
- Have I been a successful learner in this lesson?

There was little information in the lesson that could have assisted the students in answering any of these questions. The only way the students could have realistically made sense of this lesson was by drawing on their past experiences of earlier lessons. The information that was provided was random and implicit and relied on the students being passive receivers rather than active participants. For these reasons, it would be highly unlikely that the students would engage in any metacognitive behaviour by considering any of the questions. An over-reliance on the textbook questions also limited discussion of the metacognitive aspects of the lesson.

AUDITING INSTRUMENT 4.5

- The purpose of this Auditing Instrument is to complete an analysis of a recent lesson that you have taught. The lesson can be from any subject area or discipline.
- Make an audio tape of a lesson where you are introducing some new work. Ensure that you are introducing a new skill or content, as that will provide you with more information than a lesson that focusses on practice of a known skill.
- Record the whole lesson because remembering to turn the tape off, or on, during a lesson can be a problem. Select a short excerpt from the tape of about five to 10 minutes.
- Listen to the tape in order to hear what your students are hearing. This may lead to you making some adjustments in your classroom talk such as modifying repetitive expressions or changing the volume, intonation or speed of your talk.
- Make a transcript of the excerpt and review your lesson. Consider whether the students in your lesson would be able to answer the following questions:
    o   What am I supposed to be learning here?
    o   What is this lesson about?
    o   How do I participate in this lesson?
    o   What information has been provided that I need to learn?
    o   Have I been a successful learner in this lesson?
- On the basis of your reflections about whether the students would be able answer these questions, make a judgement about the success of the lesson.

In a second lesson of the 25 observed by Anstey (1993a) the students were engaged in a new, research/inquiry activity and were also Year 5 students. This enabled comparisons to be made by analysing Transcript 4.2 and Transcript 4.3, presented below.

TRANSCRIPT 4.3

T: Right, now we're going to look and introduce ourselves (sic) today to skimming. We're going to have to check what skimming is and learn the techniques of skimming so that when I open my book I am able to skim through it.

First of all, let's work out what skimming is. Well, it's a technique where you can (walks to whiteboard and writes: 1. Find out quickly) find out quickly whether there is any information in that book, in that paragraph, that you might need.

For example, you've taken this here (taps title of project 'Trains in Australia' written on whiteboard) You're looking up trains.... Instead of reading the whole chapter may take you a fair while...

(Reviewing carried out later in the lesson)

T: You don't read every sentence, right. You don't have to read every sentence or word. What do you think would be the most important sentence to read in the paragraph? (nods to student with hand up)
S: The first.
T: Right, why do you think the first...?

(A further review towards the end of the lesson)

T: You skim through, that's what skimming is (points to notes on whiteboard) You read the first sentence, read the last sentence ... So why do we skim? Why you skim (writes '4: Idea?' on whiteboard) because you need an idea of whether the information is good or not... If you were doing ... 'aha, that's what I'm looking for' or 'that's rubbish'... So that's why you skim. Right? So, what you need to ask yourself after you skim is (walks to whiteboard and writes 'Do I want it?') 'Do I want the information?'

Transcript 4.3 is different from Transcript 4.2 in that it is made up of three excerpts taken from the beginning, middle and end of the lesson, whereas Transcript 4.2 contains only one excerpt from the beginning of the lesson. However, both transcripts are representative of the whole lesson. The student talk in the second transcript was quite extensive and occurred in between the three excerpts so comparisons of the quality of student talk in the two lessons cannot be made here. Nevertheless, there are other comparisons that can be made. In the second lesson, a specific purpose (to learn about skimming) was identified at the beginning of the lesson and the metalanguage concerned with skimming was clearly defined. Teacher talk was broken up by the use of the whiteboard, where a record was compiled of the main points of the lesson. The teacher used the whiteboard as a summary of the modelling that had taken place.

By applying the same questions to the second lesson as had been done in the first lesson it is possible to make the following statements:

o   What was to be learnt was clearly defined at the start of the lesson
o   A definite purpose for the lesson was identified early
o   Skimming was specifically defined
o   Clear guidance about how, and why, to engage in skimming was provided throughout the lesson
o   Because the teacher engaged in metacognitive behaviour the students had clear directions about how to participate in skimming
o   The whiteboard summary clearly identified the important information that needed to be learnt
o   Because (a) the purpose of the lesson was identified, (b) the metalanguage was defined, and (c) the teacher modelled metacognitive behaviour, the students were given clear ideas about how to judge the success of their learning.

AUDITING INSTRUMENT 4.6

- The purpose of this Auditing Instrument is to review your previously recorded five to 10 minute excerpt and consider changes you think might be necessary to make it more successful. It is more desirable to review the excerpt after looking at both transcripts because this enables you to judge positive aspects as well as aspects that may need to be changed.
- It is important that you focus on the positive aspects of the lesson (what worked well) as well as those aspects that you think need to be changed (what didn't work so well).
- The preceding seven statements relating to Transcript 4.3 will give direction to your lesson review.
- Remember that this activity should be seen as determining what changes could be made to the lesson. It is not intended that you should be deciding whether you are a good, or poor, teacher. It is a lesson review, not a teacher review. If you approach it in this way, it will be a far more useful experience.

By comparing the seven statements above to the original questions in the first lesson it is possible to make a number of comments. While the first lesson was random in its execution, the second lesson had a clear purpose and a definite sequence. Where the first lesson was implicit, the second lesson was explicit. Because the second lesson explicitly stated what learning was to take place, supplied demonstrations supported by teacher talk, and modelled the literacy practices to be learnt, the students could be expected to successfully transfer what they had learnt to future lessons about skimming. The students in the first lesson were unlikely to be able to draw conclusions about titles, headings and sub-headings or transfer their learning to other contexts with any understanding. The first lesson encouraged students to be passive recipients while the second lesson encouraged active and flexible participation. Therefore, the pedagogy that is being employed in the first lesson does not appear to be clear to either the teacher or the students. In this sense the pedagogy was largely invisible. The pedagogy in the second lesson was highly visible. The difference between invisible pedagogies and visible pedagogies is the difference between unsuccessful and successful learning. It is important to point out here that what is being compared is one lesson against another. There is no intention to identify one teacher as 'good' and another as 'poor'. It is quite possible that the first teacher could redesign the lesson and turn it into a successful one. The second teacher had clearly defined their pedagogy, made it visible, while the first teacher had not specified a particular pedagogy so it was invisible. The use of implicit pedagogical practices is not an uncommon occurrence, as reported by Edwards-Groves (2003b).

Implicit versus explicit pedagogies

The question of implicit versus explicit practices also arises when teachers select a particular approach to literacy instruction. One such approach is that of Cambourne's (1988) theory of whole language and natural learning. The pedagogical practices that formed the basis of this approach were centred around his conditions of learning. These conditions were originally built around the idea that the processes involved in learning oral language in the home were universal and could be applied to the learning of reading and writing at school. The concept of natural learning gained traction with teachers as a reaction to the rigid, inflexible and static practices of the skills approach to literacy teaching that had been in favour since the 1960s. There were a number of criticisms of this position (see Anstey and Bull, 2004; Muspratt, Luke and Freebody, 1997), including the failure to acknowledge the rich social, cultural and linguistic diversity students brought with them from home. The work of researchers such as Bernstein, Heath and Gee, discussed in Chapter Two, all indicated that there were a range of literacy practices across social class and within different communities that led to some students, who were members of the dominant culture, being privileged while others were disadvantaged. Because the conditions of learning were seen to occur 'naturally' there was no need for explicit teaching of literacy practices and a visible pedagogy. As Delpit (1988) had argued earlier, minority students required explicit teaching practices if they were to succeed rather than being marginalised through lack of exposure to the dominant culture. There is a body of research that suggests that students' literacy learning practices are not often incorporated into those of the school (see Heath 1983; Lankshear and Knobel 2003; Gee 2004) and later research (D'warte 2014) that suggests that when they are, students are highly motivated. The issues surrounding whole language were compounded by the fact that a significant number of teachers in Australia, and elsewhere, interpreted Cambourne's position (and other proponents of whole language) to be far more implicit than was originally intended. The whole question of explicit versus implicit literacy practices can therefore be influenced not only by how a lesson is structured and planned but also by how a theory or approach is adopted by the teacher.

The idea of developing an explicit (visible) pedagogy to support student learning is not new. Research about the success of explicit pedagogy with students with reading difficulties has been reported by Bondy (1984), Paris, Cross and Lipson (1984), Brown (1985), Ellis (1986) and Brown and Kane (1988) and later by Edwards-Groves (2003b) and Edwards-Groves, Anstey and Bull (2014) with mainstream students. However, this concept of an explicit pedagogy that has been explored above should not be seen as related to direct instruction although the two concepts are sometimes used interchangeably. Direct instruction is often associated with a traditional lecture style of teaching with the teacher at the front of the class delivering a set of basic skills to the class as a whole. This approach adopts a rigid, step by step approach to teaching that follows a predetermined and linear sequence of skill acquisition that is substantially different to explicit pedagogy. Nevertheless, there is a place for direct instruction particularly when introducing a new concept. Problems with direct instruction occur when it is used as the only approach rather than in conjunction with other approaches such as discovery learning, guided investigation or negotiated learning.

REFLECTION STRATEGY 4.4

- The purpose of this Reflection Strategy is to investigate what features of your pedagogy you think are important.
- What approach to pedagogy (or pedagogies) do you employ in your classroom?
- Why are these particular pedagogical practices important to the way you teach?
- In what ways are these pedagogical practices explicit or implicit?
- How do the pedagogies and practices you employ impact on the students' learning?

The role of higher order thinking skills in the development of critical literacy

The concept of critical literacy

The concept of critical literacy has been previously discussed in Chapter Two in terms of what practices were involved in being critically literate. Kalantzis et al. (2016, p. 180) identified those practices by suggesting that '… a critically literate person identifies relevant and powerful topics, analyses and documents evidence, considers alternative points-of-view, formulates possible solutions to problems and perhaps also tries these solutions'. Kalantzis et al. (2016, pp. 74, 79, 185) also suggested that critical literacy signified analysing critically, interrogating text, reflecting, applying, interpreting, examining contradictory texts and investigating how readers are positioned by ideologies in texts, or as Kress and van Leeuwen (2006) suggested, reading between the lines. Further, Kalantzis et al. (2016) stated that critical literacy practices were grounded in an individual's lived experiences (their Literacy Identity), which were formed by their social and cultural backgrounds. These views are similar to those proposed earlier by Luke and Freebody (1999), Luke, Comber and Grant (2003) and Iyer and Luke (2010). Both Luke (1993) and Kress and van Leeuwen (2006) also pointed out, as have many others, that critical literacy practices are not confined only to print texts, but encompass multimodal texts. Critical literacy should therefore form an essential part of literacy teaching and learning. As Luke, Comber and Grant (2003) emphasised, critical literacy should not be seen as an afterthought or frill, but rather an 'entitlement' of all individuals in a democracy. As Mills (2005, p. 75) suggested, critical literacy should be seen as '... critical social practice rather than cultural transmission'.

The relationship between critical literacy and higher order thinking skills

It is important to realise that all these views about critical literacy encompass a series of practices that incorporate higher order thinking skills. Higher order thinking skills were proposed by Bloom and Krathwohl (1956) and later revised by Anderson and Krathwohl (2001). Higher Order Thinking Skills, or HOTS, as Bloom and Krathwohl defined them, involved such skills as interpreting, evaluating and analysing. These higher order thinking skills are the same as those referred to by Kalantzis, Luke, Freebody and Kress in their discussions about critical literacy. Conversely, lower order thinking skills, or LOTS, as Bloom and Krathwohl defined them, were concerned with skills such as recall, memory or retelling. In either case, teachers need to introduce students to strategies such as demonstrations, modelling through metacognition, scaffolding or monitoring to support the learning of thinking skills. In making the case for the development of strategies, and the role that metacognition plays in such development, Israel et al. (2005) suggested that the key component of strategies was that they were purposeful and intentional. They also stated that students not only need to be able to use strategies appropriately, but also they needed to be able to select the required strategy from a range of alternatives. This makes the deployment of strategies decisive in contrast to the use of activities that are automatic and applied unconsciously. This distinction is important because students', and teachers', use of higher order thinking strategies needs to be premeditated and deliberate. An important influence on strategy development is the range of texts, and the technologies by which they are delivered, that are made available by teachers in their classrooms. There needs to be a balance between fiction (narrative) and non-fiction (expository) texts. Teachers also need to be conscious of the variety of texts that they introduce so that they do not limit themselves to only those texts that form part of the literacy canon (as discussed previously in Chapter One). As Mills (2005, p. 76) pointed

AUDITING INSTRUMENT 4.7

- The purpose of this Auditing Instrument is to review your lessons to determine what part strategy development plays in teaching and learning in your classroom.
- Review your lesson planning over the last few weeks to ascertain whether strategy development was an important part of your instruction.
- Establish what kind of a balance there was between strategy development and engaging in activities.
- Do your students know a number of strategies that they can use confidently in their learning?
- Are your students able to select, from the strategies they know, those strategies that are suitable to use for particular tasks?
- Check your use of texts to establish if there is a balance across text types and delivery technologies.

out, the selection of texts only from the canon is necessary but not sufficient and needs to be balanced by texts chosen from popular culture.

In order to support students when they are required to decide which higher order thinking strategies to select to complete a particular task, it is useful to assist them in identifying the ideologies, identities and values that are being presented in a particular text. This can be achieved by posing appropriate questions that will help in the interrogation of the text. Jewitt and Kress (2008, p. 17) suggested that critical questions such as 'in whose interests?' and 'for whose benefit?' should be proposed. Anstey and Bull (2004, p. 62) suggested a series of questions that were designed to support students in developing a critical perspective. The following questions are based on those originally suggested by Anstey and Bull:

- What beliefs, attitudes or values contribute to the meaning contained in this text?
- How do these beliefs, attitudes or values relate to my own?
- Are there contradictions in the text, and if so, how do they affect my meaning making?
- Are there gaps or silences in the text and how do these affect how people or ideas are represented?
- What personal histories and experiences are valued, and which are omitted?
- Who is marginalised by this text?
- What literate practices and which strategies do I need in order to make sense of this text?
- Have I seen a text like this before, and if so, how will this help me?

There are a number of pedagogical frameworks that have been proposed in recent years that encourage the use of higher order thinking skills. The Four Resource Model originally proposed by Freebody and Luke in the early 1990s and revised in 1999 and 2003 (discussed in Chapter Two) suggested that one of the four resources (code breaker, meaning maker, text user, text analyst) that teachers and students could draw upon was text analyst. Text analyst strategies included those investigating the beliefs, attitudes and values contained in texts and have since been applied to paper, live and digital texts (see Chapters One and Two for discussion of these texts). The New London Group, which met in 1996, suggested a pedagogical framework that was reported by Cope and Kalantzis (2000) that included situated practice, overt instruction, critical framing and transformed practice that relied on higher order thinking skills such as conceptualising, analysing and applying. Lastly, the Queensland School Reform Longitudinal Study was conducted from 1998 to 2000 and reported by Land (2001) and identified areas of pedagogy that needed to be modified in order to improve student outcomes. The study outlined the Productive Pedagogies that were needed to produce an effective pedagogical framework and included the broad concerns of intellectual quality, connectedness, supportive classroom environment and recognition of difference. Within these Productive Pedagogies were such things as higher order thinking based on deep knowledge and deep understandings, problem-solving, investigating and metacognition. These frameworks, and others like them, indicate a continued interest in the application of higher order thinking skills and the critical approach that underlies critical literacy.

Higher order thinking skills and interthinking

Interthinking
The use of talk by students working in groups by using a collective, rather than an individual approach, to justify their solutions, to engage in problem-solving in learning and to develop their reasoning capabilities. Because the approach is inherently social, it enables students to share capabilities and thereby achieve more than they might be able to do individually.

In related research carried out in the U.K., the concept of **interthinking** was developed to trace the process of thinking. Littleton and Mercer (2013a, p. 111) defined interthinking as '...using talk to pursue collective intellectual activity' by combining individual intellectual capacities '... to achieve more through working together than any individual could do on their own'. They suggested that such talk could be defined as exploratory talk, sometimes called accountable or collaborative talk, (see Edwards-Groves, Anstey and Bull, 2014), as a mode of reasoning that was inherently social. Littleton and Mercer (2013a, p. 92) found that interthinking enabled groups of students to justify their solutions, to engage in problem-solving in learning and to develop their reasoning capabilities. They also found that some students came to school having already engaged in these higher order thinking skills through 'elaborate conversations' (or what the Productive Pedagogies framework termed *substantive conversations*) with their parents. Such experiences provide opportunities for students to engage in reasoned discussions that, as Littleton and Mercer suggest, provide a model for reasoning on an individual basis. As a result of several studies in what they have termed the Thinking Together research, Littleton and Mercer (2010, 2013a, 2013b) concluded that students need to learn how to talk in order to reason together and that such learning will only take place if teachers consciously teach it. They also concluded (2013a, p. 97) when students were engaged in interthinking they used exploratory talk more frequently and achieved better results in problem-solving. Interthinking embodies many of the characteristics of a multiliterate curriculum and pedagogy identified earlier in this chapter.

Cautions about critical literacy and higher order thinking skills

As Mills (2005, p. 76) pointed out, it is not enough that schools and teachers should be engaged in the teaching and learning of critical literacy. Critical literacy itself should also be subjected to a critical analysis. Just because critical literacy is being 'done', it does not mean that the social and cultural aspects of literacy are being adequately addressed. The marginalisation or silencing of certain individuals or groups may result in some students being disempowered while others are advantaged. This may be because of the adoption of particular pedagogies by the school or by the lack of access to specific strategies in the home. Schools need to be aware of how critical literacy is being operationalised in order to cater for the range of literacy identities that are to be found in everyday classrooms. Individual teachers need to be continuously monitoring how they are constructing critical literacy in their classrooms to ensure that they are not promoting certain points of view to the neglect of others. Critical literacy, by its very nature, can lead to political indoctrination or the promotion of undue influence over the views of certain students. Teachers may adopt a particular agenda, either consciously or unconsciously, that condones certain messages. As discussed before, this may be adopting a seemingly innocuous preference for traditional texts (from the literacy canon) over texts from popular culture. The teacher may also valourise particular reading positions by authorising a preferred meaning of a text.

Similarly, the mastery of higher order thinking skills does not necessarily mean that issues such as social class membership, knowledge about D/discourses or differences in home/school interactions will be overcome. Conversely, the lack of higher order thinking skills should not be used as an explanation of why certain students are not succeeding or why some homes are seen as inadequate. While the mastery of higher order thinking skills is itself a laudable objective, this should not lead to a neglect of lower order thinking skills any more than focusing on text analyst resources should lead to the neglect of code breaking or meaning making.

What is undeniable is that talk is a powerful force in teaching and learning. Talk is central to contemporary pedagogical frameworks that seek to describe how teaching and learning about literacy can be achieved and it assists this process of teaching and learning by making pedagogy visible. Talk also provides a platform from which teachers can develop their personal model of pedagogy. By using a lesson transcript, teachers can analyse the pedagogical model they have adopted through a fine-grained analysis of their teacher talk. Teacher talk is therefore central to the development of critical literacy and higher order thinking skills.

Analysing classroom talk by focussing on the functions of teacher talk and lesson structure

In the preceding section on visible and invisible pedagogies, a comparison was made between two lessons by looking at transcripts (Transcripts 4.2 and 4.3). The comparison focussed on the difference between explicit and implicit instruction. However, there are other characteristics that can be identified that enable a much more detailed analysis of teacher talk to be carried out. The research of French and MacLure (1981), Freebody, Ludwig and Gunn (1995), Ludwig and Herschell (1998), Anstey (1998), Freebody and Freiberg (2001) and Edwards-Groves, Anstey and Bull (2014) was all based on establishing a set of characteristics that could be used to analyse teacher talk. In these studies audio tapes were used to produce transcripts that recorded the oral exchanges between teacher and student or between student and student. Once teachers are familiar and comfortable with analysing audio taped, or digitally recorded lessons, they may move on to videoing lessons, which can provide further information about their body language, facial expressions or the opportunity to focus on particular students. The use of video tapes provides more detail but also requires a more complex analysis that is more time consuming because of the necessity to analyse visual, spatial and gestural information.

AUDITING INSTRUMENT 4.8

- The purpose of this Auditing Instrument is to evaluate the quality of your question and answer sequences.
- Review a tape of a lesson you have recorded and isolate some of your question and answer sequences. You may just listen to these sequences or make a series of transcripts of the sequences.
- Do you just begin a question and answer sequence or do you first explain the purpose of the lesson?
- Are logical alternative answers given by the students accepted or do you continue the sequence until you get the answer you want?
- What do you do with incorrect answers? Do you discuss with students how and why they have arrived at their answers or do you just move on to the next student?

Teacher discourse and the use of IREs

Early research by Sinclair and Coulthard (1975) and French and MacLure (1981) focussed on the question and answer sequence that formed the common type of exchange in classrooms some decades ago and is still present in classrooms today. The question and answer sequence was termed an exchange that consisted of a three-part structure. This structure was typically made up of an initiation by the teacher, most often a question, followed by a response from a student and ending in some form of feedback by the teacher. This structure was usually referred to as an IRF (initiation, response, feedback) and more commonly in recent times as an **IRE** (initiation, response, evaluation). Categorising the types of talk in this way provides a description of the flow and structure of a lesson rather than a simple summary of activities or talk that take place in a lesson.

IREs
A question and answer sequence or exchange that consists of a three-part structure. This structure was typically made up of an initiation by the teacher (I), most often a question, followed by a response (R) from a student and ending in some form of evaluation (E) by the teacher.

The following is a transcript reported in research by Bull (2003) in a Year 2 class (age seven) in a regional city in Queensland. The students were tasked with defining both fiction and non-fiction by comparing texts from each genre. They were in self-selected groups and were supplied with one stack of books that contained a mixture of fiction and non-fiction texts comprising texts about dinosaurs and dragons. They were asked to divide the texts into two piles, one fiction and one non-fiction, and then provide a definition for both genres. Transcript 4.4 below is an excerpt from the lesson that is focussed on defining fiction. Later in the lesson a similar discussion took place that addressed non-fiction.

TRANSCRIPT 4.4

GB: What is it about the words which make it fiction?
Jane: Well, with these books they have a beginning, 'Once upon a time'.
GB: And what does that tell you that it's going to be?
Jane: Fiction.
Jake: You see – if it's fiction it doesn't have paragraphs – it just keeps going.
Tricia: Well, I thought it would be fiction because I had a look at a few pages, at the words, and he threw cans at his mouth and he ate them – and dinosaurs don't do that.
GB: What makes Tricia's answer a good one?
Steven: Because if a dinosaur would eat rubbish everyone would know it – but everyone knows it doesn't.
GB: Right! Yes, Jake? (Jake is bursting to comment.)
Jake: It can't eat rubbish because it can't crunch it up in its mouth.
Jane: Dinosaurs don't eat that junk.
GB: So, what are the words telling you?
Chorus: It's not true!
GB: If it's not true it's …?
All: Fiction!

Reproduced with permission from Pearson Australia, Bull, G and Anstey M (eds) 2003, The Literacy Lexicon, 2nd ed, p.156.

There are a number of question and answer exchanges in this transcript but it is not a typical IRE sequence. It is an extended discussion that contains only one evaluative comment by the teacher (GB). Such comments are often used by a teacher to drive the lesson further and prepare students for another IRE sequence. What advances this lesson are a couple of initial questions by the teacher that are not directed to any specific students. At no time does the teacher call on a particular student to respond. The class knows, from previous lessons, that teacher questions are addressed to all students and anyone can be called upon to answer. What advances the lesson is the willingness of students to offer responses and comment on each other's answers. They do not need evaluative comments because they can carry on a sophisticated discussion without them and develop a critical perspective of their own. What this type of lesson does is to break the cycle of IREs where only the teacher gets to ask the questions. Such a cycle can lead, as Sinclair and Coulthard suggested, to a situation where the teacher has one answer in mind and rejects other plausible suggestions. When this happens, the students learn to play the 'Guess what's in my head' game. What this lesson demonstrates is that teacher talk, or discourse, can influence literacy learning because it has the potential to affect students' understandings about what literacy is, about what constitutes learning generally and what literate practices are valuable. This is not a new concern and has been addressed earlier by researchers such as Gee (1990), Baker (1991a) and Luke (1993), who all concluded that teacher talk can have a marked influence on literacy learning. As Gee pointed out, the use of a particular discourse by the teacher can advantage some students and penalise others. While IREs can limit students' learning in particular lessons (such as guided discovery), there are nevertheless certain contexts where a complex series of ideas need to be introduced where they can be useful (see Wells 1993; Cazden 2001; Alexander 2004).

The functions of classroom discourse

If, as has been argued, the use of discourse by the teacher is critical in focussing, or refocussing, the way in which literacy was practised and how literacy was learnt, then it is important to develop a method of analysis of teacher talk that goes beyond IREs. Anstey (1993a, 1998, 2003) examined the types of discourse in 25 literacy lessons by recording the lessons and then transcribing each one. She discovered that the talk had different functions or focusses and these functions impacted on the type of literate practices and literacy learning that took place. Much of the talk in the 25 lessons was directed towards management of the lesson and little information was provided about how to engage in literacy tasks or how the tasks might be useful. When the students were engaged in literate practices, the focus was on what Anstey termed *doing* literacy, that is, simply engaging in, or practising, the literate tasks. Learning *how* to complete the task or *why* it might be useful was not addressed in the lessons. As Anstey concluded, doing literacy did not add to the students' repertoire of literacy resources, nor did it support opportunities to learn about flexible and strategic literate practices. As a result of these analyses Anstey identified a set of categories that addressed the relationship between types of talk and the types of learning that are supported. Table 4.1 represents these functions of teacher talk.

The first column in Table 4.1 provides a definition of each type of teacher talk, the second column identifies the function or focus of each type of talk and the final column gives examples of the different types of talk. In the first column, the two initial categories of talk (classroom management and literacy information management) refer to managing behaviour or introducing the

Table 4.1 Functions of teacher talk

Talk type/definition	Focus/function	Example
1. Classroom management • Questions and statements to do with the social and physical functioning of the classroom • Getting the group organised, discipline • No text focus • Questions and statements to do with previous non-literacy lessons	**Organisation** • Physical, social and organizational management	• *Put your hands on your heads* • *Pens down* • *Turn around, Mandy* • *Right, OK*
2. Literacy information management • Questions and statements to do with the function and procedures of a literacy lesson, unrelated to the literacy objectives of this lesson. They contain no relevant or implicit teaching of literacy, they simply facilitate the running of the literacy aspects of the lesson • May draw attention to the text but not as a meaning system • May recall, revise, give information from previous literacy lessons	• Management of literacy tasks • Doing the ritualised behaviour of school • Procedural display	• *Read the first page* • *Write in the first box* • *What can we see on the cover?* • *The author's name is …* • *Who illustrated this book?*
3. Reconstruction • Questions and statements which construct/reconstruct/ paraphrase/rephrase the oral, written or pictorial text of the lesson • Focus on behaviour with text rather than cognitive processes - doing the task rather than informing about the task • Doing literal or text-linking activities with the text	**Doing literacy** • Implicit modelling/teaching of task • Getting the task done	• *Alunak is excited because he is going on his first seal hunt* (paraphrasing the written text) • *I think I would write two main ideas here* (focus on doing the task, implicit modelling) • *Give me three reasons archaeology is interesting* (requiring recall of written text) • *Mary says that Alunak was Jim's friend* (rephrasing oral text of lesson, i.e. student's answer)
4. Elaboration/projection • Questions and statements which model or require behaviour which involves use of knowledge beyond the text of the lesson, i.e. knowledge from students' life experience. • Focus on doing the task rather than informing about the task	• Doing literacy rather than learning about how to do literacy	• *Who would we call on to provide good weather?* • *Well, what is the order of merit?* • *What can you tell me about a magpie?*

(Continued)

Table 4.1 (Continued)

5. Informative • Questions and statements which give students information or definitions about the literacy skill/task/process but do not explain how to use this information to complete the task		• *Each paragraph has three main ideas* • *Usually the first sentence in the paragraph gives us the main idea*
6. Process • Questions or statements which explicitly explain the cognitive processes involved in the literacy task/process/skill which is the focus of the lesson.	**Learning how and when about literacy** • Cognition: How to do the task	• *What is better than guessing?* • *How would you work that out?* • *I am writing … because… .*
7. Utility • Statements or questions which explain why the literacy skill/task/process which is the focus of the lesson is useful and how it might be useful in other situations	• Social practice: The utility of the skill/process/task being learned	• *Why do we use paragraphs?* • *When we want to research a topic it is useful to look at the subheadings because they tell us where the information we want is located.* • *That is a good because you are thinking about the uses of that strategy. You skim because you need an idea of whether the information is good or not.*

Reproduced with permission from Pearson Australia, Bull, G and Anstey M (eds) 2003, *The Literacy Lexicon*, 2nd ed, pp. 114–15.

task to be completed. These two types of talk are necessary for the efficient running of a classroom but they do not teach about literacy or literate practices. They merely support the routines of the class, so teachers should try to keep these types of talk to a minimum. Bull and Anstey (1996, 1997, 2014) and Edwards-Groves, Anstey and Bull (2014) concluded that these two types of talk were quite common in classrooms where teachers had prepared their first transcript. The teachers reported surprise and consternation after analysing their transcripts, with most not realising that these two types of talk were so prevalent in their lessons. In subsequent lessons the majority of the teachers were able to minimise these types of talk. What was of interest was that teachers were not only unaware of the types of talk they were using, but just being conscious of their talk enabled them to significantly modify their talk.

Some teachers were able to establish routines more carefully before the lessons and began using techniques such as providing an overview of the lessons for the day on a display board so that students had forewarning of the routines that needed to be in place. Others devised personal contracts for students that students collected as they came to school. Anstey and Bull observed in one particularly difficult class that the students identified appropriate behaviours, which they wrote out on cards that were suspended from the ceiling. When inappropriate behaviour occurred, they drew attention to the relevant card. This routine took three to four weeks to establish and had a major impact on the behaviour of the students and minimised the amount of management/organisational talk used by the teacher. If a significant amount of management/organisational talk persists in a classroom, then it is important that teachers consider why this might be so. Sometimes it is a matter of changing classroom organisation or streamlining and making routines more explicit. It may also be that the teacher is not as confident about the content to be taught as they should be and this uncertainty is detected by the students. Some schools do not have a mentoring programme in place to support beginning teachers in developing effective behaviour management techniques. Whatever the case, it is important that the amount of these two types of talk be reduced because, although they form a necessary part of teaching, they should not predominate in teacher talk.

The next three categories of talk (reconstruction, elaboration or projection, informative) focus on doing literacy. These types of exchanges implicitly teach literacy by engaging, or practising a task without focussing on how it should be done or why it is useful. As an example of this, Anstey and Bull were working in a Year 2 class where students were writing drafts of narratives (stories). They noticed that one student was counting one, two, three, four and then putting in a full stop. This continued right through a whole page of the narrative. Another student close by was going down the right-hand edge of the page and putting a full stop at the end of each line. Investigation by Anstey and Bull revealed that in the previous year their teacher had been using commercially prepared activity books and photocopied activities that contained very short, often one line, directions for completing literacy tasks. The students had engaged in 'doing literacy' by mindlessly completing activities without realising how they should be completed or why they might be used. By using the three categories of talk (reconstruction, elaboration or projection, informative) the teacher had focussed on doing the task rather than informing about the task, or giving information about the task without explaining how to use this information to complete the task. Reconstruction talk often turns out to be repeating students' answers or not giving any explanation about why an answer is incorrect. Elaboration talk can exclude some students if they do not have the requisite general knowledge or prior experience to fall back on to assist them in completing a literacy task. If used appropriately elaboration talk can demonstrate to students how and when to draw on their literacy identities and other learning resources to develop useful literacy practices. Similarly, informative talk that provides definitions and terminology is not particularly useful unless accompanied by directions about how and when to use it. These three categories have the potential to provide useful strategies for students to learn about, and engage in, literate practices, in contrast to management/organisational talk.

The last two categories, process and utility talk, are perhaps the most important because they supply information firstly about how and when to use literacy strategies and practices, and secondly about why they should be used. They focus on literacy learning and therefore should be highly visible and explicitly demonstrated because they provide in-depth learning and understanding that supports students to transfer knowledge across different contexts and content areas of disciplines. Unfortunately, as Anstey (1993a, 1998) and Anstey and Bull (2010) reported, process and utility talk hardly ever feature in teacher talk in literacy lessons. What is interesting to note is that, as with management/organisational talk, once teachers become aware of which teacher talk is present, or absent, in their lessons they can, and do, address these issues. Process and utility talk can become an important feature of teacher talk as a result of long-term professional learning programs such as that described by Bull and Anstey (2010). What is crucial is that teachers achieve balance in their teacher talk across the categories identified by Anstey.

AUDITING INSTRUMENT 4.9

- The purpose of this Auditing Instrument is to analyse your teacher talk.
- Make an audio/digital tape of a thirty-minute literacy/English lesson, preferably one that contains new material to the students.
- Listen to the first ten minutes of the lesson to determine how you are using the Audio Semiotic System. (You may need to go back to Chapter Three to remind yourself about the codes and conventions of the Audio Semiotic System.)
- Check such codes as your intonation, pitch and volume and listen for any repetitive expressions that you use. It is important to hear yourself as your students do to judge whether there are any aspects that might be impinging on the quality of your teacher talk.
- Convert your tape to a transcript and then analyse your talk using the categories that Anstey developed. Look for imbalances across the categories, particularly comparing the amount of your management/organisational talk with process and utility talk.
- Choose one of the categories in your talk that needs addressing and teach another lesson where you attempt to modify that aspect of your talk. Record all the lesson but make a transcript of just the section of the lesson where you have attempted changes to your talk.
- Compare the two transcripts to determine what progress you have made. Keep in mind that if your talk needs to be changed significantly it will not happen straight away.

Phases of lessons

The teacher talk and interaction in any lesson will change throughout the lesson depending upon how the lesson has been planned. It is to be expected that, as a lesson is being introduced by the teacher and the students are being informed about how they will engage with it, there will be a degree of organisational talk. Hopefully there will be a minimum of management talk if routines have been firmly established. As the lesson progresses and what has to be learned has been identified, then there is an expectation that informative and utility talk will occur as the purposes of the lesson are explained. If modelling or demonstrations are to take place, then the amount of informative and procedural talk should increase. As the tasks that the students are expected to engage in change, then the type of teacher talk should change. What is critical about this relationship is that different stages of the lesson require different categories of talk if the lesson is to be successful. The implication is that teachers need to be very strategic about how they plan lessons. What has to be learnt needs to be considered, but so does the structure and sequence of the lesson and the appropriateness of the talk at each stage of the lesson. A particular lesson might contain a number of learning episodes. For example, if a certain strategy is to be introduced, then the teacher might begin with the whole class and identify the characteristics of the strategy. Following this introduction, the students might move into groups to practice identifying these characteristics and then report back to the whole class. The lesson might then conclude with a final discussion of when the strategy might be used and how it relates to other strategies that the students have previously learnt. There are therefore four parts or stages in the lesson. Anstey (1993a, 1998, 2003) termed these stages phases of the lesson. She developed an analytic technique that aided in explaining the relationship between lesson structure, discourse and literacy learning. She identified nine phases that required different types of teacher talk or discourses and different types of student interaction and behaviour. Anstey suggested that teachers need to clearly identify and explain the purpose of each lesson phase and the students need to learn to recognise them. Table 4.2 represents the ten **phases of lessons**.

Table 4.2 describes the ten categories of phases and their definitions. As can be seen from this table, the structures of lessons have the potential to vary considerably because of the number of phases and the number of possible combinations of phase types that can be incorporated into a lesson. As Anstey (1998, 2003) reported, not all phases were necessary for a successful lesson and the phases might not occur in the order in which they are represented in Table 4.2. However, she reported that the focus, guided implementation (which includes identifying, practice and transfer), review and report phases were essential for successful lesson structure, although they may not all be present in just one lesson. Further, Anstey concluded that when all four phases were present in the structure of the lesson it was likely that more process and utility talk would be used by the teacher. It is therefore important to realise that there is an important correlation between lesson structure, phases of lessons and teacher talk. The result of this relationship is that a lesson may have a logical and well-sequenced structure and contain highly relevant activities for students to engage in but still not achieve the success that is possible if the teacher talk does not support the structure. Figure 4.1 presents a possible phase structure for an explicit lesson on the teaching of skimming (presented earlier in this chapter in Transcript 4.3).

Phases of lessons
Phases refer to changes in focus or task during a lesson. Phase divisions or changes can be signalled both orally and physically. Two oral signals can be given, either an explicit statement or instruction to move on to another task or change focus (for example, 'Our next task is...') or a tag utterance, which is known and recognised by all members of the class as a signal of change (for example, OK... All right...). Physical signals can be of three kinds: a change in activity by students, physical reorganisation of the room or students moving (for example, from sitting on the floor to their desks) or use of equipment (for example, starting a film to be watched).

Table 4.2 Phases of lessons

Phase	Definition	Example statements or description of activity
Attention	How the lesson begins. Not necessarily an introduction, e.g. getting students' attention and organising for beginning of lesson	'Boys and girls, who's ready? My that is good to see'.
Focus	The part of the lesson as indicated by the teacher's tone, language, etc. where the focus of the lesson is identified. Some information may be imparted.	'Now today we are going to talk about the structure of stories'.
Guided Implementation	Where teacher and student construct, practise, or implement the knowledge which is the focus of the lesson but the activity is led by the teacher. Specific aspects of Guided Implementation: (a) *Identifying* identifying examples of new knowledge. May include writing on whiteboard or in books/laptops/iPads (b) *Practice* using new skills or knowledge learned to practice in a similar task (c) *Transferring* Using new skills or knowledge learned in a different combination or with a new or different type of task	**Identifying** Teacher leads students in identification of main idea in paragraph **Practicing** Teacher leads students in finding main idea in a new paragraph and making notes about the main idea **Transferring** Teacher leads students in using notes taken about main idea to construct a paragraph
Report	Sharing presentation of finished work/task by student	Students share answers or discuss completed work to class, as requested by Teacher
Display	Teacher displays/presents/ reads aloud/models task he or she has completed	Teacher might show work and say, 'When I was looking for information on this topic the first thing I did was...'
Unguided Implementation	Same as Guided Implementation but student must perform on own. Same sub-categories as for Guided Implementation. Independent student driven or student led work	As for Guided Implementation examples, except student led or done by student independently
Review	Teacher reviews definitions/information skills presented in previous phases at a general level. It is not a complete reworking or re-teaching of examples, but a review of what has been done and learned	Teacher might use following phrases in such a phase: 'Now what we have learned so far... First we found out that...'
Presentation of text	Teacher reads text to students, or students read text. Random exchanges between teacher and students may occur during this phase	Reading of story to class as part of a shared book activity
Coda	Teaching aspect of lesson has concluded but teacher or students may continue exchanges in some way related to topic or content of lesson	Discussing Eskimos after a reading a passage about Eskimos and answering questions has been completed in previous phases
Transition out	Signals end of lesson and tidying up or reorganisation of class for subsequent lessons	Usually signalled by activity and teacher instructions such as, 'Put your work away' or 'Forward out'

Reproduced with permission from Pearson Australia, Bull, G and Anstey M (eds) 2003, *The Literacy Lexicon*, 2nd ed, p. 117.

Teaching and learning multiliteracies 157

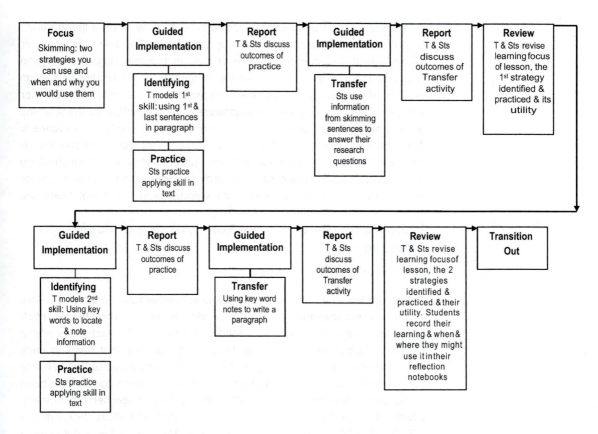

Figure 4.1 Mapping the phase structure of a lesson

T = teacher; Sts = students.

AUDITING INSTRUMENT 4.10

- The purpose of this Auditing Instrument is to investigate the phase structure of your previously recorded lesson.
- Were there clear relationships and logical sequences between the phases in your lessons?
- Did the number of changes in phases encourage literacy learning in your lessons or were there so many changes that students were more likely to engage in 'doing literacy'?
- Did your selection of phases allow you to achieve your intended learning outcomes?
- Did your selection of phases promote the teacher discourse that was best suited to achieve your intended learning outcomes?
- Compare the phase structure in your lesson with the one presented in Figure 4.1 above.

It is imperative that teachers become critically aware of the literate practices that form the basis of the teaching and learning that takes place in their classrooms. Knowledge of the types of teacher talk (discourses) and lesson structure (phases) provides a framework for this understanding. Although teacher talk and lesson phases have been presented separately in this chapter for ease of discussion, it must be emphasised that they influence the teaching and learning taking place in the classroom both individually and in tandem. Teachers need access to a range of analytical tools for examining and reflecting upon their practice and their pedagogy. Taping of lessons and constructing transcripts, although time consuming, provides one of the few ways to gather the fine-grained data that are necessary to engage with these analytical tools.

Dialogic talk and the development of a dialogic pedagogy

IREs and monologic talk

The discussion about talk has so far looked at teacher talk and its relationship to teaching and learning. As has been previously stated in this chapter, much of the talk that takes place in classrooms is based on IRE exchanges where teachers ask questions and students respond. The fact that this sequence is so common led Cazden (2001) to refer to it as the default option because she found that teachers frequently returned to it. Cazden's position has been reinforced by researchers investigating the nature of teacher talk in many countries. Research carried out by Mercer (1995) and Wells (1999) in the U.K., Harste (1993) and Nystrand (1997) in the U.S., and Baker and Freebody (1989a), Anstey (1993a) and Edwards-Groves (1998) concluded that the IRE pattern of teacher talk was common in English/literacy lessons. In a far-ranging study of talk, sometimes referred to as the 'five nations study', Alexander (2001) studied teacher talk in the U.K., France, India, Russia and the U.S. and found the IRE sequence to be common across all five countries, and particularly so in the U.K. and U.S. Solomon (2008) and Resnick et al. (2010) also found the sequence to be common in mathematics and science lessons. This type of talk has become known as **monologic talk** because it describes talk as dominated by the teacher, who acts as the source of all knowledge and provides little, or no, opportunity for student-initiated talk. It was termed *monologic talk* because it resembled a monologue by the teacher. In this type of classroom, students are passive receivers of knowledge and there is no possibility for pedagogies such as guided inquiry, problem-based learning or reciprocal teaching to occur. What has reinforced the use of traditional patterns of teacher talk such as the IREs is the standards drive that is occurring in many countries. This drive has placed teachers under added stress that has caused teachers to adopt Cazden's default position. Other stressful situations that may result in teachers adopting the default position are dealing with a difficult class or unfamiliarity with the content to be taught.

Monologic talk
Monologic talk resembles a monologue by the teacher. Talk is dominated by the teacher who acts as the source of all knowledge and provides little, or no, opportunity for student-initiated talk.

AUDITING INSTRUMENT 4.11

- The purpose of this Auditing Instrument is to determine the occurrence of monologic talk in your lessons.
- Analyse the transcript of a lesson you have taught recently to identify the occurrences of monologic talk.
- Examine each occurrence of monologic talk to see whether you are using this type of talk to introduce complex new ideas.
- Identify the number of times you use monologic talk inappropriately, to judge what sort of balance there is in the lesson.

Dialogic talk

In contrast to monologic talk, **dialogic talk** engages both teachers and students in a genuine dialogue that aims to further the process of inquiry and promote critical thinking and higher order thinking skills. Bruner (1996), Wells (1999), Mercer (2000) and Alexander (2008) all suggested that through promoting dialogic talk teachers attempt to create authentic teacher-student exchanges. This type of talk provides opportunities for both teacher talk and learner talk and promotes reciprocal talk between students and teachers. It also allows student-to-student talk and students to initiate talk. Dialogic talk encourages students to engage actively in the learning process, whereas monologic talk constructs students as passive receivers of knowledge.

Dialogic talk can take a number of different forms. Barnes (1976, 2008, 2010) and Alexander (2001, 2004, 2008) proposed that students sometimes talked their way into meaning by trying out new ways of understanding or modifying existing knowledge. By its very nature, this type of talk was indecisive and often contained incomplete thoughts as students strived to construct meaning. For these reasons Barnes termed this type of talk as exploratory. Littleton and Mercer (2013a) also referred to this type of talk as exploratory although they suggested that it had an interactive feature where students worked constructively and cooperatively in groups and adopted common, or agreed upon, meanings based on a reasoned response. In order for exploratory talk to prosper, the consensus among researchers was that both students and teachers needed to develop a tolerance for uncertainty or ambiguity. Dialogic talk is more democratic because all stakeholders get the opportunity to talk and to construct meanings cooperatively.

Other forms of talk have been proposed. Barnes (1976) asserted that presentational talk occurred when students engaged in a performance (such as a talk or debate) that was evaluated by the teacher, while Littleton and

Dialogic talk
Engages both teachers and students in a genuine dialogue that aims to further the process of inquiry and promote critical thinking and higher order thinking skills. It occurs between teacher and student, student and student and can be initiated by teacher or student.

Mercer (2013a) suggested disputational talk emerged when students disagreed with one another in an environment of competition rather than cooperation. Neither of these types of talk is dialogic and therefore the potential for developing deep understandings and a critical perspective is diminished. As Littleton and Mercer (2013a, p. 97) have suggested, exploratory talk supports more in-depth learning in school and is best able to assist students to engage in problem-solving.

AUDITING INSTRUMENT 4.12

- The purpose of this Auditing Instrument is to investigate which types of talk commonly occur in your lessons.
- Study a transcript of a recent lesson to determine the balance between monologic and dialogic talk.
- It may be useful to look at two recent lessons, one where students are in groups, and the other where there was only a whole class approach. Compare the amount of dialogic talk that occurred in the whole class lesson when compared to the lesson based on group work to see if classroom organisation has an effect.
- Do the students in your class get more opportunity to engage in dialogic or presentational talk? Which type of talk promotes more in-depth learning?
- When working in groups did the students engage more in dialogic or disputational talk? Which type of talk resulted in more learning?

Developing a dialogic pedagogy

There is general agreement in the field of research into talk that there is a far greater potential for learning with dialogic rather than monologic talk. As Barnes (1976) stated over 40 years ago, as teachers' questions became longer, so students' answers became briefer. There is a significant benefit to be gained by decreasing the amount of teacher talk and thereby allowing an increase in student talk. This does not mean that teachers should stop talking but rather that there should be a balance between teacher and learner talk because the teacher should still be a vital component in dialogic teaching. Alexander (2005) proposed that this type of teaching was based on an emerging pedagogy that drew on the potential of dialogic talk to develop students' thinking. Alexander, and later Wolfe and Alexander (2008), suggested **dialogic pedagogies** can be defined as a mutually determined construction between teacher and learner that relies on a shared accountability for learning. Wolfe and Alexander (2008, p. 6) further suggested that dialogic pedagogies were '… premised on the ability of students and teachers to establish reciprocal relationships through

Dialogic pedagogies
Those pedagogies that are based on a mutually determined construction between teacher and learner and rely on a shared responsibility for learning.

language'. Littleton and Mercer (2013a, p. 103) advocated a three-stage pedagogical model for developing talk based on teacher, joint and individual responsibility. This model is reminiscent of the three-step Gradual Release of Responsibility pedagogical framework originally proposed by Pearson and Gallagher (1983), which involved teacher modelling, Guided Implementation and independent student practice. The values that underpin these various dialogic pedagogies revolve around the recognition of the role of the teacher and teacher talk, the importance of group talk, and the utility of individual practice.

Designing a dynamic multiliterate pedagogy

Developing a dynamic pedagogy

The preceding discussions have led to the development of a model for a dialogic pedagogy. It is important to consider how such a model can become dynamic and include reference to multiliteracies. Wells (2001), Alexander (2004, 2005), Barnes (2008) and Littleton and Mercer (2013a) have explored the question of implementing a pedagogy that takes into consideration the roles of both teacher and learner. They have collectively suggested that the constructionist pedagogy is the most appropriate for addressing these considerations because it is based on the following nine understandings about what is of value in learning:

- Meaning is constructed by individuals constructing a personal view of the world, so it must be learnt by students as well as taught explicitly by the teacher
- Constructionist pedagogy advocates a student-centred, discovery learning approach where students build on current understandings to create new knowledge
- The teacher is a facilitator who supports students to make new connections between different areas of knowledge
- Learning is an active process rather than a passive one
- Learning draws heavily on an individual's literacy identity in order to relate new understandings to existing knowledge
- Learning is best achieved by engaging in authentic tasks in a community of learners
- Reflecting on the new knowledge learnt assists students to understand the processes of learning
- Learning involves critical thinking and higher order thinking skills in order to uncover new knowledge
- Constructing new knowledge is more likely to take place in a context where students feel confident to be hesitant and are prepared to make mistakes

REFLECTION STRATEGY 4.5

- The purpose of this Reflection Strategy is to review your pedagogy.
- Review your teaching practice over the last couple of weeks by analysing two of your transcripts to determine which of the nine understandings you address in your lessons.
- Undertake a similar review of your lesson planning over the last couple of weeks to determine which of the nine understandings you address in your approach to the planning of your lessons.
- What kind of changes need to be made in your practice or planning in order to address more of the understandings?

What can be drawn out of these understandings about learning is that a dialogic pedagogy must be flexible in order to cater for students adopting new roles in their learning as they enter new learning contexts. These understandings are also based on the creation of new knowledge through shared responsibilities for learning between teachers and students. This process of knowledge creation is ever-changing and therefore needs to be supported by a pedagogy that is dynamic rather than static. Students need to play a role in their own learning, where their talk, as well as the teacher's, is valued. Where this is the case, a dynamic pedagogy will flourish.

Developing a multiliterate pedagogy

A dynamic, dialogic pedagogy is necessary in order to address the increasing pace of knowledge construction and change brought about by the new technologies and globalisation, as discussed in Chapter One. In Chapter Three, the codes and conventions of the five semiotic systems, their grammar and metalanguage were presented as a way of understanding the changes brought about by the new technologies. This discussion also detailed the resources that might be drawn upon when producing or consuming (designing) the plethora of multimodal texts arising from the new technologies (see particularly Figure 3.4). These resources and semiotic systems form the basis of a multiliterate pedagogy that develops a multiliterate, active and informed student or teacher. The nine understandings that are the basis for a dynamic, dialogic pedagogy can equally be applied to a multiliterate pedagogy. This serves to illustrate the close relationship between dialogic talk and multiliteracies and the literate practices that are common to both.

Conclusion

The purpose of this chapter has been to explore classrooms as social and cultural sites that produce multiliterate practices. The relationships among literacy learning, higher order thinking skills, classroom talk and pedagogy have been explored. The different functions of teacher talk and the structure and the phases of lessons have been addressed. Finally, the concepts of dialogic talk, a dialogic pedagogy and a dynamic multiliterate pedagogy were developed.

Bibliography

Alexander, RJ 2001, *Culture and Pedagogy: International Comparisons in Primary Education*, Blackwell, Oxford.

Alexander, RJ 2004, *Talk for Learning: The Second Year*, North Yorkshire County Council, Northallerton.

Alexander, RJ 2005, *Teaching through Dialogue: The First Year*, London Borough of Barking and Dagenham, London.

Alexander, RJ 2008, *Towards Dialogic Teaching: Rethinking Classroom Talk*, 4th edn, Dialogos, York.

Anderson, LW & Krathwohl, DR (eds) 2001, *A Taxonomy for Learning, Teaching, and Assessing: A Revision of Bloom's Taxonomy of Educational Objectives*, Longman, New York.

Anstey, M 1991, 'Examining classroom talk during literacy instruction: Developing metacognitive strategies', *Australian Journal of Reading*, vol. 14, no. 2, pp. 151-60.

Anstey, M 1993a, *Quantitative and Interpretative Analyses of Classroom Talk as a Cognitive Context for Learning about Literacy*, unpublished PhD thesis, Griffith University, Brisbane, Australia.

Anstey, M 1993b, 'Examining classroom talk: Structure and talk in literacy lessons from a metacognitive perspective', *SET Research Information for Teachers*, vol. 12, no. 1, NZCER, Wellington.

Anstey, M 1993c, 'What you see is not all you get! Critical readings of illustrative text', Invited Keynote Address, Children's Book Council State Conference, Maroochydore, Queensland, Australia.

Anstey, M 1998, 'Being explicit about literacy instruction', *Australian Journal of Language and Literacy*, vol. 21, no. 3, pp. 206-21.

Anstey, M 2003 'Examining classrooms as sites of literate practice and literacy learning', in G Bull & M Anstey (eds), *The Literacy Lexicon*, 2nd edn, Pearson, Sydney.

Anstey, M & Bull, G 2004, *The Literacy Labyrinth*, 2nd edn, Pearson, Sydney.

Anstey, M & Bull, G 2006, *Teaching and Learning Multiliteracies: Changing Times, Changing Literacies*, International Reading Association, Newark.

Anstey, M & Bull, G 2010, *Report on Observation of Eighteen Reading Lessons at Anon State School*, Unpublished report.

Baker, CD 1991a, 'Classroom literacy events', *Australian Journal of Reading*, vol. 14, no. 2, pp. 103-16.

Baker, CD 1991b, 'Literacy practices and social relations in classroom reading events', in CD Baker & A Luke (eds), *Towards a Critical Sociology of Reading Pedagogy*, John Benjamins, Amsterdam.

Baker, CD & Freebody, P 1989a, 'Talk around text: Constructions of textual and teacher authority in classroom discourse', in S deCastell, A Luke & C Luke (eds), *Language Authority and Criticism: Readings on the School Textbook*, Falmer Press, London.

Baker, CD & Freebody, P 1989b, *Children's First School Books: Introductions to the Culture of Literacy*, Basil Blackwell, Oxford.

Barnes, D 1976, *From Communication to Curriculum*, Penguin, Harmondsworth.

Barnes, D 2008, 'Exploratory talk for learning', in N Mercer & S Hodgkinson (eds), *Exploring Talk in School: Inspired by the Work of Douglas Barnes*, SAGE, London.

Barnes, D 2010, 'Why is talk important', *English Teaching: Practice and Critique*, vol. 9, no. 2, pp. 7–10.

Bloom, BS & Krathwohl, DR 1956, *Taxonomy of Educational Objectives: The Classification of Educational Goals by a Committee of College and University Examiners, Handbook I: Cognitive Domain*, Longmans Green, New York.

Bondy, E 1984, 'Thinking about thinking: Encouraging children's use of metacognitive processes', *Childhood Education*, vol. 60, no. 4, pp. 234–8.

Brown, AL 1985, 'Teaching students to think as they read: Implications for curriculum reform', *Reading Education Report No. 58*, University of Illinois, Urbana.

Brown, AL & Kane, MJ 1988, 'Preschool children can learn to transfer: Learning to learn and learning from example', *Cognitive Psychology*, vol. 20, pp. 493–523.

Bruner, JS 1996, *The Culture of Education*, Harvard University Press, Cambridge.

Bull, G 2003 'An investigation of the pedagogy of literature using literature to support learning,' in G Bull & M Anstey (eds), *The Literacy Lexicon*, 2nd edn, Prentice Hall, Sydney.

Bull, G & Anstey, M 1995, *Adult Literacy Practices in Rural Families and Communities*, National Language and Literacy Institute of Australia (NLLIA), Adult Literacy Research Network Node, Queensland.

Bull, G & Anstey, M 1996, *The Literacy Teaching and Learning Practices of an Urban School and Its Community*, National Language and Literacy Institute of Australia (NLLIA), Literacy Research Network Node, Queensland.

Bull, G & Anstey, M 1997, *Investigating the Literacy Practices of School, Home and Community*, Language Australia Child/ESL Literacy Research Network Node, Queensland.

Bull, G & Anstey, M 2009, *Finding the Gaps: Navigating Sustainable Learning Futures for Indigenous Students: A Pilot Study*, report for the Department of Education, Employment and Workplace Relations (DEEWR), The Greater Toowoomba Regional Advisory Committee, Toowoomba, Queensland, Australia, available at http://www.ansteybull.com.au/media/2198/cwfinding-the-gaps-2009.pdf).

Bull, G & Anstey, M 2010, 'Using the principles of multiliteracies to inform pedagogical change', in DR Cole & DL Pullen (eds), *Multiliteracies in Motion*, Routledge, Abingdon, pp. 141–59.

Burn, A & Parker, D 2006, 'Tiger's big plan: Multimodality and the moving image', in C Jewitt & G Kress (eds), *Multimodal Literacy*, Peter Lang, New York, pp. 56–72.

Cambourne, B 1986, 'Retelling: A whole language "natural" learning activity,' in RD Walshe, P March & D Jensen (eds), *Writing and Learning in Australia*, Dellasta/Oxford University Press, Melbourne.

Cambourne, B 1988, *The Whole Story: Natural Learning and the Acquisition of Literacy in the Classroom*, Ashton Scholastic, Sydney.

Cambourne, B 1994, 'The rhetoric of "The Rhetoric of Whole Language"', *Reading Research Quarterly*, vol. 29, no. 4, pp. 330–3.

Cazden, CB 1967, 'On individual differences in language competence and performance', *Journal of Special Education*, vol. 1, pp. 135–50.

Cazden, CB 1970, 'The situation: A neglected source of social class differences in language use', *Journal of Social Issues*, vol. 26, no. 2, pp. 35-60.

Cazden, CB 1972, *Child Language and Education*, Holt, Rinehart and Winston, New York.

Cazden, CB 2001, *Classroom Discourse: The Language of Teaching and Learning*, Heinemann, Portsmouth, N. H.

Chomsky, N 1965, *Aspects of a Theory of Syntax*, MIT Press, Cambridge.

Cope, B & Kalantzis, M (eds) 2000, *Multiliteracies: Literacy Learning and the Design of Social Futures*, Routledge, London.

Delpit, L 1988, 'The silenced dialogue: Power and pedagogy in educating other people's children', *Harvard Educational Review*, vol. 58, no. 3, pp. 280-98.

D'warte, J 2014, 'Exploring linguistic repertoires: Multiple language use and multimodal literacy activity in five classrooms,' *Australian Journal of Language and Literacy*, vol. 37, no. 1, pp. 21-30.

Edwards-Groves, C 1998, *Reconceptualisation of Classroom Events as Structured Lessons: Documenting and Changing the Teaching of Literacy in the Primary School*, Unpublished PhD thesis, Griffith University, Queensland.

Edwards-Groves, C 2003a, *On Task: Focused Literacy Learning*, Primary English Teaching Association Australia (PETAA), Sydney.

Edwards-Groves, C 2003b, 'Building an inclusive classroom through explicit pedagogy: A focus on the language of teaching', in G Bull & M Anstey (eds), *The Literacy Lexicon*, 2nd edn, Pearson, Sydney, pp. 83-101.

Edwards-Groves, C, Anstey, M & Bull, G 2014, *Classroom Talk: Understanding Dialogue, Pedagogy and Practice*, Primary English Teaching Association Australia (PETAA), Sydney.

Ellis, ES 1986, 'The role of motivation and pedagogy on the generalization of cognitive strategy training', *Journal of Learning Disabilities*, vol. 19, no. 2, pp. 66-70.

Freebody, P & Freiberg, J 2001, 'Re-discovering practical reading activities in schools and homes', *Journal of Research in Reading*, vol. 24, no. 3, pp. 222-34.

Freebody, P, Ludwig, C & Gunn, S 1995, *Everyday Literacy Practices In and Out of Schools in Low Socioeconomic Urban Communities*, Commonwealth of Australia, Canberra.

Freebody, P & Luke, A 1990, 'Literacies programmes: Debates and demands in cultural contexts', *Prospect: A Journal of Australian TESOL*, vol. 11, pp. 7-16.

French, P & MacLure, M 1981, 'Teachers' questions, pupils' answers: An investigation of questions and answers in the infant classroom', *First Language*, vol. 3, no. 1, pp. 31-45.

Gee, JP, 1990, *Social Linguistics and Literacies: Ideology in Discourses*, Falmer Press, London.

Gee, JP, 1992, *The Social Mind: Language, Ideology and Social Practice*, Bergin & Garvey, New York.

Gee, JP 2004, *Situated Language and Learning: A Critique of Traditional Schooling*, Routledge, New York.

Goodman, KS 1967, 'Reading: A psycholinguistic guessing game', *Journal of the Reading Specialist*, vol. 6, pp. 126-35.

Goodman, KS 1986, *What's Whole in Whole Language?* Scholastic, Ontario.

Green, J & Weade, G 1990, 'The social construction of classroom reading: Beyond method', *Australian Journal of Reading*, vol. 13, no. 4, pp. 326-36.

Griffith, RL & Ruan, J 2005, 'What is metacognition and what should be its role in literacy instruction,' in SE Israel, CC Block, KI Bauserman & K Kinnucan-Welsch (eds), *Metacognition in Literacy Learning: Theory, Assessment, Instruction and Professional Development*, Lawrence Erlbaum, New Jersey, pp. 3–18.

Harste, J 1993, 'Literacy as curricular conversations about knowledge, inquiry and morality,' in RB Ruddell, MR Ruddell & H Singer (eds), *Theoretical Models and Processes of Reading*, International Reading Association, Newark, Delaware, pp. 1025–47.

Heath, SB 1983, *Ways with Words: Language, Life and Work in Communities and Classrooms*, Cambridge University Press, Cambridge.

Israel, SE, Bauserman, KL, Collins Block, C 2005, 'Metacognitive Assessment Strategies', *Thinking Classroom*, vol. 6, no. 2, pp. 21–8.

Iyer, R & Luke, C 2010, 'Multimodal, multiliteracies: Texts and literacies for the 21st century,' in DL Pullen & DR Cole (eds), *Multiliteracies and Technology Enhanced Education: Social Practice and the Global Classroom*, IGI Global, Hershey, New York.

Jewitt, C 2008, *Technology, Literacy and Learning: A Multimodal Approach*, Routledge, Abingdon.

Jones, A 1986, *At School I've Got a Chance: Ideology and Social Reproduction in a Secondary School*, PhD thesis, University of Auckland, New Zealand.

Kalantzis, M, Cope, B, Chan, E & Dalley-Trim, L 2016, *Literacies*, 2nd edn, Cambridge University Press, Port Melbourne.

Kress, G 2010, *Multimodality: A Social Semiotic Approach to Contemporary Communication*, Routledge, Abingdon.

Kress, G & van Leeuwen, T 1996, *Reading Images: The Grammar of Visual Design*, Routledge, London.

Kress, G & van Leeuwen, T 2006, *Reading Images: The Grammar of Visual Design*, 2nd edn, Routledge, London.

Land, R 2001, *The Queensland School Reform Longitudinal Study: Teachers' Summary*, The State of Queensland Education Department, Brisbane.

Lankshear, C & Knobel, M 2003, *New Literacies: Changing Knowledge and Classroom Practice*, Open University Press, Buckingham.

Lankshear, C & Lawler, M 1989, *Literacy, Schooling and Revolution*, 2nd edn, Falmer Press, New York.

Lenneberg, EH 1967, *Biological Foundations of Language*, Wiley, New York.

Levett, A & Lankshear, C 1990, *Going for Gold: Priorities for Schooling in the Nineties*, Daphne Brasell Associates Press, Wellington.

Littleton, K & Mercer, N 2010, 'The significance of educational dialogues between primary school children', in K Littleton & C Howe (eds), *Educational Dialogues: Understanding and Promoting Productive Interaction*, Routledge, London.

Littleton, K & Mercer, N 2013a, *Interthinking: Putting Talk to Work*, Routledge, London.

Littleton, K & Mercer, N 2013b, 'Educational dialogues', in K Hall, T Cremin, B Comber & L Moll (eds), *The Wiley Blackwell International Handbook of Research on Children's Literacy Learning and Culture*, Wiley Blackwell, Oxford.

Louden, W & Rivalland, J 1995, *Literacy at a Distance: Literacy Learning in Distance Education*, Edith Cowan University, Perth.

Ludwig, C & Herschell, P 1998, 'The power of pedagogy: Routines, school literacy practices and outcomes', *Australian Journal of Language and Literacy*, vol. 21, no. 1, pp. 67–83.

Luke, A 1993, 'The social construction of literacy in the primary school,' in L Unsworth (ed), *Learning and Teaching*, Macmillan, Sydney.

Luke, A 1995, 'When basic skills and information processing just aren't enough: Rethinking reading in new times', *Teachers College Record*, vol. 97, no. 1, pp. 95-115.

Luke, A & Freebody, P 1999, 'A map of possible practices: Further notes on the four resource model,' *Practically Primary*, vol. 4, no. 2, pp. 5-8.

Luke, A, Comber, B & Grant, H 2003, 'Critical literacies and cultural studies,' in G Bull & M Anstey (eds), *The Literacy Lexicon*, 2nd edn, Pearson, Frenchs Forest, pp. 15-35.

MacNeill, N, Cavanagh, RE & Silcox, S 2003, 'Pedagogic principal leadership', *Management Education*, vol. 17, no. 4, pp. 14-17.

Martin, JR 1985, *Factual Writing: Exploring and Challenging Social Reality*, Deakin University Press, Geelong.

Martin, JR 1992, *English Text: System and Structure*, Benjamins, Amsterdam.

Mercer, N 1995, *The Guided Construction of Knowledge: Talk amongst Teachers and Learners*, Multilingual Matters, Clevedon.

Mercer, N 2000, *Words and Mind: How We Use Language to Think Together*, Routledge, London.

Mills, KA 2005, 'Deconstructing binary oppositions in literacy discourse and pedagogy', *Australian Journal of Language and Literacy*, vol. 28, no. 1, pp. 67-82.

Muspratt, S, Luke, A & Freebody, P (eds) 1997, *Constructing Critical Literacies: Teaching and Learning Textual Practice*, Allen & Unwin, Melbourne.

National Board for Professional Teaching Standards, viewed on 12 May 2017, http://www.nbpts.org/sites/default/files/ATLAS/atlas_onepager.pdf.

Nystrand, M 1997, *Opening Dialogue: Understanding the Dynamics of Language and Learning in the English Classroom*, Teachers College Press, New York.

Paris, SG, Cross, DR & Lipson, MY 1984, 'Informed strategies for learning: A program to improve children's reading awareness and comprehension', *Journal of Educational Psychology*, vol. 76, no. 6, pp. 1239-52.

Pearson, PD & Gallagher, MC, 1983, 'The instruction of reading comprehension', *Contemporary Educational Psychology*, vol. 8, no. 3.

Resnick, LB, Michaels, S & O'Connor MC, 2010, 'How (well-structured) talk builds the mind', in DD Press & RJ Sternberg (eds), *Innovations in Educational Psychology*, Springer, New York, pp. 163-94.

Sinclair, J & Coulthard, M 1975, *Towards an Analysis of Discourse: The Language of Teachers and Pupils*, Oxford University Press, London.

Smith, F 1978, *Reading*, Cambridge University Press, Cambridge.

Smith, F 1982, *Understanding Reading: A Psycholinguistic Analysis of Reading and Learning to Read*, Holt, Rinehart and Winston, New York.

Solomon, Y 2008, *Mathematical Literacy: Developing Identities of Inclusion*, Routledge, New York.

Street, BV (ed.) 1993, *Cross-cultural Approaches to Literacy*, Cambridge University Press, Cambridge.

Taylor, D 1983, *Family Literacy: Young Children Learning to Read and Write*, Heinemann, Exeter.

Tough, J 1976, *Listening to Children Talking*, Ward Lock Educational, London.

Vygotsky, LS 1962, *Thought and Language*, MIT Press, Cambridge.

Wells, G 1993, 'Reevaluating the IRF sequence', *Linguistics and Education*, vol. 5, pp. 1-37.

Wells, G 1999, *Dialogic inquiry: Towards a Sociocultural Practice and Theory of Education*, Cambridge University Press, Cambridge.

Wells, G (ed) 2001, *Action, Talk and Text: Learning and Teaching through Inquiry*, Teachers College Press, New York.

Wolfe, SE & Alexander, RJ 2008, 'Argumentation and dialogic teaching: Alternative pedagogies for a changing world', *Beyond Current Horizons Project*, Department for Children, Schools and Families, U.K.

5 Exploring literature: Engaging with multimodal texts and new literacies

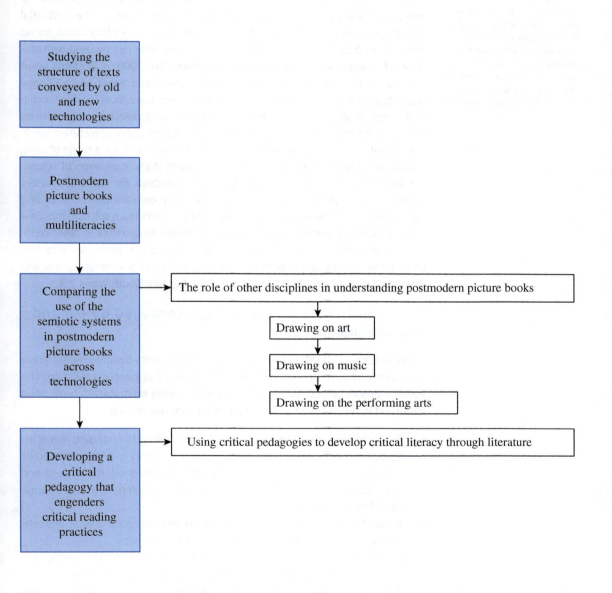

Postmodern Picture book
The postmodern picture book manipulates the characteristics of a traditional picture book (for example, plot, characters, setting, format, sequencing, illustrative material) to interrupt reader expectations and create multiple readings and meanings.

This chapter will demonstrate how the study of literature, conveyed by a range of technologies, develops students' higher order thinking skills and critical literacy, together with understandings about the way texts are constructed to achieve particular purposes and meanings. There will be a discussion about the ways in which students might investigate how the semiotic systems, individually and in combination, convey meaning. Given the desire to focus on a range of semiotic systems, this chapter will focus on picture books, and in particular **postmodern picture books**, together with their translation and interpretation to other technologies, music, film and animation, in order to explore their potential role in the development of students' multiliterate practices. Picture books are no longer limited to the province of beginning readers; they can be used with students of all ages. As author and illustrator Shaun Tan (2002, p. 2) stated when asked about the audience for his picture books, 'There is no reason why a 32-page illustrated story can't have equal appeal for teenagers or adults as they do for children. After all, other visual media such as film, television, painting or sculpture do not suffer from narrow preconceptions of audience. Why should picture books?' Just as authors and illustrators identify their work as written for a range of ages, school curricula identify picture books for in-depth study in all levels of schooling. As early as 1999 the *National Curriculum Handbook for Primary Teachers* advocated the use of picture books because they broaden perspectives and extend thinking. (Whether current iterations of this curriculum still hold this view is debateable; see Gardner's analysis [2017]). Similar to curricula in other countries the Australian Curriculum English Years K-10 is often accompanied by recommended lists of picture books for study at each level (for example, *Suggested Texts for the English K-10 Syllabus*, Board of Studies New South Wales 2012).

Studying the structure of texts conveyed by old and new technologies

In the preceding chapters the need to ensure students become multiliterate in all semiotic systems and with all technologies has been established. The specific practices necessary to an individual being multiliterate have been identified in full in Chapter Two and can be summarised as:

- being *flexible* and capable of actively responding to changing literacies by being able to design, adopt, and sustain mastery over new strategies
- having a *repertoire of practices* that can be designed, redesigned and used appropriately for different purposes and audiences and in a range of different contexts
- understanding and employing *traditional and new communication technologies* and the semiotic systems conveyed by them
- recognising how *social and cultural diversity* affect literate practices
- being *critically literate* by understanding that no text is neutral and every literate practice requires reflective and analytical problem solvers able to evaluate and produce a variety of multimodal texts

Given the prominence of new technologies and semiotic systems in these practices it may seem inappropriate to suggest that exploring literature would aid the development of multiliterate practices, particularly if any definition of literature is limited to paper technology. However, literature includes multimodal texts such as film and plays, and many traditional paper texts in literature incorporate the Visual and Spatial Semiotic Systems. Even paper text that does not contain visual elements can be regarded as multimodal. According to Kress (2000, p. 184), such texts contain punctuation marks that give direction as to how the text should be read (e.g. through intonation, pause and stress) and therefore such texts have audio elements that accompany the print.

As literature is conveyed by a range of technologies and an increasing range of options are available in production and consumption, the ways of consuming and producing literature have become broader and continue to evolve. EBooks have sound effects and touch screen options not available in print, and picture books are sometimes presented as live performances accompanied by orchestras. The advances in technology have also influenced the production of paper texts. The variety of media used, its colour and texture can be reproduced with greater accuracy and the design and the format of books can be varied with cut-outs, split pages, flaps and fold out pages easily employed in more cost-effective ways. In *The Viewer,* written by Gary Crew and illustrated by Shaun Tan (1997), cut-outs show the views through a view master or kaleidoscope and in *Little Mouse's Big Book of Fears* by Emily Gravett (2007), cut-outs show evidence of where little mouse has been. In *Home* (2006) and *Sandswimmers* (1999) by Narelle Oliver, actual photographs have been combined with collage, linocut, rubbings, pastel, pencil and watercolour, which previously could not have been reproduced without advances in printing techniques. Some books, such as *Requiem for a Beast* by Matt Ottley (2007), even have an accompanying CD-ROM as part of the book, which provides music which he has written as well as songs played and sung by Aboriginal people. All these advances mean that publishers are able to embrace the creative ideas of authors and illustrators and produce challenging and innovative books.

Literature provides opportunities for students to interact with, and respond to, social and cultural diversity. Literature provides authentic texts and artefacts of society and culture, portraying historical events and social comment on times past and present. As early as 1976 Bader described literature as a social, cultural and historical document and more recently Marriott suggested that they are not simply a crutch to developing adult reading skills but 'complicated and potent' (2009, p. 1) and 'contain a network of beliefs, values and social practices which are explicitly espoused or more often implicitly sustained within the text' (2009, p. 4). The complexity of the issues, beliefs and values addressed in these books, combined with the developments in multimodality and technologies, require the use of sophisticated literacy practices to engage with them in critical ways. Furthermore, as artefacts, that is, authentic products of culture and society at a particular time and in a particular context, they provide contextualising information and background for study in other disciplines such as history, studies of society and psychology.

The perennial issues of war and immigration have been explored in picture books across continents since the 1960s. At the height of the cold war Janet Charters (1962) wrote *The General* (illustrated by Michael Foreman) about a general who sent his army back to their homes to make a better country rather than going to war. He was later visited by the generals from the East and West, who could see the positive impact of this decision. It was republished in 2010 because of its continued relevance and environmental themes. Raymond Briggs' (1982) comic style book *When the Wind Blows* showed the impact of nuclear war in graphic detail as a couple gradually die from radiation sickness. *Archie's War* by Marcia Williams (2007) provides the perspective of the first world war through the scrapbook of a 10-year-old boy and *The Enemy* by David Cali and Serge Bloch (2007) provides a first-person account or fable about two lonely soldiers facing each other across a deserted battlefield, wondering if they are the only soldiers left and how they can end the war. It explores the question of just who is the enemy. *Tagged* by Gary Crew and Steve Woolman examines post-traumatic stress after the Vietnam War, as a boy searching for his dog comes across a homeless veteran and the veteran shares his story. *The House that Baba Built: An Artist's Childhood in China* by Ed Young (2011) tells the story of war in China through the eyes of a boy.

The realities of immigrating to another country by choice or through famine or persecution have been explored positively by Hest (1997) in *When Jessie Came Across the Sea* and in a more confronting way by Tan (2006) in *The Arrival*. A controversial policy in Australia regarding how people arrived and whether they should be turned back when arriving 'illegally' by boat gave rise to the 'protest' picture book *Home and Away*, written by John Marsden and illustrated by Matt Ottley (2008).

Personal issues are also explored through literature, such as depression in *The Red Tree* by Tan (2001), the death or leaving of a parent in *Mending Lucille* by Poulter and Davis (2008), and fear in *Parachute* by Parker and Ottley (2013). Once again the complexities of these topics, their application to multiple age groups and the unique ways in which they have been presented through traditional and other technologies, makes them excellent vehicles for practicing and developing multiliterate practices.

Apart from developing multiliteracies there are other reasons to engage students with picture books. Little expense is needed in accessing picture books, as most school libraries already have a good collection and increasingly authors and illustrators of these books have websites where images from them can be accessed together with the authors' and illustrators' comments about the books. Anecdotal evidence from early childhood teachers indicates that an increasing number of students come to school with little or no knowledge of, or contact with, children's literature because of the increasing availability of technology. While young children are frequently able to use iPads and mobile phones before coming to school, an increasing number have no idea how to manipulate or interact with a book. Nevertheless, research by Styles and Noble (2009, p. 127) indicates that young children move easily between the modes or semiotic systems and respond to images, particularly gestural elements, very early. It would seem therefore an optimum point at which to build on this ability and provide students with a language for talking about the semiotic systems and assist them in making more strategic moves and meaning making between them.

Finally, while looking at all the semiotic systems in literature and picture books it is important to note the role of the linguistic (language) in developing students' multiliterate practices. Picture books are a resource that provides a rich vocabulary and variety of sentence structures and styles of writing, unlike the sanitised and regulated introduction of vocabulary and sentence structure in commercially produced reading scheme materials, designed specifically to teach reading. High stakes testing such as the Australian National Assessment Plan Literacy and Numeracy (NAPLAN) often indicates vocabulary and sentence structure in writing as an area that needs improvement and an analysis of student responses in the NAPLAN reading tests (2011-2013) indicated that many students in Years 7 and 9 (aged approximately 12 and 14) were challenged by questions requiring higher order thinking, inference, analysis or evaluation. Using the authentic texts of literature, particularly picture books, which engage students in accessing and using these skills and provide rich writing models, can only assist with students' development in these areas.

Postmodern picture books and multiliteracies

In Chapter One the issues that inform the need for multiliterate practices and changes to literacy pedagogy were discussed. These included rapid change in all aspects of life, particularly workplaces, globalisation and advances in technology, all of which contribute to an indeterminate future. The term *postmodern* has been used to characterise 'the changes, tendencies and/or developments that have occurred in philosophy, literature, art and music in reaction to these rapid changes' (Pantaleo and Sipe 2008, p. 1). These trends in the arts were often manifested in works that questioned, critically revisited and engaged in irony or parody, indicating an uneasiness about what constitutes authority and legitimacy in changing times (Fleiger 1991). A particular type of picture book is one such manifestation and has been identified as the postmodern picture book. It has specific characteristics which require more of the reader than previous picture books and is therefore particularly suitable for students to engage in, and develop, multiliterate practices. In Table 5.1 the characteristics of the postmodern picture book have been summarised by drawing on the work of Anstey (2002), Anstey and Bull (2006), Bull and Anstey (2010), Pantaleo and Sipe (2008), Nikolejava and Scott (2001), Watson (2004) and Lewis (2001). In addition, Table 5.1 provides examples of how these characteristics might be realised in a postmodern picture book.

The descriptions of the ways in which these characteristics might be realised in a postmodern picture book in Table 5.1 indicate that these books are more demanding of the consumer/producer and require more sophisticated

Table 5.1 Characteristics of postmodern picture books and how they might be realised

Characteristics	How the characteristics might be realised
1. Non-traditional or radical ways of using plot, character or setting.	Challenges the expectations of the consumer/producer and therefore requires different readings and meanings. Because the plot, character or setting is presented in novel or unexpected ways, attention is drawn to the author's purposes in constructing an alternative telling. Draws attention to the place of the plot, character or setting in the narrative and how the changes affect the resolution of the narrative.
2. Unusual uses of narrator's voice, including unreliable narrators and blurring of distinctions among author, narrator and reader	Unusual uses of the narrator's voice (or an unreliable narrator who does not behave in expected ways) position the consumer/producer to read a book in particular ways and from the point of view of a particular character. This may be achieved through any of the semiotic systems present (e.g. linguistic, visual, audio)
3. Indeterminacy or lack of resolution, including incomplete narratives in written or illustrative text, plot, character or setting	Requires the reader/viewer to construct some of the written or illustrative text to make meaning through the plot, character or setting. Focuses attention on the gaps or silences in the book and how these are used to foreground or marginalise particular issues or characters.
4. Pastiche of illustrative styles or texts	Pastiche of styles draws attention to the style of illustration, the medium used, the dominant elements in illustration, balance and layout of illustration, form of address or person, use of narrative and/or expository genre, features of vocabulary and use of rhyme, rhythm or repetition.
5. New and unusual design and layout, including non-linear or non-sequential organisation.	This focuses the attention of the consumer/producer on size and shape of illustrations (whether regular or irregular), including use of portrait or landscape, range of page layouts, placement and balance of text and image, variation of page design in terms of size or shape and design of font. In the case of books delivered via new technologies, it may facilitate, or even require, different forms of interaction and control of the text by the consumer/producer.
6. Contesting discourses between illustrative and written text, including multiple perspectives, playfulness, irony and parody	Challenges the consumer/producer to consider or create alternative readings and meanings. All of the techniques (contesting discourses, irony, parody, etc.) focus attention on features of the book such as plot, theme, characterisation or setting in new ways that require the consumer/producer to consider alternative ways of consuming the text.
7. Intertextuality	Requires the consumer/producer to draw on previous experiences in both their school world and lifeworld. Expects the consumer/producer to access and use background knowledge in novel ways to access the multiple meanings in the book.
8. Multiple and ambiguous readings and meanings	Focuses the attention of the consumer/producer on the meanings and themes in the book and how they are realised. Requires the consumer/producer to attend to the different audiences of the book, consider the purpose for which the book might have been written and what the author/illustrator might be trying to achieve. Focuses attention on aspects of the social, cultural, economic or political contexts in which the book was produced.
9. Self-conscious or self-referential texts that refer to themselves as texts	The conscious construction of the book focuses attention on particular details about plot, theme, characterisation or setting. It challenges and engages the consumer/producer to construct meaning in new and different ways.

REFLECTION STRATEGY 5.1

- The purpose of this Reflection Strategy is to identify some of the characteristics of postmodern picture books in a range of picture books.
- Using the list of postmodern (and other) picture books presented at the end of this chapter, select at least five that you can access from a local library or bookstore (the online store 'Book Depository' is useful for books published in countries other than your own) and read and examine them carefully. Try to identify some of the characteristics of a postmodern picture book present in each book.
- Think about how those characteristics contribute to the book, its impact and the ways in which it challenges the consumer of the text. What are the implications for engaging your students with these books?

REFLECTION STRATEGY 5.2

- The purpose of this Reflection Strategy is to consider how the 12 understandings about text presented in Chapter Two might be developed through postmodern picture books.
- Examine the 12 understandings from Chapter Two, which are re-presented below, and revisit Table 5.1 which identifies the characteristics of the postmodern picture book and the ways in which they are realised in picture books. Think about how engaging with books that have these characteristics might develop some of the 12 understandings about text. It may be useful to look at the books used in Reflection Strategy 5.1 to assist with this process.
- One strategy that may help you with this task would be to create a table with the understandings on one side and the characteristics and the ways they are realised in the other and match those that are related.
  1. All texts are multimodal
  2. All texts are consciously constructed and have a particular purpose
  3. No text is neutral
  4. Texts can be interactive, linear or non-linear
  5. Texts can be designed for dissemination via multiple technologies
  6. Texts may be intertextual
  7. The reader/viewer actively constructs the meaning of the text
  8. The reader/viewer produces a hypertext when using hyperlinks
  9. The social and cultural background of individuals influences the production of, and engagement with, text
  10. A text may have several possible meanings
  11. Multimodal texts require readers/viewers to consciously differentiate the focus of their attention across the semiotic systems
  12. Texts will continue to change

understandings about the processes of consuming or producing a text. A pervading theme among the characteristics is to challenge conventions, recreating the concepts of book and picture book in multiple ways. These challenges to convention are indicative of change and as such require consumers/producers to be active rather than passive, to take responsibility for making meaning and to engage in critical thinking and other higher order thinking skills. Coping with change and being able to respond to it in productive and strategic ways is one of the overarching needs for a multiliterate person. As Coats (2008, p. 79) stated, 'the project of postmodern picture books is to reveal their own processes, the goal of revelation is empowerment for the reader; they deliver a strong invitation and even an expectation that readers will participate in meaning making.' These demands make the postmodern picture book a perfect site for engaging students in multiliterate practices, accustoming them to being challenged and introducing them to the codes and conventions of the semiotic systems.

Plummer (2016) pointed out that postmodern picture books of the late 20th and 21st centuries are not the only books that exhibit *postmodern* characteristics and that some books published long before the term *postmodern* was coined challenged the conventions of picture books. She used the term 'playful' to describe these pre-postmodern books, and suggested that playful texts 'disrupt our expectations' and play on words and images in much the same way children engage in make-believe, where the everyday world, common sense and rules are challenged or left behind (Plummer 2016, p. 65). Regardless of when books are published and the labels used to describe them, the selection of a range of authentic texts, that require a deeper engagement, either through challenging conventions or exhibiting the traditional qualities of a variety of literature, is essential to developing students with the knowledge, skills and strategies to survive in the future. As Plummer (2016, p. 65) stated, 'In much the same way that make-believe play depends upon the ability to step outside oneself and take on other roles,

REFLECTION STRATEGY 5.3.

- The purpose of this Reflection Strategy is to explore some books that exhibit postmodern characteristics. Find the picture books mentioned in Table 5.2 or other picture books that explore or challenge the concept of books and/or reading with traditional or paper or other technologies. (Your friends and colleagues or local town or school librarian may be able to help you find books other than those mentioned.)
- Read the books and examine them carefully. Identify the ways in which they explore the concepts of reading/consuming, picture books and the difference between reading paper texts and reading texts delivered by other technologies.

- Identify the semiotic systems present and consider what each contributes to the ways in which the concepts about reading/consuming are developed or commented upon.
- Identify the characteristics of postmodern picture books that are present in each book and how they are realised.

playful (or postmodern?) texts ask the reader to participate in a process of conceptual reframing ... accompanied by the subversion of conventional narrative practices.' This is exactly what students will need to do as texts, and the acts of consuming and producing them, continue to change.

The following group of texts described in Table 5.2 contains a range of texts that might be defined as postmodern. They have been selected because they challenge and explore the concepts about picture books, narratives and the semiotic systems books contain.

Table 5.2 A group of books that explore the concept of picture book

Publication details and book description	How this book explores and/or challenges the concept of book
Black and White, David Macaulay 1990 Houghton Mifflin, New York Tells the story of an interruption in commuter train services and the impact on people's lives.	• A sign warns the reader on the verso that the book contains a number of stories that may not occur simultaneously and both words and pictures need careful inspection. • Verso is on first opening and imprint page on last page. • Layout of pages is unusual and changes at critical points in the story. Common format is four framed images with narrative per double page spread, each image using different illustrative style and media. • Illustrative styles remain constant and appear to indicate a different story. • Each framed image or story contains different characters and settings.
The Book with No Pictures, B J Novak 2014, Penguin, New York The book has no pictures and instructs the reader to read it aloud.	• The reader is given instruction as to how to read the book. • The book contains the oral responses/commentary of the reader, who is not comfortable reading the book because it has no pictures. • Colour, font and layout of words varies with 'read aloud' content. • The book emphasises the Audio Semiotic System because it has to be read aloud. It plays with language and sound, using nonsense words, size of font, layout and colour that may suggest how the words might be said aloud (volume, pitch, intonation, stress, modulation). • There is no conventional narrative (plot or story).
It's a Book, Lane Smith 2010, Walker Books Australia, Newtown. A monkey and a jackass have a conversation about a book the monkey is reading. The jackass has a laptop, the monkey a book. The jackass asks what the book can do…	• The conversation humorously reveals the differences between consuming/producing a paper narrative book and a computer. (Jackass asks if a book can text, tweet, scroll or use Wi-Fi, produce sound.) • Introduces possible differences and purposes of texts delivered by different technologies. (The jackass suggests there are too many words in the book and 'fixes' it by summarising and retyping it on his computer in SMS; jackass offers to recharge book when he has finished.) • There are visual and linguistic puns around 'mouse'. • The jackass ends up reading the book for hours (clock shows passage of time).

(Continued)

Table 5.2 (Continued)

Look, A BOOK! Libby Gleeson and Freya Blackwood 2011, Little Hare Books, Richmond. Two children, who live in a low socioeconomic area find a book and as they take it home, taking great care to look after it, embark on an imaginary adventure.	• The format and cover of the book resemble a very old publication with simulated red cloth binding and cover illustration resembling a colour plate set into the binding. • The cover appears worn and stained and the book resembles the book the children find, as illustrations include the book as it actually appears. • The children repeat typical librarian or parent statements about caring for the book as they take it home. • Although the children are talking about caring for the book as they take it home the illustrations show them on an imaginative adventure as though they are simultaneously entering the book and its story. • The final illustrations shows the book being read 'again and again' at home with an adult and other friends and each time another adventure appears in the illustrations.

THEORY INTO PRACTICE 5.1

- The purpose of this Theory into Practice strategy is to explore the books you examined in Reflection Strategy 5.3 with your students. The purpose is for both you and your students to know more about their reactions to, and understandings about, unconventional books and the ideas within them.
- Over a period of time read these books with your students and discuss with them how they view them. The following questions might stimulate conversations. You may have other questions stimulated by your previous examination of the books. Depending upon the age and prior experience of your students you may wish to investigate the books in groups, as whole class discussions or a combination of both.
    - o What is your initial reaction to a quick look through this book? Do you want to read it or not? What are your reasons for your answer?
    - o What do you think this book is saying about picture books? What evidence is there that supports your ideas?
    - o What do you think it is saying about reading? What evidence is there that supports your ideas?
    - o Why do you think the author/illustrator wrote this book?
    - o Has reading this book changed/influenced your thoughts about how you read and what you attend to when you read? If so, how?
    - o Has reading this book changed/influenced your thoughts about reading picture books or what picture books are and their purpose? If so, how?
- You may wish to review some of the information in Chapter Four about classroom talk to help inform the way in which you discuss the books with your students.
- You may find the journal article 'It's not all Black and White' by Anstey (2002), which discusses multiliteracies and postmodern picture books and in particular student reactions to the book (*Black and White* by David Macaulay) informative and helpful in planning your lesson. It is available through QR code 5.1.

QR code 5.1 Link to 'It's not all Black and White' (https://www.researchgate.net/publication/250055512_It%27s_Not_All_Black_and_White_Postmodern_Picture_Books_and_New_Literacies)

Comparing the use of the semiotic systems in postmodern picture books across technologies

As stated previously, some picture books, including those that exhibit postmodern characteristics, have now been converted to film or animation. They are also delivered via live performances and some authors and illustrators have written music to accompany them. These changes in components, format and delivery enable students to compare the effect of delivery via different technologies, for example, the addition of sound and music. In this way students develop a better understanding about how the selection and use of different semiotic systems and their associated codes and conventions, affect meaning making, which in turn informs them about the processes of consuming and producing text.

The role of other disciplines in understanding postmodern picture books

The fact that postmodern picture books cross the boundaries of technology and media means that they are informed by a range of disciplines within the arts, specifically music, art and the performing arts. Therefore, it is appropriate to examine how these disciplines might inform students' understandings about postmodern picture books in all their forms.

Drawing on art

Clark (1960, p. 69) described four phases of appreciating a work of art which can be summarised as follows:

- Phase One – Impact: gaining a general impression of the picture as a whole, the subject matter and composition.
- Phase Two – Scrutiny: carefully looking at the whole picture taking time to examine it from a purely aesthetic perspective, considering the emotions it engenders and whether it appeals.
- Phase Three – Recollection: looking at the picture and making connections with previous experiences and asking questions of it, thinking.
- Phase Four – Renewal: Looking more deeply, fitting reactions to it with previous knowledge and formulating a response based on memory, imagination and thought.

When studying young children's reactions to picture books Arizpe and Styles (2003, p. 44), pointed out that without impact (Phase One) there is no engagement and therefore subsequent phases cannot occur. They also found that careful scrutiny (Phase Two) and recollection (Phase Three) takes time and concentration, as the picture has to be looked at several times, firstly to examine all the detail and then to relate to past experiences and knowledge. The issues of time and looking several times that Arizpe and Styles raised are important. There are 32 pages in a picture book, potentially 32 'works of art', in Clark's terms. This is before other semiotic systems, such as the linguistic and possibly music or sound effects, are considered. The implications for planning students' engagement with picture books are that there need to be multiple passes through the books and time allowed for scrutiny, in combinations of individual, group or whole class work. Some guidance about what to think about during scrutiny and recollection may also need to be taught. The issue of what should be taught and how students should be guided in responding to art has been the subject of some debate in the areas of visual arts and is often discussed as visual literacy. There is general agreement that a syntax (a set of codes and conventions or grammar) is necessary to talk about Art (Dondis 1973; Allen 1994), but, similar to the teaching of literacy, there is much debate about how it should be taught.

Raney (1998, 1999) suggested that it is important that the teaching of a syntax (the codes and conventions of the Visual Semiotic System) should not be taught in the static way that linguistic grammar has been taught, because it implies that the codes, and their conventions for use, are fixed. This is very similar to current views about the teaching of the codes and conventions of the semiotic systems in literacy education, which were discussed in Chapter Three. It also reinforces the need to teach the codes and conventions of the semiotic systems and therefore the arts curriculum, and teachers of the arts are useful resources for literacy teaching. In primary school, where teachers are mostly responsible for teaching all areas of the curriculum, it opens up the possibilities of integrating and cross-teaching the arts and English curricula. Raney also stated that not simply decoding, but context and prior experience, needed to be considered: 'our relationship to the visual world (should be) in terms of choice, habit, passion or delight... the driving force is prior expectations of meaning set up by the social fields in which an object is encountered' (1998, p. 39). Raney's (1998, 1999) discussion of visual literacy and the art curriculum emphasised the influence of historical, cultural and artistic contexts of both the artwork and its viewer in meaning making. Her discussion of the issues of context and the viewer's background experiences (lifeworld) reflect current beliefs about the teaching of literacy, multiliteracies and the codes and conventions of the semiotic systems in previous chapters.

THEORY INTO PRACTICE 5.2

- The purpose of this Theory into Practice is to use the ideas of Clark and Raney, in conjunction with the knowledge about teaching the semiotic systems provided in Chapter Three, as one way to guide students' viewing of a picture book.

- Explain to students that today they are going to approach a picture book in a different way. The goal is to interrupt the normal focus of a picture book in an English lesson and, rather than viewing the book as something to be read and comprehended, view it as a work of art from which to make meaning. Explain that at the end of the lesson there will be discussion about if, and how, focussing on the book as a work of art influenced their consumption of the book and meaning making.
- Use the following questions and sequence to view a picture book. Depending upon the age of the students and the experience they have with the semiotic systems and picture books, change the language of the questions and work as a whole class, in groups and individually at different stages of the lesson. You may wish to refer back to Chapter Four and its discussion of how classroom talk shapes students' learning and meaning making and the discussion of students' lifeworld and prior experience in Chapter Two for assistance in planning the lesson.
- Phase One: Impact. Look at the whole book, its subject matter, format and layout. Focus on the images rather than the linguistic text. What are your initial reactions to this book and why? Do you feel you want to look further (and why)? What questions about the book come into your mind as you look at it? What do you want to know more about and investigate further and why? What do you wonder about?
- Phase Two: Scrutiny. Questions to guide further scrutiny of each page and image. What is the style of illustration, the media used? What dominates the image or immediately attracts the eye and why? What codes and conventions of the Visual Semiotic System do you immediately see used and why do you immediately see them? How does this influence your meaning making? (This could be repeated/alternated with Gestural and Spatial Semiotic Systems, depending upon age and experience of students and the book.)
- Phase Three: Recollection. What experiences have you had that you remember or draw upon when you look at the images and make sense of them? (Have you seen similar styles of illustration/format/layout /use of colour/space, other books by the author or illustrator or on the same topic, etc.?) Is the subject matter familiar or unfamiliar? How do these things influence your meaning making? What do they make you think about and how do they influence how react to in the image?
- Phase Four: Renewal. Read the words in the book. As well as their meaning or what they say, think about where they are placed, use of font, colour, size, the presence or absence of words on every page or image. Think about whether they change your perceptions or meaning making about the book and why.
- Discuss with the students whether this approach made them look at the picture book differently and if so, how. What did it make them focus upon and how did it influence their meaning making?
- Discuss how knowledge about art can help with meaning making in English.

Drawing on music

As has been stated previously many picture books have been made into film or animation or have had music composed and added as a CD accompanying the book. The availability of some picture books as film or as animated versions provides the opportunity for comparative study. Students can examine how the plot, setting and characters have been translated, whether original illustrations have been used or new ones created and how all these factors compare with the original book. The addition of visual codes and conventions applicable to film (see Chapter Three) can be examined to see how codes, such as camera angles, focus, framing, lighting and editing, foreground particular meanings and how these meanings compare with the original book. The availability of audio brings in an aural interpretation of characters' speech. Investigations can be made into how the aural element of speech affects meaning making and interpretation of the character and why particular pitch, timbre and accent may have been selected. Examination of the images of the character and their actions in the picture book may provide clues and students could also consider other voices for the character and why they would or wouldn't work. These types of investigation and discussion all contribute to students' understanding about character development and plot and the relationships between character and plot, as well as elaborating their understandings about the different semiotic systems and how they can be used to make meaning. In addition, sound effects and music provide another level of interpretation for comparison with the original picture book. The CD of the animated film of Shaun Tan's picture book *The Lost Thing* (Ruhemann and Tan 2010) provides extra material that demonstrates particular sound effects, together with alternatives. The use of the extra material that is frequently found on film CDs provides a rich source for students to view and discuss. It assists in the development of understandings about the complexity of interpreting a picture book for film. Examples that include alternatives, such as those on *The Lost Thing* CD, are particularly useful as they provide a source for immediate comparison and discussion. A more detailed explanation of the whole process of converting *The Lost Thing* to film, including links to the film trailer and interviews with those involved in the creation of the film, can be found on Shaun Tan's website at QR Code 5.2.

QR Code 5.2 Discussion about making the picture book *The Lost Thing* into film (http://www.shauntan.net/film1.html)

While the Audio Semiotic System provides codes and conventions that relate to sound and voice (see Chapter Three), the music curriculum and teachers of music can provide more detailed information about these codes and conventions, together with guidance about response to music. Drawing upon these resources may assist when planning for students to examine picture books that have music accompanying them and also film versions of the books. Ellis and Simons (reported in Barton and Unsworth 2014) found the simultaneous presentation of images and music produced physiological and emotional stimulation, and that certain structural features stimulated particular reactions. For example, major keys had a positive association while minor keys had a negative association. However, it should be remembered that the codes and conventions of the Audio Semiotic System are mediated by the culture and prior experiences of the consumer. Barton and Unsworth (2014, p. 17) elaborated on the work of Ellis and Simons and others and developed an analytical framework for musical soundtracks that specifically assists consideration of how music influences the interpretation of images.

It includes tonal features, rhythmic features, articulation and dynamics and timbral features. They then used the framework to examine how the musical soundtrack for the animated film of *The Lost Thing* (Ruhemann and Tan 2010) contributes to interpretation of the images. Barton and Unsworth (2014) concluded that music should be included in the repertoire of resources that students develop to produce and consume multimodal texts.

On fairly rare occasions an author or illustrator may also be a composer and actually compose the music to accompany their illustrations. One illustrator, artist and composer who engages in this process is Matt Ottley. On his website Ottley provides insights into the process of composing illustrations and music, and interestingly the process does not always start with the illustrations. Two video clips show excerpts from a workshop run in Western Australia, where the author of the picture book, Matt Ottley, and the Western Australian Symphony Orchestra explore the process of composition with students. These excerpts provide useful insights into one person's process when composing multimodal texts and also demonstrate the ways in which the concepts about picture books and their production are continually being challenged and changed. A link to this material and Matt Ottley's website is provided in QR Code 5.3.

QR Code 5.3 Matt Ottley talks about composing images and music (http://mat-tottley.com/composition/the-sound-of-picture-books/)

Drawing on the performing arts

The performing arts are a powerful way of helping students to respond to picture books. Arizpe et al. (2008, pp. 212–13) reported how students spontaneously acted out, performed and improvised on postmodern picture books as they encountered ambiguities and disruptions to anticipated meaning. Anderson, Kauffman and Short (1998) reported how students used drama and art to respond to images and themes in picture books and further explore issues such as gender, class, ethnicity and prejudice. Laycok (1998) found that dramatising picture books enabled students from other cultures and for whom English was a second language, to enter into and respond to ideas and themes in picture books. These findings provide evidence that drama and the performing arts can assist students in exploring meanings in postmodern picture books.

The drama or performing arts curriculum and teachers of drama can be a valuable source to further inform such explorations and a way of assisting students to transfer and use knowledge across disciplines. The collaborative nature of performance and the influence of social, cultural and historical contexts in performance further reinforce the multiliterate understandings, knowledge and skills that are necessary for students to participate in society. The semiotic systems inform drama and drama informs student knowledge and understandings of how the semiotic systems can be combined and recombined to make and convey meaning. The Gestural Semiotic System informs the use of facial expression, costume, props, posture and movement. The Spatial Semiotic System informs the use of space and the Audio Semiotic System informs the use of voice, music and sound effects. The actual planning and interpretation of the drama involves detailed exploration of character, relationships, plot and setting, all of which inform the consumption and production of text. Knowledge about drama and the performing arts can also assist students in responding to film and performance versions of picture books.

Developing a critical pedagogy that engenders critical reading practices

In Reflection Strategy 5.2, the 12 understandings about text from Chapter Two were re-presented. Review of these understandings, particularly numbers 2, 3, 7, 9, 10, 11 and 12, reveals the necessity for students to be able to engage in critical reading (consumption) practices in order to understand how the construction of texts shapes meaning, in particular, ideology, beliefs and attitudes. Therefore, it is imperative pedagogies that develop critical reading practices are developed and employed. Anstey (2008, p. 153) referred to the investigation of postmodern picture books as similar to an archaeological dig, requiring the use of a variety of tools and perspectives and multiple examinations of the artefact in question: the postmodern picture book. She developed a model for investigating postmodern picture books by drawing upon research into a literary response to picture books and the sociocultural basis of theories about literacy pedagogy together with the Four Resource Model (Anstey 2008, pp. 155–58). The model she developed was intended for use by researchers, students and teachers. It was designed to:

- inform research methodology by providing a framework for investigation that could be modified to suit the particular inquiry
- assist students to investigate postmodern texts in order to better understand how they are constructed and how they can shape meaning
- assist teachers in designing learning experiences that foreground the constructed nature of text and the need for critical investigation of how meaning has been constructed and the multiple readings possible

Table 5.3 has revisited this model, updating and further developing and modifying it to address the current concepts about multiliteracies, multimodal texts, semiotic systems and their codes and conventions together with the rapid and continuous changes in what constitutes text and the technologies by which text is conveyed. It has been reframed as 'A model for engaging with text' and is intended for use with any text, not just children's literature or postmodern picture books. It should be noted that the model is not meant to be exhaustive and complete: it is a prompt that teachers can use for planning engagement with texts. Teachers can also use it to develop conversations with students about how they go about consuming a text. Teachers and students or groups of students can also work collaboratively to develop prompts for use when consuming text.

Table 5.3 A model for engaging with multimodal text

Pre-engagement with text: Focus on purpose
- What is your purpose? Why are you investigating this text?
- What are your expectations of the text, in terms of:
  o the technology by which it is conveyed,
  o how it is to be used,
  o its content,
  o the text types or genres, format and features that might be present,
  o the semiotic systems and codes and conventions that might be present, and
  o any ideologies, beliefs, attitudes or biases that might be present?
- What will you need to do with this text; what are your responsibilities as a consumer of text, in order to fulfil your purpose?

Use steps two, three and four as needed, that is, only if they are relevant and useful to fulfilling your purpose for engaging with, and or investigating, this text

Step one: Focus on code-breaker practices	Step two: Focus on meaning maker practices
Engage in an in-depth familiarisation with the text and how it works. Scan the physical, technological and interactive, features of the text and identify the semiotic systems present. Develop a comprehensive knowledge of these features and how they work prior to further specific investigations.	Engage with and identify the meanings in this text and how they are realised. *Structure of text* • What text types or genres are used (e.g. narrative, persuasive, report, explanation, procedure) and how does their use contribute to meaning making? • Is there one or more text type or genre present? • What prior knowledge or experiences about the text type do you have that might assist your meaning making? • What are the purposes of the text type/s or genre/s? • What structural features and conventions are present for the text type/s genre/s (e.g. in narrative - title, orientation, complication, resolution)? • How are the semiotic systems and their codes and conventions used to support the text type or genre?

Physical features and form
• How are these realised in the technology by which the text is conveyed?
  o Paper - size, format (e.g. portrait, landscape, square), manipulation of pages: (e.g. cut-outs, half pages, foldouts), page layouts employed, (e.g. double page spread), quality of paper (e.g. shiny, thick, thin, textured), semiotic systems present and available for use.
  o Digital - screen format, placement of text/images on the screen (e.g. what is above and below the fold), semiotic systems present and available for use, interactive devices (e.g. hyperlinks, search engine, chat facility, links to other users), ability to customise your use of the text (e.g. save links, parts of text or images to your device for future use).
  o Live - Content and organisation of three-dimensional space (e.g. chairs, tables, stage), placement of those present in relation to one another, behavioural and/or interactive expectations of those present (specified or implied), semiotic systems present and available for use. (Some of this may not be possible to consider before a live interaction and may have to occur during interaction.)
	Text features
	• How do the physical, technological and interactive features of the text contribute to the meanings you make?
	• Have you encountered/used any of these features before and does this knowledge and experience help your meaning making?
	• Are there experiences from your lifeworld that will help your meaning making (e.g. do you know something about the content from another experience?)
	Semiotic systems
	• How do the semiotic systems and the codes and conventions present interact to make meaning? Do they enhance, oppose, complement or mirror one another?
	  o Are the semiotic systems used in this way throughout the text or do their interactions and roles change, and how does this affect your meaning making?

(Continued)

Table 5.3 (Continued)

Semiotic systems
• Those present, dominant codes and conventions
  o Which of the semiotic systems (Linguistic, Visual, Audio, Spatial, Gestural) are present and available for use via the technology by which the text is conveyed?
  o Which semiotic system is dominant (used most)?
  o Which codes and conventions within each semiotic system present are dominant?	

Step three: Focus on text user practices
Consider who might use this text, the purpose for which the text might be used and how it would be used.
Use
• Have I used a text for this purpose before and is there knowledge and experience I can draw upon that will assist me in this context?
• Does the purpose of this text mean that there are particular behaviours or social or cultural conventions that should be observed when using it?
• How should this text be used in this context?
Text features and semiotic systems
• How has the purpose and use of this text shaped its physical, technological and interactive features?
• Would you use these features differently if you were using the text for a different purpose?
• How do these features, and the way they have been used, shape meaning making?
• How has the purpose and use of the text shaped the ways in which the semiotic systems present, together with their codes and conventions, have been brought together and employed?
• How does the way the semiotic systems and their codes and conventions have been used shape meaning making?
	Step four: Focus on text analyst practices
	Engage in a critical examination and evaluation of the meanings present, their origins, authenticity, authority and relevance to the context and purpose for which the text is being used.
	Context and origins
	• Does the text reflect any social, cultural, economic or political features of the time and context in which it was produced?
	• Are there multiple meanings or themes available and how are they made available and what are they?
	• What are the origins of the text?
	  o What are the commercial or political origins of the text and do these influence the ideas, beliefs, attitudes and values being presented?
	  o Who produced the text and what interests, attitudes, values and beliefs are evident in this text?
	  o What authority or credentials does the producer of the text have regarding the content and meanings presented?
	Text features and semiotic systems
	• How do the physical, technological and interactive features shape or portray any social, cultural, economic or political ideologies, attitudes, values and beliefs present in this text?
	• How do the semiotic systems, together with their codes and conventions, shape or portray any social, cultural, economic or political ideologies, attitudes, values and beliefs present in this text?
	  o Have particular semiotic systems or particular codes and conventions been used more than others to shape or portray these meanings, (for example, camera angles, lighting, framing and editing)?
	  o Are there meanings, values, attitudes, beliefs or ideas that have been marginalised, silenced or misrepresented in the text?
	  o How are particular beliefs and positions foregrounded in the text (for example, repetition in sound and image, volume, colour)?
	• What do you think about the way this text presents these ideas, and what alternatives are there?
	• Having engaged with the text, what actions are you going to take?

The main goal of the model is to address how the producers of the text have conveyed meaning through multiple semiotic systems and technologies and to focus on how this has been achieved. Therefore, many of the questions in Table 5.3 ask the consumer to consider how all the parts of the text convey meaning, singly and in combination. In addition, the goal is to encourage the active consumer of the text to use all semiotic systems present – the physical, technological and interactive features of the text, together with their lifeworld experiences and current purpose and context – to make meaning.

While the model presented in Table 5.3 may seem exhaustive and complex, it simply reflects the types of thinking and conversations with oneself the active consumer would have as they engage with the text in order to fulfil their purpose. It comprises metacognitive prompts. However, novice consumers need to actually have these prompts modelled, develop further prompts of their own and practice active engagement with text, before these prompts become automatic and part of their repertoire of metacognitive practices. Hence the need for a critical pedagogy to develop these practices.

The model has an extensive pre-engagement step that requires the consumer to focus on their purpose in engaging with the text and what their expectations are regarding its technology, content, how it is to be used, the semiotic systems present and the genres or text types that might be encountered. The complexity of this pre-engagement step is necessary with multimodal texts delivered by multiple technologies, as texts are increasingly complex and constantly changing. It is simply not enough to use the typical pre-reading activity that dominates shared book sessions and focusses on looking at the cover of the book, the title, author and any pictures present on the cover. Consumers of text need to be considering not simply what the text might be about, but its physical, technological and interactive features which affect how they will engage with it and what their responsibilities will be as a consumer using the text to fulfil their purpose. Therefore, thinking about the topic and potential content (which is essentially all the shared book example just given does) is simply not adequate in order to be an active multiliterate consumer.

Although all four foci of the Four Resource Model are addressed in the model for engaging with text, only those that are relevant to fulfilling one's purpose would be used. Nevertheless, any active engagement with text would normally require code breaking and meaning making and some critical engagement (text analyst) practice. Text user practices may only be used, together with code-breaking and meaning making, in specific contexts for specific purposes, such as completing a set of instructions in order to make or build something.

Using critical pedagogies to develop critical literacy through literature

As stated at the beginning of this chapter, literature includes paper, live and digital texts and often the same piece of literature is produced and delivered in all these forms. Therefore, literature provides the ideal opportunity for students to develop critical literacy skills across paper, live and digital texts and learn more about the affordances of these different delivery technologies as they examine how the semiotic systems, together with the physical, technological and interactive features of the text, combine to convey meaning. It is particularly useful to start such investigations with a known piece of children's literature where students are familiar with the plot, characters and setting, for example, a fairy tale such as *Cinderella* or *The Three Little Pigs*. This enables students to focus on how the text has been constructed to convey meaning, rather than on comprehending and remembering the plot. Furthermore, as many of these tales have been retold over time, by different authors, illustrators and producers of text, there is opportunity to compare how these different producers and technologies have conveyed meaning and to engage in critical analysis of the different versions.

Students can use their critical literacy skills to examine whether 'good' and 'bad' fairy tale characters have been constructed in particular ways and whether the settings and plot have been changed. Students can also consider whether the different versions of the fairy tale reflect the social and cultural context of the time and if this contributes to differences among the meanings conveyed. Consideration of how 'good' and 'bad' characters have been constructed may also lead to examination of stereotypes and whether particular physical characteristics portrayed through the Gestural and Audio Semiotic Systems convey attitudes and values associated about physical characteristics (for example, the unkind 'bad' step-sisters of Cinderella are often portrayed as very thin, having warts and hair on their faces, very fat or older). Consideration could be given as to whether repeated use of such portrayals may shape people's attitudes toward people with these characteristics in negative ways.

There are many postmodern versions of fairy tales available that present the plot from a different perspective or alter the number of characters and settings for events in different ways. Examination of these versions enables students to understand more about the genre of narrative, the importance of character development and the development of plot and setting. This informs their writing and production knowledge and skills, as well as their skills and knowledge about consuming text. From a critical literacy perspective students can consider why the postmodern version, or any rewritten version of a fairy tale, has been constructed. This enables students to explore understandings about texts being products of society, their cultural basis and the idea that no text is neutral. This is an important concept for students because as narrative is used for entertainment and leisure, it is often consumed without critical engagement and the values, beliefs and attitudes present are absorbed without question.

REFLECTION STRATEGY 5.4

- The purpose of this Reflection Strategy is to use the model for engaging with multimodal text to practice critical engagement with a fairy tale. This Reflection Strategy will also provide knowledge and strategies that can then be used in Theory into Practice 5.3.
- Choose a fairy tale to investigate. Find two versions, preferably delivered via different technologies, for example, a paper version and a digital version. You may wish to use the bibliography of postmodern (and other) picture books at the end of this chapter for assistance. If choosing a digital version, try to use film or cartoon rather than an eBook. Links to three versions of The Three Little Pigs are provided via QR Code 5.4. Searching the name of any fairy tale on YouTube will locate cartoon and film versions of other fairy tales.

QR Code 5.4 Three links to cartoon and puppet versions of *The Three Little Pigs*
1. The original 1933 cartoon version (https://www.youtube.com/watch?v=SKxWJP_LH7A)

2. A 2008 version (https://www.youtube.com/watch?v=4F8vWWcTPnE)

3. A puppet version in French to a Lady Gaga song (https://www.youtube.com/watch?v=1qxnpzOz_hg)

- Using the model for engaging with multimodal picture books, analyse the two versions of the fairy tale you have chosen, with a focus on characterisation. That is, examine the fairy tale to see how the main characters have been portrayed through all semiotic systems and technologies.
    o This will involve pre-engagement and the selection of relevant questions from Step One, code breaker practices; Step Two, meaning maker practices and Step Four, text analyst practices. N.B. Each of these steps will require at least one pass through the whole text.
    o When addressing the selected questions focus only on how each applies to characterisation, as that is the focus of this task. For example, the question from Step Four, text analyst practices, 'How do the semiotic systems, together with their codes and conventions, shape or portray any social, cultural, economic or political ideologies, attitudes, values and beliefs present in this text?', would be addressed in terms of how the semiotic systems have been used to portray the character and if this portrayal may contribute to negative associations in society generally or reinforce stereotypes (e.g. if you are fat, you are ugly; if you wear black, you are bad; if you are blonde, blue-eyed and slender, you are beautiful).

- Compare the similarities and differences in characterisation between the two versions. While much of this comparison will be addressed through Steps One and Two, the reasons for the similarities and differences involve the text analyst practices of Step Four. For example, the question from Step Four text analyst practices, 'Does the text reflect any social, cultural economic or political features of the time and context in which it was produced?', would be relevant. Alternate or postmodern versions of the fairy tales produced and published more recently may have less gendered roles and/or may reflect the ways in which young people grow up and leave home in ways more relevant to current times than fairy tales from previous eras.
- If you have addressed this task carefully, revisiting the text and questions several times, then you will realise that asking students to do such a task in one session, with limited access to the text, would be tedious and difficult for them. It will also be apparent that such investigations must be modified to address the students' knowledge about the codes and conventions of the five semiotic systems. Translating this task into a lesson in Theory into Practice 5.3 may assist you with these issues.

THEORY INTO PRACTICE 5.3

- The purpose of this Theory into Practice task is to assist students to compare how the character of the wolf is constructed in two versions of *The Three Little Pigs*. This will be achieved by examining how each of the semiotic systems contributes to the development of the wolf's character. Find two traditional (i.e. not postmodern) versions of the story of *The Three Little Pigs*, one paper (picture book) and one digital (cartoon or short film).
- Explain to the students that over the next few days they are going to investigate how each of the semiotic systems contributes to the development of a character and how we, as the consumers, perceive the character because of the way it has been constructed. Explain that the story to be used is one with which they are familiar so they can concentrate on their investigations.
- Before showing students either book or cartoon/film revise with students the plot of *The Three Little Pigs* completing a summary students can refer to later. Identify the main characters and their actions and once again create a summary students can refer to later.
- Discuss how the actions of the characters make the students, as consumers of the text, feel about each character. Focus only on recalled actions; do not refer to the two versions to be examined. The students will probably identify the wolf character as not very likeable and possibly bad or evil. Explain that they are going to be investigators and see if there are things in the text, in addition to his actions, that reinforce our feeling that he is not a good character.

- Before examining the book or film use some of the pre-engagement questions in the model for engaging with a multimodal text, as follows:
  o What are we focussing on in this book? (the wolf and how he is portrayed as bad)
  o Remember we are investigating to see how we perceive him as bad from things in the text other than his actions. So what might we focus on? (see the sample table for taking notes for examples)
  o Apart from focussing on the wolf, himself, what else might we examine? (lighting, sound effects, music when he appears, the timbre of his voice, how other characters react when he appears)
- Using either the paper or cartoon/film version of the story, read through/watch the whole text in order to become familiar with it. Depending upon your students' age, experience and knowledge about the semiotic systems and constructing multimodal texts such as film or cartoon, the rest of the lesson could be completed in a variety of ways:
  o Start with whole class joint analysis and construction of tabular summary with a selection of codes from one semiotic system with which students are familiar. Examine the second text in a later lesson using group work, with different groups looking at different semiotic systems with which they are familiar and constructing a tabular summary of their findings (supply table for summary)
  o Group work with each group working on a semiotic system with which they are familiar, providing a table for summarising investigations
  o Teacher and students work out a table for summarising an investigation of how one semiotic system portrays the wolf's character and then students apply it individually or in groups. Repeat with each semiotic system over several days. Students conduct investigations with second text independently
- When students have analysed both texts and reported back their findings, summarise their findings in tabular form so they can compare how the semiotic systems and any other factors were used to portray the wolf's character.
- Discuss their findings firstly by comparing how each semiotic system was used in each text.
  o Discuss whether some codes or semiotic systems were dominant and contributed more to building the character of the wolf
  o Discuss the additional semiotic systems or additional codes that were available in the digital text. Ask the students how these additional codes and semiotic systems contributed to the character of the wolf
  o Ask the students to consider the similarities and differences in the use of the semiotic systems to portray the character of the wolf in the two texts (possibly use a comparative table) and draw conclusions about the effectiveness of the portrayal of the wolf in each text
  o Ask the students to consider whether they would do anything differently and get them to explain what they would do and why.
- Finally remind the students of their purpose and ask them what they have discovered from their investigation about where and how they gain information about a character when consuming a text. Ask them to consider how they would use what they have discovered when developing and portraying a character in a multimodal text they are producing. (This could be done as a discussion or as a reflection if students regularly used a reflection book to write about their learning and how they might use it.)

Conclusion

The purpose of this chapter was to demonstrate how the study of literature, conveyed by a range of technologies, develops students' higher order thinking skills and critical literacy, together with understandings about the way texts are constructed to achieve particular purposes and meanings.

It has been demonstrated that because literature, and in particular picture books, cross the boundaries of age groups and technologies as they are translated into music, film, and animation, they are the perfect vehicle for developing understandings about how texts are constructed. They facilitate investigations of the interaction of the physical, technological and interactive features, together with the semiotic systems and the consumer's own knowledge and experiences, in making meaning. As authentic products of their time, society and culture, that draw on art, music and performing arts, they are a rich source for developing critical literacy practices and provide a context for study in other disciplines such as history, studies of society and psychology. In addition, postmodern picture books challenge and demand more of the consumer and are therefore excellent for developing and practicing multiliterate practices as they force the consumers to rethink traditional conventions and become active consumers.

Bibliography

Allen, D 1994, 'Teaching visual literacy: Some reflections on the term', *Journal of Art and Design Education*, vol. 13, pp. 133–43.

Anderson, C, Kauffman, G & Short, KG 1998, 'Now I think like an artist: Responding to picture books', in J Evans (ed), *What's in the Picture? Responding to Illustrations in Picture Books*, Paul Chapman Publishing, London, pp. 146–65.

Anstey, M 2002, 'It's not all Black and White: Postmodern picture books and teaching new literacies', *Journal of Adolescent and Adult Literacy*, vol. 45, no. 6, pp. 444–56.

Anstey, M 2008, 'Postmodern picturebooks as artefact: Developing tools for an archaelogical dig', in LR Sipe & S Pantaleo (eds), *Postmodern Picturebooks: Play Parody and Self-referentiality*, Routledge, London, pp. 147–63.

Anstey, M & Bull, G 2006, *Teaching and Learning Multiliteracies*, International Reading Association, Newark.

Arizpe, E & Styles, M 2003, *Children Reading Pictures: Interpreting Visual Texts*, Routledge Falmer, London.

Arizpe, E & Styles, M with K Cowan, L Mallouri & M Wolpert 2008, 'The voices behind the pictures: Children responding to postmodern picturebooks', in LR Sipe & S Pantaleo *Postmodern Picturebooks: Play Parody and Self-referentiality*, Routledge, London, pp. 207–22.

Australian Curriculum Assessment and Reporting Authority (ACARA) 2014, *Foundation to Year 10 Australian Curriculum English*, viewed 28 July 2017, https://www.australiancurriculum.edu.au/f-10-curriculum/english/?strand=Language&strand=Literature&strand=Literacy&capability=ignore&priority=ignore&elaborations=true.

Bader, B 1976, *American Picturebooks from* Noah's Ark *to* The Beast Within, Macmillan, New York.

Barton, G & Unsworth, L 2014, 'Music, multiliteracies and multimodality: Exploring the book and movie versions of Shaun Tan's *The Lost Thing*', *Australian Journal of Language and Literacy*, vol. 37, no. 1, pp. 3-20.

Board of Studies New South Wales 2012, *Suggested Texts for the English K-10 Syllabus*, Board of Studies, NSW, Sydney.

Briggs, R 1982, *When the Wind Blows*, Penguin Books, London.

Bull, G & Anstey, M 2010, *Evolving Pedagogies: Reading and Writing in a Multimodal World*, Curriculum Corporation, Melbourne.

Cali, D & Bloch, S 2007 *The Enemy*, Wilkins Farago, Albert Park.

Charters, J 1961, *The General*, Routledge and Kegan Paul, London.

Charters, J 2010, *The General*, Walker Books, London.

Clark, K 1960, *Looking at Pictures*, John Murray, London.

Coats, K 2008, 'Postmodern picturebooks and the transmodern self', in S Pantaleo & LR Sipe (eds), *Postmodern Picturebooks: Play, Parody and Self-Referentiality*, Routledge, New York, pp. 75-88.

Crew, G 1997, *The Viewer*, Lothian, Melbourne.

Crew, G & Woolman, S 1997, *Tagged*, Era, Flinders Park.

Department for Education and Employment, 1999, *The National Curriculum Handbook for Primary Teachers in England*, viewed 18 July 2017, http://www.educationengland.org.uk/documents/pdfs/1999-nc-primary-handbook.pdf.

Dondis, DA 1973, *A Primer of Visual Literacy*, MIT Press, Cambridge.

Fleiger, J 1991, *The Purloined Punch Line: Freud's Comic Theory and the Postmodern Text*, The Johns Hopkins University Press, Baltimore.

Gardner, P 2017, 'Worlds apart: A comparative analysis of discourses of English in the curricula of England and Australia', *English in Australia*, doi: 10.1111/eie.12138, viewed 20 July 2017, http://onlinelibrary.wiley.com/journal/10.1111/(ISSN)1754-8845.

Gleeson, L & Blackwood, F 2011, *Look, A BOOK!*, Little Hare Books, Richmond.

Gravett, E 2007, *Little Mouse's Big Book of Fears*, Macmillan, London.

Hest, A 1997, *When Jessie Came Across the Sea*, Walker Books, London.

Kress, G 2000, 'Design and transformation: New theories of meaning' in B Cope & M Kalantzis (eds), *Multiliteracies: Literacy Learning and the Design of Social Futures*, Routledge, London.

Laycock, L 1998, 'A way into a new language and culture', in J Evans (ed), *What's in the Picture? Responding to Illustrations in Picture Books*, Paul Chapman Publishing, London, pp. 79-95.

Lewis, D 2001, *Picturing Text: The Contemporary Children's Picturebook*, Taylor and Francis, London.

Macaulay, D 1990, *Black and White*, Houghton Mifflin, New York.

Marriott, S 2009, 'Picture books and the moral imperative', in J Evans (ed), *What's in the Picture? Responding to Illustrations in Picture Books*, Paul Chapman Publishing, London, pp. 1-24.

Marsden, J & Ottley, M 2008, *Home and Away*, Lothian, Melbourne.

Nikolejava, M & Scott, C 2001, *Words About Pictures: The Narrative Art of Children's Picture Books*, University of Georgia Press, Athens.

Novak, BJ 2014, *The Book with No Pictures*, Penguin, New York.

Oliver, N 2006, *Home*, Omnibus Books, Malvern.

Ottley, M 2007, *Requiem for a Beast: A Work for Image, Word and Music*, Lothian, Hachette, Sydney.

Pantaleo, S & Sipe, LR (eds) 2008, *Postmodern Picturebooks: Play, Parody and Self-Referentiality*, Routledge, New York.

Parker, D & Ottley, M 2013, *Parachute*, Little Hare, Richmond.

Plummer, A 2016, *Playful Texts and the Emergent Reader: Developing Metalinguistic Awareness*, Equinox, Sheffield.

Poulter, JR and Davis, S 2008, *Mending Lucille*, Lothian, Sydney.

Queensland Curriculum and Assessment Authority 2014, *Beyond NAPLAN: Using Reading Data to Improve Students' Performance in Higher-order Questioning*, Queensland Curriculum and Assessment Authority, South Brisbane.

Raney, K 1997, *Visual Literacy: Issues and Debates*, Middlesex University Press, London.

Raney, K 1998, 'A matter of survival: On being visually literate', *The English and Media Magazine*, vol. 39, pp. 37–42.

Raney, K 1999, 'Visual literacy and the art curriculum,' *Journal of Art and Education* vol. 18, no. 1, pp. 41–7.

Ruhemann, A & Tan, S 2010, *The Lost Thing* (DVD PAL), Madman Entertainment, Australia.

Smith, L 2010, *It's a Book*, Walker Books, Newtown.

Styles, M and Noble, K 2009, 'Thinking in action: Analysing children's multimodal responses to multimodal picturebooks', in J Evans (ed), *Talking Beyond the Page: Reading and Responding to Picturebooks*, Routledge, Abingdon, pp. 118–33.

Tan, S 2001, *The Red Tree*, Lothian, South Melbourne.

Tan, S 2002, *Picture Books. Who are they for?*, viewed 19 June 2017, http://www.shauntan.net/comments1.html.

Tan, S 2006, *The Arrival*, Lothian, Melbourne.

Watson, K 2004, 'The postmodern picture book in the secondary classroom', *English in Australia*, no. 140, pp. 55–7.

Williams, M 2007, *Archie's War*, Walker Books, London.

Young, E 2011, *The House that Baba Built: An Artist's Childhood in China*, Little Brown, New York

An initial bibliography of postmodern picture books (and other) picture books from the U.S., U.K. and Australia

Ahlberg, J & A 1986, *The Jolly Postman or Other People's Letters,* Heinemann, London.

Baillie, A & Harris W 1996, *DragonQuest*, Scholastic, Gosford.

Baillie, A & Tanner, J 1988, *Drac and the Gremlin*, Viking Kestrel, Melbourne.

Baker, J 2010, *Mirror*, Walker Books, London.

Base, G 1996, *The Discovery of Dragons*, Viking, Australia.

Briggs, R 1982, *When The Wind Blows*, Penguin, London.

Browne, A 1983, *Gorilla*, Walker Books, London.

Browne, A 1989, *The Tunnel*, Julia MacRae, London.

Browne, A 1990, *Changes*, Julia MacRae, London.

Browne, A 1991, *Willy's Pictures*, Candlewick, Cambridge, MA.

Browne, A 1992, *Zoo*, Random House, London.

Browne, A 1997, *Willy the Dreamer*, Walker Books, London.
Browne, A 1998, *Voices in the Park*, Picture Corgi Books, London.
Bunting, E & Diaz, D 1994, *Smoky Night*, Harcourt Brace Jovanovich, San Diego.
Burningham, J 1977, *Come Away from the Water, Shirley*, Jonathan Cape, London.
Burningham, J 1978, *Time to Get Out of the Bath, Shirley*, Jonathan Cape, London.
Burningham, J 1999 *Whadayamean*, Jonathan Cape, London.
Cali, D & Bloch, S 2007, *The Enemy*, Wilkins Farago, Albert Park.
Charters, J 1961, *The General*, Routledge and Kegan Paul, London.
Charters, J 2010, *The General*, Walker Books, London.
Child, L 2000, *Beware of the Storybook Wolves*, Scholastic, New York.
Child, L 2002, *Who's Afraid of the Big, Bad Book?* Hyperion, New York.
Crew, G 1994, *The Watertower*, Era, Melbourne.
Crew, G 1997, *The Viewer*, Lothian, Melbourne.
Crew, G 1999, *Memorial*, Lothian, Melbourne.
Crew, G 2004, *Beneath the Surface*, Hodder, Sydney.
Crew, G & Woolman, S 1997, *Tagged*, Era, Flinders Park.
Cresp, G 1999, *The Biography of Gilbert Alexander Pig*, Puffin Books, Ringwood.
Dr Seuss with Prelutsky, J & Smith, L 1998, *Hurray for Diffendoofer Day*, Alfred A Knopf, New York.
French, F 1986, *Snow White in New York*, Oxford University Press, Oxford.
Gleeson, L 2009, *Clancy and Milly and the Very Fine House*, Little Hare Books, Prahan, Victoria.
Gleeson, L & Blackwood, F 2011, *Look, A BOOK!*, Little Hare Books, Richmond.
Graham, B 2008, *How to Heal a Broken Wing*, Walker Books, London.
Graham, B 2006, *Wolves*, Simon and Schuster, New York.
Graham, B 2008 *Spells*, Macmillan, London.
Graham, B 2012, *Wolf Won't Bite*, MacMillan, London.
Gravett, E 2007, *Little Mouse's Big Book of Fears*, Macmillan, London.
Greeder, A 2007, *The Island*, Allen and Unwin, Crows Nest.
Hathorn, L 1994, *Way Home*, Random House, Sydney.
Heffernan, J & Sheehan, P 2005, *The Island*, Scholastic, Gosford.
Hest, A 1997, *When Jessie Came Across the Sea*, Walker Books, London.
Jeffers, O 2006, *The Incredible Book Eating Boy*, Philomel Books, New York.
Jennings, P 1990, *Grandad's Gifts*, Viking, Melbourne.
Kitamura, S 1987, *Lily Takes a Walk*, Happy Cat Books, Bradfield Essex.
Macaulay, D 1987, *Why the Chicken Crossed the Road*, Houghton Mifflin, Boston.
Macaulay, D 1990, *Black and White*, Houghton Mifflin, New York.
Macaulay, D 1995, *Shortcut*, Houghton Mifflin, Boston.
Marsden, J 1998, *The Rabbits*, Lothian, Melbourne.
Marsden, J & Ottley, M 2008, *Home and Away*, Lothian, Melbourne.
McGuire, R 1997, *What's Wrong with This Book?*, Viking, New York.
Millard, G 2009, *Isabella's Garden*, Walker Books, London.
Muntean, M 2006, *Do Not Open This Book!*, New York, Scholastic.
Norling, B 2002, *The Stone Baby*, Lothian, Melbourne.
Novak, BJ 2014, *The Book with No Pictures*, Penguin, New York.
Oliver, N 1999, *Sandswimmers*, Lothian, Melbourne.
Oliver, N 2006, *Home*, Omnibus Books, Malvern.

Ottley, M 2007, *Requiem for a Beast: A Work for Image, Word and Music*, Lothian, Sydney.
Parker, D & Ottley, M 2013, *Parachute*, Little Hare, Richmond.
Planet Dexter (eds) 1999, *This Book Really Sucks*, Penguin Putnam, New York.
Poulter, JR & Davis, S 2008, *Mending Lucille*, Lothian, Sydney.
Prap, L 2003, *Why?* Wilkins Farago, Elwood.
Riddle, T 2000, *The Singing Hat*, Penguin, Ringwood.
Riddle, T 2005, *Irving the Magician*, Viking, Melbourne.
Riddle, T 2008, *Nobody Owns the Moon*, Penguin, Melbourne.
Rogers, G 2009, *The Hero of Little Street*, Allen and Unwin, Crows Nest.
Scieszka, J & Johnson, S 1991, *The Frog Prince Continued*, Viking, London.
Scieszka, J & Smith, L 1989, *The True Story of the Three Little Pigs*, Puffin, Melbourne.
Scieszka, J & Smith, L 1992, *The Stinky Cheese Man and Other Fairly Stupid Tales*, Viking Penguin, Melbourne.
Scieszka, J & Smith, L 1995, *Maths Curse*, Viking Penguin, Melbourne.
Smith, L 2010, *It's a Book*, Walker Books, Newtown.
Silvey, C 2007, *The World According to Warren*, Fremantle Arts Centre Press, Fremantle.
Tan, S 2000, *The Lost Thing*, Lothian, Melbourne.
Tan, S 2001, *The Red Tree*, Lothian, Melbourne.
Tan, S 2006, *The Arrival*, Lothian, Melbourne.
Trivizas, E 1993, *The Three Little Wolves and the Big Bad Pig*, Heinemann, London.
Thompson, C 1993, *Looking for Atlantis*, Knopf, New York.
Thompson, C 2005, *The Short and Incredibly Happy Life of Riley*, Lothian, Melbourne.
Van Allsburg, C 1995, *Bad Day at Riverbend*, Houghton Mifflin, Boston.
Weisner, D 1991, *Tuesday*, Clarion, New York.
Weisner, D 2001, *The Three Pigs*, Houghton Mifflin, New York.
Wild, M 1989, *The Very Best of Friends*, Margaret Hamilton Books, Sydney.
Wild, M 1995, *Old Pig*, Allen and Unwin, St Leonards.
Wild, M 2000, *Fox*, Allen and Unwin, St Leonards.
Wild, M 2006, *Woolvs in the Sitee*, Penguin, Melbourne.
Wild, M 2009, *Harry and Hopper*, Omnibus/Scholastic, Gosford.
Williams, M 2007, *Archie's War*, Walker Books, London.
Young, E 2011, *The House that Baba Built: An Artist's Childhood in China*, Little Brown, New York.

6 Assessment and evaluation of pedagogy, practice and planning in the multiliterate and multimodal classroom

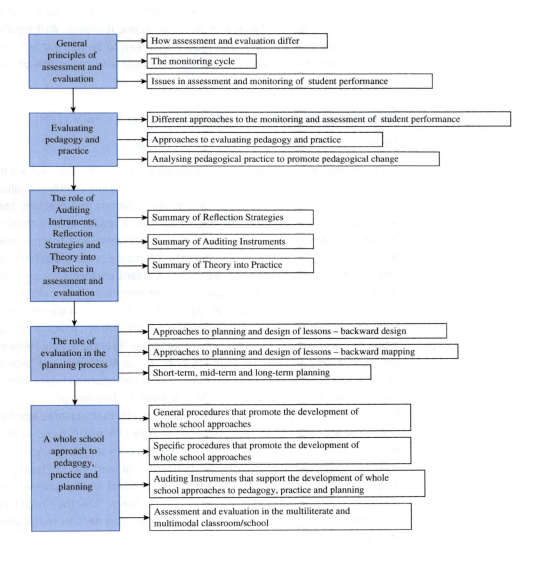

The focus of this chapter is the assessment and evaluation of literacy teaching and learning. The chapter will begin by defining assessment, evaluation and monitoring and will then examine the assessment of student performance and the evaluation of pedagogy, practice and planning. The Reflection Strategies, Auditing Instruments and Theory into Practice tasks that have been outlined throughout this book will be revisited to explore how these tasks relate to assessment and evaluation.

Note regarding Chapter Six: This chapter draws on the work of previous chapters in **Foundations of Multiliteracies: Reading, Writing and Talking in the 21st Century**. *The reader will need to be familiar with the other five chapters in order to fully understand and make use of this content.*

General principles of assessment and evaluation

How assessment and evaluation differ

For the purposes of discussion, in this chapter the term *assessment* will be employed when student performance is examined, while the term *evaluation* will refer to the investigation of teacher pedagogy and practice. This approach has been adopted initially to assist the reader of this chapter in differentiating between discussions about student and teacher performance. This distinction is also important because when assessment is addressed it is often limited to measuring student performance and limits or neglects, any discussion about teacher pedagogy. This omission is sometimes the result of a focus on standardised testing as a way of examining student performance and sometimes occurs through a lack of recognition of the importance of teacher evaluation. In a recent article Medwell (2012), in a very thorough discussion of both the Australian and English context, foregrounded student assessment and national and international standardised testing, but gave little attention to teacher performance. This is by no means an isolated example; research that explores teacher pedagogy and practice is far less common (see Edwards-Groves, Anstey and Bull, 2014). Understanding the relationship between assessment and evaluation can give direction to the teaching and learning of literacy to a teacher, or a school. Developing knowledge about what practices and pedagogies are being employed, when to use them, how they might be used and why they are important, can support teachers in monitoring their performance.

Pedagogy, practice and planning 199

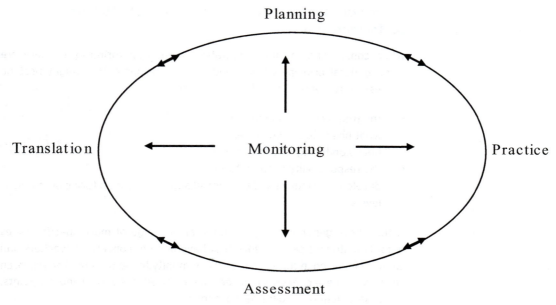

Figure 6.1 The monitoring cycle

The monitoring cycle

A monitoring cycle was suggested by Anstey and Bull (1989) and Anstey (1991) as a way of exploring the relationship between the learning and teaching of literacy. This relationship is represented in Figure 6.1.

As can be seen from Figure 6.1, monitoring is a constant process that is recursive in nature and involves accessing information from a number of sources. A range of assessment and evaluation practices provides information about student and teacher performance. The assessment practices provide the teacher with information about planning the teaching and learning that is to come. In this sense, it is future oriented. These assessment practices also give the teacher direction about which literacy practices to employ. Constant monitoring of evaluation provides information about which pedagogies to enact and translation enables the teacher to measure the success (or otherwise) of particular pedagogies. This process of translation in turn informs the teacher about what practices are appropriate and what types of planning are needed to allow these practices to develop. This constant monitoring and review ensures that the teacher is continually thinking about the appropriateness of literacy learning and teaching – what is being done and why.

Issues in assessment and monitoring of student performance

When considering the implementation of the monitoring cycle there are some general principles that need to be considered that might best be addressed from a school-wide perspective:

- the frequency of monitoring
- what needs to be monitored
- how monitoring is to take place
- the responsibility for monitoring
- developing a logical and sequenced approach to monitoring across year levels

Within these general principles, there are a range of more specific issues regarding student performance that have been of concern to teachers and all those involved in the educational community for some time. The research addressing these concerns has been summarised in the following dot points. The assessment of student performance:

- has traditionally focussed on the measurement of student knowledge and skills but has not been concerned with students' use of strategies or processes. Such assessment needs to incorporate texts that are conveyed by digital technologies and not be confined to those texts conveyed by paper technologies (Hartman, Morsink and Zheng 2010)
- must be concerned not only with the final product of learning but also with the process of how that learning takes place (Wiggins and McTighe 2005)
- should not rely only on standardised testing at the national level (such as NAPLAN, National Assessment Program for Literacy and Numeracy, in Australia) or at the international level (such as PIRLS, Progress in International Reading Literacy Study, or PISA, Programme for International Students Assessment) but also draw on teacher assessment (Medwell 2012)
- does not always address the more complex skills and processes associated with multimodal texts (Kress 2010; Hartman, Morsink and Zheng, 2010; Kalantzis et al. 2016)
- should have a balance among diagnostic, formative and summative assessment that are typically carried out before, during and after learning (Kalantzis et al. 2016)
- as measured using diagnostic assessment, is often determined by standardised tests that compare students with other students rather than finding out what students already know and what they need to learn in the future (van Kraayenoord 2003)
- is sometimes assessed using multiple choice items where a particular answer is required that does not allow for different interpretations of a text (Wagner 2008)

- sometimes results in a mismatch between standardised testing assessment and teacher assessment (Nicholas 2015; Kemmis 2005)
- when it focusses on standardised testing, can lead to teachers spending more time on teaching to the test rather than being concerned with student learning, leading to less attention being given to pedagogy and practice (Au 2009; van Kraayenoord 2003)
- is increasingly generating assessment data gathered by the use of standardised tests to address the issue of accountability, whereas once teachers were more concerned with collecting a broad range of data about students' strengths and weaknesses (van Kraayenoord 2003)
- can lead to a focus on summative assessment to the neglect of diagnostic, and particularly formative, assessment (Harlen 2005; Kalantzis et al. 2016). The development of computer-adaptive assessment, at this point, seems to be following in the same direction, as Kalantzis et al. (2016, p. 516) report that these types of tests '... remain primarily retrospective and judgemental'
- needs to incorporate data collected through student self-assessment as well as teacher judgement (Anstey 1991; Dargusch 2014)
- should encompass both static and dynamic types of assessment, particularly when the teachers' approach to teaching and learning is dynamic (Hartman, Morsink and Zheng 2010; Kress 2010)
- is not necessarily accurately measured by high-stakes standardised testing at the state or national level. Medwell (2012) referenced the ACARA report on the NAPLAN testing for 2011, which stated that the average scales scores achieved by Year 5 students across all domains measured varied significantly and consistently depending on where the students lived. There was a difference of 146 in the scores, dependent on whether the students lived in metropolitan, provincial, remote or very remote areas
- should aim to monitor and assess students' capabilities before, during and after their engagement in the learning process so that the students can transfer their learning to new settings (Bates 2014; Kalantzis et al. 2016)
- should include students' self-assessment (Anstey 1991; Carr 2005; Biesta 2013)

While the preceding issues about assessing and monitoring student performance are not meant to be definitive, they nevertheless provide some information about the complexity of the process. Teachers are becoming increasingly aware of these issues as they become more concerned about the balance between assessment and teaching and increasingly concerned about the possibility of assessment driving teaching and learning. When state-wide and national testing are perceived as high-stakes testing, it is more likely that teachers' practice will be affected. As van Kraayenoord (2003) and Kalantzis et al. (2016) suggest, increasing attention to test scores by parents, administrators, politicians and the media has caused added stress to teachers and reinforced the likelihood that teachers' practices will change. The purposes of classroom literacy assessment and monitoring in addressing improved literacy teaching and learning may be incompatible with these various calls for accountability. This tension produced by mounting calls for accountability has been reinforced by the increasing amount of time students spend undergoing testing and the increasing time spent by teachers preparing students for test taking (van Kraayenoord 2003).

Different approaches to the monitoring and assessment of student performance

Many of the issues surrounding the assessment of student performance can be ameliorated, at least in part, by the instigation of particular approaches to assessment. Masters (2014, p. 4) described three general approaches to assessment which could '… provide powerful messages to students not only about their own learning, but also about the nature of learning itself' and have the potential to 'shape student, parent and community beliefs about learning'. The first approach, which Masters described as 'providing success', involved students in assessment tasks that were aligned to students' capabilities and were therefore likely to be completed successfully. The underlying theory behind this approach was that, by achieving success, students would increase their engagement and confidence and so find learning more pleasurable. Masters (2014, p. 4) identified a number of problems with this approach, including (a) a lack of challenge, (b) minimising learning in order to keep students comfortable, (c) sending a message that successful learning can be achieved by minimal effort and (d) encouraging students to believe that they are entitled to easy work and praise.

The second approach Masters identified was judging performance against standards based on the belief that by reporting performance against standards, achievement levels would somehow be raised. As Masters (2014, p. 5) stated, the attraction of this approach was that it provided explicit statements about student performance that were in line with what the general community, and politicians in particular, thought the characteristics of learning should be and what schools should be aiming for in students' competencies. As Masters suggested, this approach was no better at assisting students to understand the link between effort and success than the first approach, nor did it provide challenge in the assessment tasks. Masters quoted the research by Wiliam (2007) and others that identified the differences in attainment by advanced students and less advanced students, which persisted throughout the years of school. While both groups of students may be making progress from year to year, the difference gap of between five and six years between the groups is maintained from one year to the next. No amount of standardised testing changes it. It is a case of the rich get richer and the poor get poorer. Masters quoted Grenny et al. (2013), who suggested that the only sane response of students to repeated reminders that they are performing below average, is to drop out of school. At the same time, advanced students are achieving higher grades with limited effort and can develop a belief that they are smart. This second approach was intended to raise achievement levels but, in practice, it often has the opposite effect for both advanced and less advanced students.

The third approach to assessment outlined by Masters was termed *growth over time*, where students' learning was assessed and then challenging targets were set for further learning. The underlying belief in this approach is that all students can make progress over time if they are sufficiently motivated with authentic learning experiences and high expectations. Each student is set a realistic learning goal at the time of assessment. Once this goal has been achieved, then further assessment determines a future learning task. This type of assessment provides learning goals for students and teaching goals for teachers and is what Masters called a 'growth mindset'. Assessment directed towards a growth mindset gathers information to inform individual learning targets rather than standardised year-level expectations and allows teachers to monitor progress over time. All students are challenged to improve performance because there is a more explicit relationship between effort and success based on the quality of the learning they have achieved.

The first and second approaches to assessment as outlined by Masters are more closely aligned to **diagnostic** and **summative assessment**, or *before and after assessment*, as suggested by Kalantzis et al. (2016). The third approach, or *growth mindset*, is more closely related to **formative assessment**, or *during assessment* as Kalantzis et al. (2016) suggested, and has far more potential to adequately address the issues related to measuring student performance. Because formative assessment takes place during learning, it is undertaken at the point of learning and is therefore much more likely to occur in a growth mindset approach to assessment. Any programme or framework for assessment needs to give careful consideration to both the types of assessment employed and the approach to assessment that is undertaken.

Evaluating pedagogy and practice

Over the years, much has been written about the assessment of student performance. However, little has been written about the evaluation of teacher pedagogy and practice in literacy. There is a significant amount of research that addresses the effectiveness of teacher pedagogy in relation to student performance and has been reported in a synthesis of research by Goe (2007), Goe, Bell and Little (2008), Goe and Stickler (2008) and in an extensive review of U.S., U.K. and Australian work in the area by Little, Goe and Bell (2009). Much of this reported research has been concerned with measuring the success of teacher effectiveness by quantifying change in student achievement. It is important that teachers understand this relationship between teacher effectiveness and

Diagnostic assessment
Assessment, often based on the use of standardised tests, that is designed to find out what students know so that the appropriate skills, strategies and processes can be taught. It is conducted before learning takes place and can provide information to both teachers and students.

Formative assessment
Assessment, usually based on teacher judgement or teacher-designed tests, that takes place while students are engaged in learning. Because it takes place during learning, it provides feedback to students and also assists in the development of future learning for both students and teachers.

Summative assessment
Assessment that provides information to students, teachers, parents and the general community after the learning has taken place. It is backward looking because it is designed to measure what students have learned. Various programs of state and national testing are also summative where the focus is sometimes on comparing student with student, school with school or state with state rather than on measuring what learning has taken place.

student achievement, but this knowledge does not assist teachers in analysing the nature of their pedagogy or why they do what they do. Other research in the area looks at the effectiveness of pedagogy in higher education (Moon 2014) or in other discipline areas (Quellmalz and Haertel 2008). There have also been attempts to link the literacy levels of preservice teachers (Moon 2014) and recent graduates (Exley et al. 2016) with a degree of pedagogical knowledge.

A recent review of attempts to correlate teacher levels of literacy with teacher effectiveness investigated a number of tests, including the Literacy and Numeracy Test for Initial Teacher Education Students (LANTITE) in Australia, the Program for International Student Assessment (PISA) and the Programme for the International Assessment of Adult Competencies (PIAAC) (Freebody and Freebody 2017). The data from these tests indicated that Australia out-performed all other countries except Japan in proficiency on literacy tests. This is an interesting result because Australian students have been consistently out-performed by other countries, notably Scandinavian, in OECD tests. This led Freebody and Freebody (2017, p. 6) to conclude that these high-performing students '... were taught by a teaching force that was, on average, reliably less proficient on literacy tests'. The theory that links teacher effectiveness with student performance would seem, if not entirely unproven, tenuous at best and is at odds with other reviews of effective literacy teaching (Pressley and Allington 2015).

Approaches to evaluating pedagogy and practice

The seminal paper written by the New London Group (1996) and subsequently taken up in Australia by Cope and Kalantzis (2000) focussed attention on what pedagogy might look like, particularly if it was to cater for active and informed citizens in the 21st century. The term *multiliteracies* was suggested as a way of formulating a new pedagogical approach that complemented, but also augmented, existing traditional approaches to pedagogy. This new concept of literacy, in part, grew out of a consideration of 'new literacies' first proposed by Buckingham (1993) and later taken up by many others, including Coiro et al. (2008) in the U.S. and Newfield et al. (2003) in South Africa. It was based on a recognition of the impact on literacy of the plethora new technologies, together with the social and cultural diversity that was a feature of the late 20th century and 21st century, in the developed countries. Both the New London Group (1996) and Cope and Kalantzis (2000, 2015) took these developments into consideration by proposing a much broader definition of literacy that went beyond language alone to incorporate visual, audio, spatial and gestural meaning making systems or, as they termed them, modes. Anstey and Bull (2006), Bull and Anstey (2010a) and Edwards-Groves, Anstey and Bull (2014) referred to these meaning making systems as semiotic systems (see Chapters Three and Four) and discussed in detail how they required new pedagogical approaches.

Concurrent with the development of these new approaches to pedagogy, Freebody and Luke (1990, 2003) and Luke and Freebody (1999a, 1999b) developed earlier concepts of the 'four roles of the reader' that they later referred to as the Four Resources Model. Initially, these roles were said to describe, as the model suggested, four roles that the reader could engage with to make meaning. Later, as the model focussed on the resources that the reader could draw on, it became the foundation of the Literate Futures project in Queensland, Australia (Anstey 2002). In this context, it came to be seen as a set of four pedagogical resources that teachers could implement in their teaching about the new literacies and multiliteracies and it was applied by teachers in the field to listening, speaking and writing as well as reading. This focus on pedagogy was also adopted in Queensland by two other projects, the Productive Pedagogies Project (Lingard et al. 2001; Lingard, Hayes and Mills 2003) and the New Basics Project (Luke et al. 2000) both of which grew out of the Queensland School Reform Longitudinal Study. The Productive Pedagogies project was predicated on a knowledge of students learning styles and teachers' repertoires of practice to support engagement with 20 pedagogies such as higher-order thinking, substantive conversations, metalanguage and the problem-based curriculum. The New Basics Project was based on an integrated framework of pedagogy, assessment and curriculum and was centred around intellectually engaging and real-world 'rich tasks'. For all this attention on pedagogy, there are still some issues surrounding the relationship of pedagogy, assessment and practice. A number of researchers in the area, including Coiro et al. (2008) and Brown, Lockyer and Caputi (2010), report that teachers have difficulties with adjusting their assessment and practice when implementing a multiliterate pedagogy.

Analysing pedagogical practice to promote pedagogical change

Early in 2002 Anstey and Bull developed a professional learning and development program that addressed the relationship of multiliterate pedagogy, assessment and practice, which was designed to promote pedagogical change (Bull and Anstey 2004, 2005). This was entitled The Multiliteracies Professional Development Program, and involved classroom teachers in long-term, individually tailored professional learning, development and dialogue (PD). The teachers in the programmes, which ran for one, two or three years as determined by the teachers, were drawn from state, Catholic or independent school systems. In some forms of the programme teachers were drawn from a cluster of schools and at other times a whole school staff, including the principal, was involved. Anstey and Bull developed a 26-item reflection tool, the Multiliteracies Matrix, which was designed to define the concept of multiliteracies and to support participants to deliberate on their multiliterate pedagogy. Participants were then required to develop their own action plan, designed to change their pedagogy, based on a number of items they had chosen from the Multiliteracies Matrix (see Bull and Anstey [2010b]) and the complementary volume, *Elaborating Multiliteracies through Multimodal Texts: Changing Classroom Practices and Developing Teacher Pedagogies*, for details about the Multiliteracies Professional Development Program). The programme provided five days of

PD about pedagogical approaches and change in pedagogy spread over the life of the programme. At the conclusion of the programme each participant was required to give a presentation detailing the changes in their knowledge and practice about pedagogy based on evidence they had collected. The programme was judged by participants to be relevant, successful and enjoyable (see Bull and Anstey 2010b) and resulted in significant increases in teachers' knowledge about pedagogy. What is interesting to note is that the participants needed to be continually reminded that their individual projects were designed to evaluate change in pedagogical approach rather than the assessment of student performance. Throughout all of the programmes conducted, it became clear that teachers were very familiar with student assessment but had limited knowledge about the nature of pedagogy or of how to go about changing, assessing or monitoring their pedagogical approach. This outcome was in line with the findings of Coiro et al. (2008) and Brown, Lockyer and Caputi (2010) about the difficulties that teachers have with understanding the relationships among pedagogy, assessment and curriculum.

The role of Auditing Instruments, Reflection Strategies and Theory into Practice in assessment and evaluation

Chapter Six has explored the different types of assessment and evaluation and the issues that affect both the assessment of student performance and the evaluation of teacher pedagogy. It is useful now to revisit the approach taken to assessment and evaluation that has been undertaken throughout the previous five chapters as a process of review.

SUMMARY OF REFLECTION STRATEGIES

- Those strategies that were directed towards assessment of student performance were 1.6 and 2.7.
    o As an example, Reflection Strategy 1.6 stated: 'The purpose of this Reflection Strategy is to consider how well you know your students in terms of their use of, and access to, technology.'
- Those strategies that were directed towards evaluation of pedagogical approach were:

    1.1, 1.2, 1.3, 1.5, 1.8
    2.1, 2.3, 2.4, 2.5, 2.6
    3.1, 3.2, 3.3
    4.1, 4.2, 4.3, 4.4, 4.5

    o As an example, Reflection Strategy 4.2 stated: 'The purpose of this Reflection Strategy is to make judgements about the quality of your approach to pedagogy.'
- There were six Reflection Strategies that did not address either assessment or evaluation.

SUMMARY OF AUDITING INSTRUMENTS

- The instrument that was directed towards assessment of student performance was 3.2.
  - As an example, Auditing Instrument 3.2 stated: 'The purpose of this Auditing Instrument is to gauge your students' current metacognitive awareness. You can use this information together with the information you gathered about your own metacognitive awareness in Reflection Strategy 3.2 to inform your planning and practice.'
- Those Auditing Instruments that were directed towards evaluation of pedagogical approach were:

    2.1
    3.1
    4.1, 4.2, 4.3, 4.4, 4.5, 4.6, 4.7, 4.8, 4.9, 4.10, 4.11, 4.12

- There were two Auditing Instruments that did not address either assessment or evaluation.

SUMMARY OF THEORY INTO PRACTICE

- The Theory into Practice strategies that were directed towards assessment of student performance were:

    1.1, 1.2
    2.1, 2.3, 2.4, 2.5, 2.6, 2.7
    3.1, 3.3, 3.4, 3.5, 3.6, 3.7
    5.1, 5.2

  - As an example, Theory into Practice 1.1 stated: 'The purpose of this Theory into Practice strategy is to explore the social and literate practices of your students through discussion. In this way, you will get to know more about your students' literacies and it may also help the students to broaden their understanding of literacy and literate practice.'
- Those Theory Into Practice strategies that were directed towards evaluation of pedagogical approach were:

    1.3, 1.4
    2.1, 2.2, 2.3, 2.4, 2.5, 2.6, 2.7
    3.1, 3.2

  - As an example, Theory into Practice 1.3 stated: 'The purpose of this Theory into Practice task is to consider the implications of the concept of literacies, literate practice and literacy as social practice for your teaching practices.'
- 2.1, 2.2, 2.3, 2.4, 2.5, 2.6, 2.7 Theory into Practice strategies address both assessment of student performance and evaluation of pedagogical approach.

A summary of Reflection Strategies, Auditing Instruments and Theory into Practice strategies indicates that far more strategies are directed towards the evaluation of pedagogical approaches than towards the assessment of student performance. This has been an intentional choice since this book addresses the notions of multiliteracies and multimodal pedagogies together with the fact that teachers have more difficulty examining their pedagogy than assessing student performance. This choice was not intended to undervalue assessment of student performance but rather to indicate the interconnectedness of assessment to the evaluation of pedagogical approaches.

The role of evaluation in the planning process

When considering how to go about the planning process it is important to realise that planning, practice and pedagogy are closely related to one another. Any adjustment in pedagogical approach will result in changes to teacher practices that will, in turn, demand a change to planning. Similarly, if a teacher changes the way they plan, then this will necessitate the employment of different practices and a modification of pedagogical approach. As soon as one changes, then the other two must change, irrespective of whether assessment or evaluation is being targeted. As well as this relationship, there are a number of other considerations.

Approaches to planning and design of lessons – backward design

There are two general approaches to planning that were proposed by Wiggins and McTighe (2005) in their discussions of understanding by design and what they termed *backward design*. These two approaches are represented in Figure 6.2 and have been derived from the definition of backward design suggested by Wiggins and McTighe (2005, p. 338). They suggested that many teachers started their lesson planning, or design, process with the 'means', such as textbooks, prescribed curriculum or favourite approaches, rather than with 'the desired results', or what the students need to learn. For the purposes of this book, the former (which Wiggins and McTighe call 'backward design') has been termed *content-driven* and the latter, *student-driven*.

In the content-driven approach to planning, the design process begins with reference to the prescribed curriculum, which may be derived from local, state or national documents. Content and resources are then selected in order to plan a lesson that will address the curriculum statements and finally a check is made to determine whether the desired learning outcomes for the students have been achieved. In this approach to lesson planning, the essential question that drives the design process revolves around what content needs to be covered. In the student-driven approach, the essential

Pedagogy, practice and planning 209

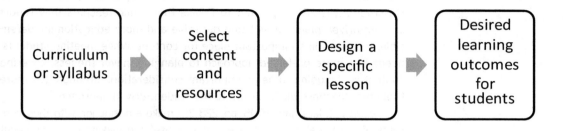

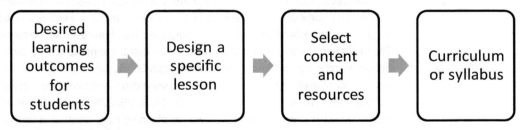

Figure 6.2 Understanding by design and backward design

question that instigates the design process is based on the question of what it is that students need to learn and be able to do. A specific lesson is then planned and content and resources are selected to support the lesson design and finally the curriculum is consulted to determine which prescribed content has been covered.

While there are many different ways in which teachers may plan their lessons, the content and student-driven approaches have been reported by

Wiggins and McTighe (2005) and by Bull and Anstey (2004, 2005, 2010a) as being the most common designs found in teacher planning. Interestingly, in the long-term, action learning projects incorporating multimodality, pedagogy and talk reported by Bull and Anstey (2010b), the majority of teachers indicated a clear preference for student-driven planning. However, this preference was not always followed up in the day-to-day practice in the classroom. It is also important to realise that, while teachers may report *student-driven* planning as being desirable and more educationally defensible, there is still an important place for content. While meeting students' needs is a more preferred approach to planning, never-the-less, covering content is still going to be an important consideration, although it is more likely that teachers will be drawn to the student-driven approach.

Wiggins and McTighe (2005, pp. 228–35) make a distinction with their concepts of 'coverage' and 'uncoverage' that is useful in making decisions about which approach is more suitable for a particular learning context. Essentially, the difference between designing lessons to cover or uncover is the difference between surface and deep understanding. As Wiggins and McTighe suggest, coverage implies that teachers design lessons to cover content with little regard to student understanding or engagement. They further suggest that these lessons are taught because teachers feel under pressure to address the content that is mandated by the curriculum or syllabus and are often accompanied by comments from teachers such as, 'I know I taught it but I'm not sure that they learnt it' or, 'I think I was the only one who covered the content'. Conversely, uncoverage implies the pursuit of deep learning and understanding where lessons are deliberately designed to focus on explicit teaching from an inquiry perspective. In this approach students still learn core content by exploring possibilities and alternatives and purposeful involvement in higher order thinking skills rather than engaging in rote learning that serves no purpose other than covering the content. The important question to resolve might not be that there needs to be a balance between content-driven and student-driven approaches, but rather how the covering of content might be achieved. Teachers involved in long-term action research, such as that detailed by Bull and Anstey (2004, 2005, 2010b), have consistently reported that student-driven approaches to planning have resulted in increased learning at deeper levels of understanding, accompanied by a greater degree of engagement and enjoyment by the students. The teachers also reported higher levels of success and satisfaction with pedagogical approaches that are based on student-driven approaches to planning. While backward design, as it has been presented here, is primarily designed to evaluate the pedagogical approach used by the teacher, it also addresses the assessment of student performance. In both the content-driven and student-driven approaches illustrated in Figure 6.2, there is a place for designing specific lessons where student assessment will necessarily be included. This will provide further information about the success, or otherwise, of either approach by allowing comparison of the level of student performance and how it relates to the two different pedagogical approaches.

Approaches to planning and design of lessons – backward mapping

Backward mapping is another technique that can aid in the design of lessons. It is not another term for backward design, but rather a more fine-grained approach to the design of day-to-day lesson planning. It is based on the premise that teachers are experts in the tasks that they devise for students to engage in. Because teachers are experts in these tasks and have engaged in them over the longer term, they can successfully complete the tasks automatically, with little conscious thought about the necessary processes involved. On the other hand, students can be regarded as novices who require explicit modelling of the processes. Backward mapping requires the teacher to take a step back (hence the term) and complete the task themselves while consciously recording each step in the process. The teacher works backward from the known answer and completes the task. This is a metacognitive activity, sometimes referred to as a 'think aloud', where the teacher has to consciously think about their thinking as they complete the task. While this is a deceptively simple task where the teacher completes the task before asking the students to engage in it, it does prove difficult for some teachers who have been 'automatically' engaging in the task over a considerable period of time. However, in order to design a lesson that will support students to successfully complete the task, the teacher will have to engage in explicit modelling of the task. In order to construct an explicit model using backward design it can be useful to ask yourself a number of questions (a) *before* you begin the task (involving predicting how you might go about the task), (b) *during* engagement with the task (synthesising the different processes you are engaging in), and (c) *after* you have completed the task (reflecting about the processes you used). The following questions, which are by no means intended to be definitive, might be useful in engaging in the 'before, during and after' exercise:

- What did you do?
- Where did you start?
- Why did you start there?
- Did you back track, and if so, why?
- What did you think about?
- What decisions did you make?
- What knowledge did you need to draw upon?
- Why did you do these things?

Some of the reasons why such questions might be asked include a selection, or all, of the following:

- There is a need to identify the knowledge, skills and processes necessary to complete the task.

- There is a need to focus on making the thinking processes transparent to teachers and students through developing the metacognitive skills of both students and teachers.
- Explicit teacher modelling of tasks is essential.
- There needs to be a clearly identified purpose for engaging in the task.
- Ideally the task to be completed should be drawn from the real world of the students.
- Appropriate metalanguage should be identified to use when modelling tasks for students.
- Students should be encouraged to use the appropriate metalanguage when engaging in tasks.
- The lesson design should be based on teaching strategies that the students are familiar with.

Backward mapping assists in the planning of individual lessons whereas backward design is more concerned with the pedagogical approach that the teacher is implementing. In this way, backward mapping provides more fine-grained detail to support teachers in designing particular lessons while backward design assists teachers in developing appropriate pedagogy. Therefore, backward mapping is more suitable for short-term planning while backward design is more appropriate for mid-term or long-term planning.

Short-term, mid-term and long-term planning

Whether to use backward design or backward mapping depends on the type of planning that the teacher is engaged in. Short-term planning, or planning at the lesson or short sequence of lessons level, usually involves backward mapping or a similar technique. This technique is more appropriate in this situation because the teacher is more likely to be focusing instruction on a particular activity or strategy that will support student learning. With mid-term planning over a period of several weeks, or long-term planning over a unit, term or semester period, teachers are often more concerned with the balance of pedagogical approaches. This is not to say that the use of particular planning techniques is purely governed by the length of time in the planning period because teachers will undoubtedly be introducing certain activities or strategies during mid and long-term planning. What is being suggested here is that teachers carefully consider which type of technique is more suitable for which type of planning, considering the focus of student learning. It is also important to keep in mind the balance between student learning and the covering of content and how this impacts on lesson design.

A whole school approach to pedagogy, practice and planning

Consideration of pedagogy, practice and planning during short, mid and long-term planning should not be seen as only the province of an individual teacher in a particular classroom. As students progress through their school career they move from class to class, from teacher to teacher and across a range of subjects or disciplines. There is potential for students to encounter a range of different approaches during any, or all, of these changes. This can be beneficial for certain students because a particular approach to pedagogy, practice or planning implemented by a teacher might be especially appropriate. What works for one student does not necessarily work for all, so some diversity of approaches can be seen as educationally sound. However, there is also the potential for confusion if there is little, or no, continuity across the school. Sometimes a teacher becomes known for the use of a particular strategy that requires students not only to learn a new strategy but also to unlearn a previous one from a different class or teacher. Finding a balance between diversity and individual preference is more likely to be achieved if a school-wide programme or school strategy is adopted.

General procedures that promote the development of whole school approaches

Which particular approach to planning is taken at the whole school level is not as important as constructing a concisely thought out, comprehensive and logical framework. There are four general considerations that can assist in the design and development of a framework for a multiliterate and multimodal strategy that is more likely to be successful.

1. Developing a community of learners. The development of a community of learners within a school has received growing attention from researchers such as Bull and Anstey (1994, 2000) Comber and Kamler (2005), Stoll et al. (2006) and Gordon (2008). The formation of a community of learners within the school requires that all teachers are involved in discussions about what form the school strategy and policies might take. The role of the community of learners is to devise an agreed upon framework that is formed through a consensus of opinions from the whole staff about what is desirable. It is important to realise that consensus does not mean a unanimous decision where everyone agrees. Some differences and disagreements will occur and will need to be carefully dealt with over time. This type of collegial activity is the direct opposite of what is sometimes referred to as the 'silo' approach, where each teacher acts autonomously and makes their own decisions without reference to what instruction has come before and what will follow, about their class. This silo approach often tends to create divisiveness among staff and confusion for the students. Some schools find it easier to develop a community of learners because the majority of staff are collegial. However, it is not a straightforward process and takes time, requires insightful leadership and an understanding of the change

process as suggested by such researchers as Calabrese (2002) and Fullan (1993, 1999, 2001, 2007).

2. Cooperative planning. One of the ways of promoting a community of learners is to encourage cooperative planning, as reported by Gillies and Boyle (2010). In its simplest form, cooperative planning involves two or more teachers who are teaching classes at the same year level engaging in various types of lesson design as a group process. This process is firstly directed towards eliminating the presence of silos and secondly to demonstrate to teachers that more can be achieved by the group than by the sum of individual efforts. It parallels the advantages gained by placing students in group work, as highlighted by Littleton and Mercer (2013). Once the grade groups have been operating successfully, teachers can be encouraged to extend cooperative planning by forming networks across year levels. This process has the advantage, not only of eliminating the silo effect, but also making teachers aware of the sequence of learning from one year level to another. This then demonstrates the value of a whole school approach.

3. Collaborative learning and negotiated learning. Cooperative planning can lead to collaborative learning, where various planning techniques can be shared among the groups or networks of teachers. This allows for tasks to be divided around the groups and for individual teachers to take responsibility, or leadership, for particular subject areas. Developing teacher expertise in discipline areas and in leadership provides important support for developing whole school frameworks and strategies. Apart from developing teacher expertise, this leads to benefits such as improved student learning because of the development of deeper teacher understanding. Collaborative learning can also involve students learning in the same types of contexts as teachers and is more likely to be successful when negotiated learning has occurred. Negotiated learning results from students being given a role in the planning of lessons and making some decisions about what is to be learned and how it is to be learned. In this situation, the teacher will retain overall control of the planning process, as there will always be some non-negotiables. Commitment to, and involvement in, the process of shared lesson design from both teachers and students can provide important stimulus for the development of whole school approaches to pedagogy and practice.

4. Parents and the wider community. As has been previously discussed in Chapter Two, drawing on the school-based world and lifeworld resources of students can have a positive effect on learning. Analogous to this process, when teachers engage in short, mid or long-term planning they can draw on the resources available from parents and the wider community, as suggested in the research of Bull and Anstey (1994) and Fuller and Hood (2005). This process can then not only inform the development of whole school approaches, but also provide authentic educational experiences for students, drawn from their day-to-day life.

Specific procedures that promote the development of whole school approaches

There are some specific considerations that a school can implement that will support the four general procedures mentioned above. Some schools begin the process of developing a whole school approach by addressing the general procedures first, as reported by Bull and Anstey (2007), while others begin the process by establishing the specific procedures first.

- People in the school, may it be the principal or a group of key teachers, give priority to the establishment of a whole school approach. Sometimes the priority is driven by the principal (a top-down approach); at other times the priority is addressed by a group of teachers (a bottom-up approach) and at other times again by a combination of all stakeholders, as reported by Anstey and Bull (2005). The latter two approaches have, in practice, been more successful in producing change, while the top-down approach can frequently lead to teacher resistance.
- Commitment by the school to joint ownership in the designing of a whole school approach will produce greater change in practice because the teachers will more likely be committed to the process if they feel they have some influence over it.
- During the design of the whole school approach, the school can commit to addressing the issue of school renewal, where a focus on the challenge of dealing with change is often necessary.
- Creation of leadership positions within the school, to be responsible for promoting the whole school approach. This might take the form of a literacy coordinator to promote a school-wide literacy strategy or a key teacher to manage pedagogical change.
- Establishment of a group of teachers, led by a curriculum coordinator, to devise a developmental sequence of literacy skills and strategies throughout the school.
- Formation of a committee to oversee a uniform approach to student assessment throughout the school.
- Structuring of a monitoring program that oversees the regular evaluation of teacher pedagogy.
- Reaching out to other schools, networks or clusters to investigate what other whole school approaches have been designed.
- Developing a shared vision for literacy across the school that is based on a well-thought-out theoretical stance rather than a smorgasbord of different approaches to the teaching and learning of literacy.
- Formulation of a community profile so that the school has well-defined knowledge of the clients that it serves.
- The school provides leadership and support for professional learning and development.

It is not expected that every school would attempt to implement all of the specific procedures that have been identified above. Nor is it advisable to introduce a number of the suggestions concurrently, but rather select one or two procedures to promote gradually over time. However, the four general procedures mentioned earlier do lend themselves to being implemented together in a shorter timeframe. It is up to the individual school to decide which approaches and procedures are relevant to their particular context and which attract the required support from the teaching and administrative staff.

Auditing Instruments that support the development of whole school approaches to pedagogy, practice and planning

In the case of pedagogy, once a common approach has been decided to be implemented throughout the whole school, then it is advisable to devise an auditing instrument that can be applied reasonably simply while still providing enough information to the individual teacher to encourage a degree of uniformity throughout the school. The following example, based on the Four Resource Model, provides a number of questions that can be asked when teachers are selecting and using texts and other resources, ensuring a uniformity of pedagogical approach. The questions would need to be adjusted to suit the age of the students in each particular year level. Not all four of the resources would be dealt with at once and not all questions would be asked of each text. However, as the students (and the teachers) become more familiar with the Four Resource Model, then more questions would be dealt with concurrently. As students progress to the upper primary/elementary year levels, then they would increasingly be expected to address all four resources when consuming text.

AUDITING INSTRUMENT 6.1

Code breaker – How do I crack this code?

- How do I crack this text?
- How does it work?
- Is there more than one semiotic system operating here? If so, how do they relate?
- What are the codes and conventions used?
- How do the parts relate singly and in combination?

Meaning maker – What does this mean to me?

- How are the ideas in this text sequenced – do they connect to one another?
- Is the text linear or nonlinear, interactive or noninteractive?

- How does this affect the way I make meaning?
- How will my purpose for reading/viewing and the context in which I am reading/viewing influence my meaning making?
- Are there other possible meanings and readings/viewings of this text?

Text user – What do I do with this text?

- What is the purpose of this text, and what is my purpose in using it?
- How have the uses of this text shaped its composition?
- What should I do with this text in this context?
- What will others do with this text?
- What are my options or alternatives after reading/viewing?

Text analyst – What does this text try to do to me?

- What kind of person, with what interests and values, produced this text?
- What are its origins?
- What is the author/producer of this text trying to make me believe or do?
- What beliefs and positions are dominant or silenced in the text?
- What do I think about the way this text presents these ideas and what alternatives are there?
- Having critically examined this text, what action am I going to take?
- The 'so what?' factor.

Considering teacher practice, a number of simple auditing instruments can be employed to assist teachers in achieving a sequential approach to content, skills and strategies across the school.

In the case of reviewing assessment procedures, a simple instrument can be used. This instrument can identify whether an individual teacher is using a variety of assessment techniques and can also determine if there is a common approach throughout the school. There needs to be a position taken by the school on which of the following techniques are suitable, or whether

AUDITING INSTRUMENT 6.2

What is the balance that you have achieved with technologies?

- Print technologies (e.g. newspaper, novel, magazine)
- Live technologies (e.g. person-to-person, play, concert)
- Digital (e.g. mobile phone, computer, iPad)

AUDITING INSTRUMENT 6.3

What is the balance that you have achieved with the semiotic systems?

- Linguistic (e.g. grammar, vocabulary, sentence structure)
- Visual (e.g. colour, vector, viewpoint)
- Audio (e.g. volume, pitch, tone)
- Gestural (e.g. facial expression, proximity, gaze)
- Spatial (e.g. position, distance, framing)

other assessments are required because of social or cultural factors within the school community or because there are significant numbers of 'at risk' students or students with behavioural problems.

AUDITING INSTRUMENT 6.4

What is the balance that you have achieved with assessment techniques?

- Standardised tests
- Teacher designed tests
- Student self-assessment
- Assessment of skills, processes, knowledge, attitudes
- Student profiles that include work samples, conference records, anecdotal notes from a variety of language modes (reading, writing, listening, speaking)
- Assessment of students' engagement with semiotic systems and technologies

There are other issues that are possibly best addressed in the context of the various teacher groups, such as year level groups, teacher networks based on common interests or a community of learners that have been established in the school. One such issue revolves around the types of planning that the school has decided are appropriate and the relationship between these types of planning. Decisions need to be made as to which combination of short-term (lesson), mid-term (unit, theme) and long-term (semester, year) planning is going to be implemented and how it is going to be sequenced. Another issue relates to whether a programme of teacher evaluation is to be put in place, and if so, who will be responsible for conducting it and whether it will involve lesson observations or audiotaping or videotaping of lessons and preparation and analysis of transcripts.

Assessment and evaluation in the multiliterate and multimodal classroom/school

Finally, there are a number of questions that can to be asked about how multiliteracies and multimodality will be approached at the classroom and school level. The questions below are not meant to be a definitive list, nor is there an expectation that all the questions will need to be addressed. However, there are a number of important considerations that need to be taken into account and widely discussed throughout the school so that the approach is not adopted merely because it is the next new thing. There needs to be a clear and explicit rationale for adopting an approach that addresses multiliteracies and multimodality.

- Is there a clearly defined and shared vision of multiliteracies at the classroom and school level?
- Is there a clearly defined and shared vision of multimodality at the classroom and school level?
- Are the strategies, processes and concepts involved in multiliteracies and multimodality defined at a deep or surface level?
- Has there been an in-depth investigation into why the multiliterate and multimodal approach to literacy teaching and learning is more appropriate for your school than other approaches?
- Is there general agreement in the school about why multiliterate and multimodal pedagogical approaches are being introduced? Are the advantages and challenges clearly understood?
- Has the whole school framework been explicitly designed for each year level?
- How will you determine whether the introduction of a multiliterate and multimodal pedagogical approach has been a success?
- Are there processes in place that will allow modification of the approach if it is not meeting expectations?
- What professional learning and development has been organized to ensure that all the teachers are conceptually at the same level with regard to multiliteracies and multimodality?
- Are there plans to engage teachers in action research about multiliteracies and multimodality that is based on the collection of data and evidence to determine progress by both teachers and students?

Conclusion

The purpose of this chapter has been to explore the assessment of student performance and the evaluation of teachers' pedagogy, practice and planning. The approach in this chapter has been to relate assessment to student performance and evaluation to the measurement of teacher performance although the terms *assessment* and *evaluation* are often used interchangeably in other places.

The issues surrounding assessment have been investigated and a monitoring cycle has been proposed. Different approaches to the monitoring and assessment of student performance were explored, as were the different approaches to evaluating pedagogy. The Reflection Strategies, Auditing Instruments and Theory into Practice tasks that have been described throughout the preceding five chapters in this book have been reviewed in order to relate them to either assessment or evaluation. Finally, a whole school approach to assessment and evaluation in the multiliterate and multimodal classroom/school were explored.

It is important to realise that, while assessment and evaluation have been discussed in the last chapter in this book, this should not be taken to mean that assessment and evaluation in the multiliterate and multimodal classroom should be relegated to the final phase of considerations about classroom instruction. Assessment and evaluation should be seen as integral parts, and continuous processes, in the planning, practice and pedagogy of multiliteracies and multimodality.

Bibliography

Anstey, M 1991, *Blueprint for Assessment*, Ashton Scholastic, Sydney.

Anstey, M 2002, *Literate Futures: Reading*, Department of Education, State of Queensland.

Anstey, M & Bull, G 1989, 'From teaching to learning: Translating monitoring into planning and practice', in E Daly (ed), *Monitoring Children's Language Development*, Australian Reading Association, Carlton South, Melbourne.

Anstey, M & Bull, G 2005, 'One school's journey: Using multiliteracies to promote school renewal', *Practically Primary*, vol. 10, no. 3, pp. 10-13.

Anstey, M & Bull, G 2006, *Teaching and Learning Multiliteracies: Changing Times, Changing Literacies*, International Reading Association, Newark.

Au, W 2009, *Unequal by Design: High-Stakes Testing and the Standardisation of Inequality*, Routledge, New York.

Bates, K 2014, 'Assessment in a testing time', *Practically Primary*, vol. 19, no. 2, pp. 10-12.

Biesta, G 2013, 'Knowledge, judgement and the curriculum: On the past, present and future of the idea of the practical', *Journal of Curriculum Studies*, vol. 45, no. 5, pp. 684-96.

Brown, I, Lockyer, L & Caputi, P 2010, 'Multiliteracies and assessment practice', in DR Cole & DL Pullen (eds), *Multiliteracies in Motion: Current Theory and Practice*, Routledge, New York.

Buckingham, D 1993, 'Towards new literacies, information technology, English and media education', *The English and Media Magazine*, Summer, pp. 20-5.

Bull, G & Anstey, M 1993, *Report on a Three-year Literacy Study at Surat State School*, Language and Literacy Research Unit (LLRU), Faculty of Education, University of Southern Queensland, Queensland.

Bull, G & Anstey, M 1994, *A Study of the Literacy Attitudes and Practices in the Ravenshoe State School and Community*, Language and Literacy Research Unit (LLRU), Faculty of Education, University of Southern Queensland, Queensland.

Bull, G & Anstey, M 2000, *Report on the Harristown State High School Literacy Project*, Vols. 1 to 4, Centre for Literacy and Children's Literature in Education (CLEAR), Faculty of Education, University of Southern Queensland, Queensland, Australia.

Bull, G & Anstey, M 2004, *Inala Multiliteracies Project Report*, submitted to Mark Campling Principal, Forest Lakes State School for Inala Cluster of Schools, Brisbane, Queensland.

Bull, G & Anstey, M 2005, *Townsville Multiliteracies Project Report*, submitted to Janelle Pepperdene, Co-ordinator Townsville LDC (Literacy) and Melinda Webb, Education Advisor, Literacy-Productive Pedagogies, Townsville, Queensland.

Bull, G & Anstey, M 2007, *Moreton Bay College Multiliteracies Project Report*, Anstey & Bull Consultants in Education, Toowoomba, Queensland.

Bull, G & Anstey, M 2010a, *Evolving Pedagogies: Reading and Writing in a Multimodal World*, Education Services Australia, Carlton South.

Bull, G & Anstey, M 2010b, 'Using the principals of multiliteracies to inform pedagogical change', in DR Cole & DL Pullen (eds), *Multiliteracies in Motion: Current Theory and Practice*, Routledge, New York.

Calabrese, RL 2002, *The Leadership Assignment: Creating Change*, Allyn and Bacon, Boston.

Carr, W 2005, 'The role of theory in the professional development of an educational theorist', *Pedagogy, Culture and Society*, vol. 13, no. 3, pp. 333-46.

Coiro, J, Knobel, M, Lankshear, C, & Leu, DJ (eds) 2008, *Handbook of New Literacies Research*, Lawrence Erlbaum Associates, New York.

Cole, DR & Pullen, DL (eds) 2010, *Multiliteracies in Motion: Current Theory and Practice*, Routledge, New York.

Comber, B & Kamler, B (eds) 2005, *Turn-around Pedagogies: Literacy Interventions for At-risk Students*, Primary English Teaching Association (PETA), Newtown.

Cope, B & Kalantzis, M (eds) 2000, *Multiliteracies: Literacy Learning and the Design of Social Futures*, Routledge, London.

Cope, B & Kalantzis, M (eds) 2015, *A Pedagogy of Multiliteracies: Learning by Design*, Palgrave, London.

Dargusch, J 2014, 'Teachers as mediators: Formative practices with assessment criteria and standards', *Australian Journal of Language and Literacy*, vol. 37, no. 3, pp. 192-204.

Edwards-Groves, C Anstey, M & Bull, G 2014, *Classroom Talk: Understanding Dialogue, Pedagogy and Practice*, PETAA, Newton.

Exley, B, Honan, E, Kervin, L, Simpson, Wells, M & Muspratt, S 2016, 'Surveying the field: Primary school teachers' conceptions of the literacy capabilities of recently graduated primary school teachers', *Practical Literacy: The Early and Primary Years*, vol. 21, no. 2, pp. 39-42.

Freebody, P & Luke, A 1990, 'Literacies programmes: Debates and demands in cultural contexts', *Prospect: A Journal of Australian TESOL*, vol. 11, pp. 7-16.

Freebody, P & Luke, A 2003, 'Literacy as engaging with new forms of life: The Four Roles Model' in G Bull & M Anstey (eds), *The Literacy Lexicon*, 2nd ed, Pearson, Frenchs Forest.

Freebody, S & Freebody, P 2017, 'Australian teachers' literacy levels: Comparisons from OECD international Survey of Adult Skills', *ALEA Hot Topics*, Australian Literacy Educators' Association.

Fullan, M 1993, *Change Forces: Probing the Depths of Educational Reform*, Falmer Press, New York.

Fullan, M 1999, *The Meaning of Educational Change*, Teachers College Press, New York.

Fullan, M 2001, *Leading in a Culture of Change*, Jossey-Bass, San Francisco.

Fullan, M 2007, *The New Meaning of Educational Change*, 4th edn, Teachers College Press, New York.

Fuller, R & Hood, D 2005, 'Utilising community funds of knowledge as resources for school learning', in B Comber & B Kamler, *Turn-around Pedagogies: Literacy Interventions for At-risk Students*, Primary English Teaching Association (PETA), Newtown.

Gillies, RM & Boyle, M 2010, 'Teachers' reflections on cooperative learning: Issues of implementation', *Teaching and Teacher Education*, vol. 26, no. 4, pp. 933–40.

Goe, L 2007, *The Link Between Teacher Quality and Student Outcomes: A Research Synthesis*, National Comprehensive Center for Teacher Quality, Washington, DC.

Goe, L & Stickler, LM 2008, *Teacher Quality and Student Achievement: Making the most of recent research*, National Comprehensive Center for Teacher Quality, Washington, DC.

Goe, L, Bell, C & Little, O 2008, *Approaches to Evaluating Teacher Effectiveness: A Research Synthesis*, National Comprehensive Center for Teacher Quality, Washington, DC.

Gordon, SP (ed.) 2008, *Collaborative Action Research: Developing Professional Learning Communities*, Teachers College Press, New York.

Grenny, J, Patterson, K, Maxfield, D, McMillan, R & Switzer A 2013, *Influence: The New Science of Leading Change*, McGraw Hill, New York.

Harlen, W 2005, 'Teachers' summative practices and assessment for learning: Tensions and synergies', *The Curriculum Journal*, vol. 16, no. 2, pp. 207–23.

Hartman, DK, Morsink, PM & Zheng, J 2010, 'From print to pixels: The evolution of cognitive conceptions of reading comprehension', in EA Baker (ed), *The New Literacies, Multiple Perspectives on Research and Practice*, The Guilford Press, New York, pp. 131–64.

Kalantzis, M & Cope, B and the Learning by Design Group 2005, *Learning by Design*, Common Ground, Altona.

Kalantzis, M, Cope, B, Chan, E & Dalley-Trim, L 2016, *Literacies*, 2nd edn, Cambridge University Press, Cambridge.

Kemmis, S 2005, 'Knowing practice: Searching for saliences', *Pedagogy, Culture and Society*, vol. 13, no. 3, pp. 391–426.

Kress, G 2010, *Multimodality: A Social Semiotic approach to Contemporary Communication*, Routledge, Abingdon.

Lingard, B, Hayes, D & Mills, M 2003, 'Teachers and productive pedagogies: Contextualising, conceptualising, utilising', *Pedagogy, Culture and Society*, vol. 11, no. 3, pp. 397–422.

Lingard, B, Ladwig, J, Mills, M, Bahr, M, Chant, D & Warry, M 2001, *The Queensland School Reform Longitudinal Study*, Education Queensland, Brisbane.

Little, O, Goe, L & Bell, C 2009, *A Practical Guide to Evaluating Teacher Effectiveness*, National Comprehensive Center for Teacher Quality, Washington, DC.

Littleton, K & Mercer, N 2013, *Interthinking: Putting Talk to Work*, Routledge, London.

Luke, A & Freebody, P 1999a, 'A map of possible practices: Further notes on the four resources model', *Practically Primary*, vol. 4, no. 2, pp. 5–8.

Luke, A & Freebody, P 1999b, *Further Notes on the Four Resources Model*, viewed 21 March 2017, http://kingstonnetworknumandlitteam.wikispaces.com/file/view/Further+Notes+on+the+Four+Resources+Model-Allan+Luke.pdf.

Luke, A, Matters, G, Barrett, R & Land, R 2000 'New Basics Project technical paper', viewed 21 March 2017, http://works.bepress.com/gabrielle_matters/30/.

Masters, G 2014, 'Towards a growth mindset in assessment', *Practically Primary*, vol. 19, no. 2, pp. 4–7.

Medwell, J 2012, 'An Introduction to Assessing English', in R Cox (ed), *Primary English Teaching: An Introduction to Language, Literacy and Learning*, Hawker Brownlow, Moorabbin. (English version originally published by SAGE, London, 2011.)

Moon, B 2014, 'The literacy skills of secondary teaching undergraduates: Results of diagnostic testing and a discussion of findings', *Australian Journal of Teacher Education*, vol. 39, pp. 111–13.

New London Group 1996, 'A pedagogy of multiliteracies: Designing social futures', *Harvard Educational Review*, vol. 66, no.1, pp. 60–92.

Newfield, D, Andrew, D, Stein, P & Maungedzo, R 2003, 'No number can describe how good it was: Assessment issues in the multimodal classroom', *Assessment in Education*, vol. 10, no. 1, pp. 61–81.

Nicholas, M 2015, 'Informed assessment: Self-doubt and reflecting on practice', *Literacy Learning: The Middle Years*, vol. 23, no. 1, pp. 7–13.

Pressley, M & Allington, R L 2015, *Reading Instruction that Works: The Case for Balanced Teaching*, The Guilford Press, New York.

Quellmalz, ES & Haertel, GD 2008, 'Assessing new literacies in science and mathematics', in J Coiro, M Knobel, C Lankshear & DJ Leu (eds), *Handbook of Research on New Literacies*, Routledge, New York, pp. 941–72.

Stoll, L, Bolam, R, McMahon, A, Wallace, M & Thomas, S 2006, 'Professional learning communities: A review of the literature', *Journal of Educational Change*, vol. 7, no. 4, pp. 221–58.

van Kraayenoord, CE 2003, 'Literacy Assessment', in G Bull & M Anstey (eds), *The Literacy Lexicon*, 2nd edn, Prentice Hall, Sydney.

Wagner, T 2008, *The Global Achievement Gap: Why Even Our Best Schools Don't Teach the New Survival Skills Our Children Need and What We Can Do About It*, Basic Books, New York.

Wiggins, G & McTighe, J 2005, *Understanding by Design*, Pearson, New Jersey.

Wiliam, D 2007, 'Once you know what they've learned, what do you do next? Designing curriculum and assessment for growth', in R Lissitz (ed), *Assessing and Modeling Cognitive Development in School*, JAM Press, Maple Grove.

FULL BIBLIOGRAPHY

Alexander, RJ 2001, *Culture and Pedagogy: International Comparisons in Primary Education*, Blackwell, Oxford.
Alexander, RJ 2004, *Talk for Learning: The Second Year*, North Yorkshire County Council, Northallerton.
Alexander, RJ 2005, *Teaching Through Dialogue: The First Year*, London Borough of Barking and Dagenham, London.
Alexander, RJ 2008, *Towards Dialogic Teaching: Rethinking Classroom Talk*, 4th edn, Dialogos, York.
Allen, D 1994, 'Teaching visual literacy: Some reflections on the term', *Journal of Art and Design Education*, vol. 13, pp. 133–43.
Anderson, C, Kauffman, G & Short, KG 1998, 'Now I think like an artist: Responding to picture books', in J Evans (ed), *What's in the Picture? Responding to Illustrations in Picture Books*, Paul Chapman Publishing, London, pp. 146–65.
Anderson, LW & Krathwohl, DR (eds) 2001, *A Taxonomy for Learning, Teaching, and Assessing: A Revision of Bloom's Taxonomy of Educational Objectives*, Longman, New York.
Anstey, M 1991a, 'Examining classroom talk during literacy instruction: Developing metacognitive strategies', *Australian Journal of Reading*, vol. 14, no. 2, pp. 151–60.
Anstey, M 1991b, *Blueprint for Assessment*, Ashton Scholastic, Sydney.
Anstey, M 1993a, *Quantitative and Interpretative Analyses of Classroom Talk as a Cognitive Context for Learning about Literacy*, unpublished PhD thesis, Griffith University, Brisbane.
Anstey, M 1993b, 'Examining classroom talk: Structure and talk in literacy lessons from a metacognitive perspective', *SET Research Information for Teachers*, vol. 12, no. 1, NZCER, Wellington.
Anstey, M 1993c, 'What you see is not all you get! Critical readings of illustrative text', Invited Keynote Address, Children's Book Council State Conference, Maroochydore, Queensland, Australia.
Anstey, M 1998, 'Being explicit about literacy instruction', *Australian Journal of Language and Literacy*, vol. 21, no. 3, pp. 206–21.
Anstey, M 2002a, 'It's not all Black and White: Postmodern picture books and teaching new literacies', *Journal of Adolescent and Adult Literacy*, vol. 45, no. 6, pp. 444–56.
Anstey, M 2002b, *Literate Futures: Reading*, AccessEd, Department of Education, State of Queensland, Coorparoo.
Anstey, M 2003 'Examining classrooms as sites of literate practice and literacy learning', in G Bull & M Anstey (eds), *The Literacy Lexicon*, 2nd edn, Pearson, Sydney.
Anstey, M 2008, 'Postmodern picturebooks as artefact: Developing tools for an archaelogical dig', in LR Sipe & S Pantaleo (eds), *Postmodern Picturebooks: Play Parody and Self-referentiality*, Routledge, London, pp. 147–63.
Anstey, M 2009, 'Multiliteracies: The conversation continues: What do we really mean by "multiliteracies" and why is it important?' *Reading Forum*, vol. 24, no. 1, pp. 5–15.
Anstey, M & Bull, G 1989, "From teaching to learning: Translating monitoring into planning and practice', in E Daly (ed), *Monitoring Children's Language Development*, Australian Reading Association, Carlton South, Melbourne.
Anstey, M & Bull, G 2004, *The Literacy Labyrinth*, 2nd edn, Pearson, Sydney.
Anstey, M & Bull, G 2005, 'One school's journey: Using multiliteracies to promote school renewal', *Practically Primary*, vol. 10, no. 3, pp. 10–13.
Anstey, M & Bull, G 2006, *Teaching and Learning Multiliteracies: Changing Times, Changing Literacies*, International Reading Association, Newark.

Anstey, M & Bull, G 2010, *Report on Observation of Eighteen Reading Lessons at Anon State School*, Unpublished report.
Anstey, M & Bull, G 2016, 'Pedagogies for developing literacies of the visual', *Practical Literacy: The Early and Primary Years*, vol. 21, no.1, pp. 22-4.
Applebee, AN 1981, *Writing in the Secondary School*, National Council for the Teaching of English, Urbana.
Arizpe, E & Styles, M 2003, *Children Reading Pictures: Interpreting Visual Texts*, Routledge Falmer, London.
Arizpe, E & Styles, M with K Cowan, L Mallouri & M Wolpert 2008, 'The voices behind the pictures: Children responding to postmodern picturebooks', in LR Sipe & S Pantaleo (eds), *Postmodern Picturebooks: Play Parody and Self-referentiality*, Routledge, London, pp. 207-22.
Au, W 2009, *Unequal by Design: High-Stakes Testing and the Standardisation of Inequality*, Routledge, New York.
Australian Curriculum Assessment and Reporting Authority (ACARA) 2014, Foundation to Year 10 Australian Curriculum English, viewed 28 July 2017, https://www.australiancurriculum.edu.au/f-10-curriculum/english/?strand=
Australia's Future Workforce? 2015, Report from CEDA (Committee for Economic Development of Australia), viewed 22 February 2017, http://adminpanel.ceda.com.au/FOLDERS/Service/Files/Documents/26792~Futureworkforce_June2015.pdf.
Bader, B 1976, *American Picturebooks from Noah's Ark to The Beast Within*, Macmillan, New York.
Baker, CD 1991a, 'Classroom literacy events', *Australian Journal of Reading*, vol. 14, no. 2, pp. 103-16.
Baker, CD 1991b, 'Literacy practices and social relations in classroom reading events', in CD Baker & A Luke (eds), *Towards a Critical Sociology of Reading Pedagogy*, John Benjamins, Amsterdam.
Baker, CD & Freebody, P 1989a, 'Talk around text: Constructions of textual and teacher authority in classroom discourse', in S deCastell, A Luke & C Luke (eds), *Language Authority and Criticism: Readings on the School Textbook*, Falmer Press, London.
Baker, CD & Freebody, P 1989b, *Children's First School Books: Introductions to the Culture of Literacy*, Basil Blackwell, Oxford.
Baker, CD & Freebody, P 2008, 'Exploratory talk for learning', N Mercer & S Hodgkinson (eds), *Exploring Talk in School: Inspired by the Work of Douglas Barnes*, SAGE, London.
Baker, EA (ed) 2010, *The New Literacies, Multiple Perspectives on Research and Practice*, The Guilford Press, New York.
Balanskat, A & Engelhart, S 2015, *Computing our Future: Computer programming and coding, priorities, school curricula and initiatives across Europe*, European Schoolnet, Belgium, viewed 28 February 2017, http://fcl.eun.org/documents/10180/14689/Computing+our+future_final.pdf/746e36b1-e1a6-4bf1-8105-ea27c0d2bbe0.
Barnes, D 1976, *From Communication to Curriculum*, Penguin, Harmondsworth.
Barnes, D 2008, 'Exploratory talk for learning' in N Mercer & S Hodgkinson (eds), *Exploring Talk in School: Inspired by the Work of Douglas Barnes*, SAGE, London.
Barnes, D 2010, 'Why is talk important', *English Teaching: Practice and Critique*, vol. 9, no. 2, pp. 7-10.
Barton, D, Hamilton, M & Ivanic, R 2000, *Situated Literacies: Reading and Writing in Context*, Routledge, London.
Barton, G & Unsworth, L 2014, 'Music, multiliteracies and multimodality: Exploring the book and movie versions of Shaun Tan's The Lost Thing', *Australian Journal of Language and Literacy*, vol. 37, no. 1, pp. 3-20.
Bates, K 2014, 'Assessment in a testing time', *Practically Primary*, vol. 19, no. 2, pp. 10-12.
Bean, TW & Dunkerly-Bean, J 2015, 'Expanding conceptions of adolescent literacy research and practice: Cosmopolitan theory in educational contexts', *Australian Journal of Language and Literacy*, vol. 38, no. 1, pp. 46-54.
Bearne, E & Wolstencroft, H 2007, *Visual Approaches to Teaching Writing: Multimodal Literacy 5-11*, Paul Chapman Publishing, London.
Bee, B 1990, 'Teaching to empower: Women and literacy', *Australian Journal of Reading*, vol. 13, no. 1, pp. 53-9.
Benedikt, C & Osborne, M 2013, *The Future of Employment: A working paper*, Oxford Martin Programme of Technology and Employment, Oxford Martin School University of Oxford, Oxford, viewed 22 February 2017, http://www.oxfordmartin.ox.ac.uk/downloads/academic/The_Future_of_Employment.pdf.
Bernstein, B 1960, 'Language and social class' in *Class, Codes and Control, Vol. 1, Theoretical studies towards a sociology of language*, Routledge and Kegan Paul, London.
Bernstein, B 1961, 'Social structure, language and learning' in *Educational Research*, vol. 3, pp. 163-76.

Bernstein, B 1962a, 'Linguistic codes, hesitation phenomena and intelligence', in *Class, Codes and Control, Vol. 1, Theoretical studies towards a sociology of language*, Routledge and Kegan Paul, London.
Bernstein, B 1962b, 'Social class, linguistic codes and grammatical elements', in *Class, Codes and Control, Vol. 1, Theoretical studies towards a sociology of language*, Routledge and Kegan Paul, London.
Bernstein, B 1964, 'Elaborated and restricted codes: Their origins and some consequences', in Ethnography and Speech, Monograph Issue of *American Anthropologist*, March.
Bernstein, B 1971, *Class, Codes and Control, Vol. 1, Theoretical studies towards a sociology of language*, Routledge, London.
Bernstein, B 1973, *Class, Codes and Control, Vol. 2, Applied studies towards a sociology of language*, Routledge, London.
Bernstein, B 1975, *Class, Codes and Control, Vol. 3, Towards a theory of educational transmission*, Routledge, London.
Bernstein, B 1990, *Class, Codes and Control, Vol. 4, The structuring of pedagogical discourse*, Routledge, London.
Bezemer, J & Kress, G 2016, *Multimodality, Learning and Communication: A Social Semiotic Frame*, Routledge, London.
Biesta, G 2013, 'Knowledge, judgement and the curriculum: On the past, present and future of the idea of the practical', *Journal of Curriculum Studies*, vol. 45, no. 5, pp. 684-96.
Bloom, BS & Krathwohl, DR 1956, *Taxonomy of Educational Objectives: The Classification of Educational Goals, by a Committee of College and University Examiner, Handbook I: Cognitive Domain*, Longmans Green, New York.
Board of Studies New South Wales 2012, *Suggested Texts for the English K-10 Syllabus*, Board of Studies, NSW, Sydney.
Bondy, E 1984, 'Thinking about thinking: Encouraging children's use of metacognitive processes', *Childhood Education*, vol. 60, no. 4, pp. 234-8.
Bourdieu, P 1986, 'The struggle for symbolic order', (trans J Bleicher), *Theory, Culture and Society*, vol. 3, no. 3, pp. 35-51.
Briggs, R 1982, *When the Wind Blows*, Penguin Books, London.
Brown, AL 1978, 'Knowing when, where and how to remember: A problem of metacognition', in R Glaser (ed), *Advances in Instructional Psychology, Vol. 1*, Lawrence Erlbaum, Hillsdale.
Brown, AL 1985, 'Teaching students to think as they read: Implications for curriculum reform', *Reading Education Report No. 58*, University of Illinois, Urbana.
Brown, AL & Kane, MJ 1988, 'Preschool children can learn to transfer: Learning to learn and learning from example', *Cognitive Psychology*, vol. 20, pp. 493-523.
Brown, AL & Palincsar, AS 1982, 'Inducing strategic learning from texts by means of informed, self-control training', *Topics in Learning and Learning Disabilities*, April, pp. 1-17.
Brown, I, Lockyer, L & Caputi, P 2010, 'Multiliteracies and assessment practice', in DR Cole & DL Pullen (eds), *Multiliteracies in Motion: Current Theory and Practice*, Routledge, New York.
Bruner, JS 1996, *The Culture of Education*, Harvard University Press, Cambridge.
Buckingham, D 1993, 'Towards new literacies, information technology, English and media education', *The English and Media Magazine*, Summer, pp. 20-5.
Bull, G 2003 'An investigation of the pedagogy of literature using literature to support learning,' in G Bull & M Anstey (eds), *The Literacy Lexicon*, 2nd edn, Prentice Hall, Sydney.
Bull, G & Anstey, M 1993, *Report on a Three-year Literacy Study at Surat State School*, Language and Literacy Research Unit (LLRU), Faculty of Education, University of Southern Queensland, Queensland.
Bull, G & Anstey, M 1994, *A Study of the Literacy Attitudes and Practices in the Ravenshoe State School and Community*, Language and Literacy Research Unit (LLRU), Faculty of Education, University of Southern Queensland, Queensland.
Bull, G & Anstey, M 1995, *Adult Literacy Practices in Rural Families and Communities*, National Language and Literacy Institute of Australia (NLLIA), Adult Literacy Research Network Node, Queensland.
Bull, G & Anstey, M 1996, *The Literacy Teaching and Learning Practices of an Urban School and Its Community*, National Language and Literacy Institute of Australia (NLLIA), Literacy Research Network Node, Queensland.
Bull, G & Anstey, M 1997, *Investigating the Literacy Practices of School, Home and Community*, Language Australia Child/ESL Literacy Research Network Node, Queensland.

Bull, G & Anstey, M 2000, *Report on the Harristown State High School Literacy Project*, Vols. 1 to 4, Centre for Literacy and Children's Literature in Education (CLEAR), Faculty of Education, University of Southern Queensland, Queensland.

Bull, G & Anstey, M 2004, *Inala Multiliteracies Project Report*, submitted to Mark Campling Principal, Forest Lakes State School for Inala Cluster of Schools, Brisbane, Queensland.

Bull, G & Anstey, M 2005, *Townsville Multiliteracies Project Report*, submitted to Janelle Pepperdene, Co-ordinator Townsville LDC (Literacy) and Melinda Webb, Education Advisor, Literacy-Productive Pedagogies, Townsville, Queensland.

Bull, G & Anstey, M 2007, *Moreton Bay College Multiliteracies Project Report*, Anstey & Bull Consultants in Education, Toowoomba, Queensland.

Bull, G & Anstey, M 2009, *Finding the Gaps: Navigating Sustainable Learning Futures for Indigenous Students: A Pilot Study*, report for the Department of Education, Employment and Workplace Relations (DEEWR), The Greater Toowoomba Regional Advisory Committee, Toowoomba, Queensland, available at http://www.ansteybull.com.au/media/2198/cwfinding-the-gaps-2009.pdf).

Bull, G & Anstey, M 2010a, *Evolving Pedagogies: Reading and Writing in a Multimodal World*, Education Services Australia, Carlton South.

Bull, G & Anstey, M 2010b, 'Using the principals of multiliteracies to inform pedagogical change', in DR Cole & DL Pullen (eds), *Multiliteracies in Motion: Current Theory and Practice*, Routledge, New York, pp. 141-59.

Bull, G & Anstey, M 2013, *Uncovering History Using Multimodal Literacies: An Inquiry Process*, Education Services Australia, Carlton South.

Burn, A & Parker, D 2006, 'Tiger's big plan: Multimodality and the moving image', in C Jewitt & G Kress (eds), *Multimodal Literacy*, Peter Lang, New York, pp. 56-72.

Calabrese, RL 2002, *The Leadership Assignment: Creating Change*, Allyn and Bacon, Boston.

Cali, D & Bloch, S 2007 *The Enemy*, Wilkins Farago, Albert Park.

Cambourne, B 1986, 'Retelling: A whole language "natural" learning activity,' in RD Walshe, P March & D Jensen (eds), *Writing and Learning in Australia*, Dellasta/Oxford University Press, Melbourne.

Cambourne, B 1988, *The Whole Story: Natural Learning and the Acquisition of Literacy in the Classroom*, Ashton Scholastic, Sydney.

Cambourne, B 1994, 'The rhetoric of "The Rhetoric of Whole Language"', *Reading Research Quarterly*, vol. 29, no. 4, pp. 330-33.

Carr, W 2005 'The role of theory in the professional development of an educational theorist', *Pedagogy, Culture and Society*, vol. 13, no. 3, pp. 333-46.

Carrington, V & Robinson, M (eds) 2009, *Digital Literacies: Social Learning and Classroom Practices*, SAGE, London.

Carson, KP and Stewart, GL 1996, 'Job analysis and the sociotechnical approach to quality: A critical examination', *Journal of Quality Management*, vol. 1, pp. 49-64.

Cazden, CB 1967, 'On individual differences in language competence and performance', *Journal of Special Education*, vol. 1, pp. 135-50.

Cazden, CB 1970, 'The situation: A neglected source of social class differences in language use', *Journal of Social Issues*, vol. 26, no. 2, pp. 35-60.

Cazden, CB 1972, *Child Language and Education*, Holt, Rinehart and Winston, New York.

Cazden, CB 2001, *Classroom Discourse: The Language of Teaching and Learning*, Heinemann, Portsmouth.

Charters, J 1961, *The General*, Routledge and Kegan Paul, London.

Charters, J 2010, *The General*, Walker Books, London.

Chomsky, N 1965, *Aspects of a Theory of Syntax*, MIT Press, Cambridge.

Clark, K 1960, *Looking at Pictures*, John Murray, London.

Coats, K 2008, 'Postmodern picturebooks and the transmodern self', in S Pantaleo & LR Sipe (eds), *Postmodern Picturebooks: Play, Parody and Self-Referentiality*, Routledge, New York, pp. 75-88.

Coffin, C and Derewianka, BM 2009, 'Multimodal layout in school history books: The texturing of historical interpretation', in G Forey & G Thompson (eds), *Text Type and Texture: In Honour of Flo Davies*, Equinox Publishing, London, pp. 191-215.

Coiro, J, Knobel, M, Lankshear, C, & Leu, DJ (eds) 2008, *Handbook of New Literacies Research*, Lawrence Erlbaum Associates, New York.

Cole, DR & Pullen, DL (eds) 2010, *Multiliteracies in Motion: Current Theory and Practice*, Routledge, New York.

Comber, B & Kamler, B (eds) 2005, *Turn-around Pedagogies: Literacy Interventions for At-risk Students*, Primary English Teaching Association (PETA), Newtown.

Cope, B & Kalantzis, M (eds) 2000, *Multiliteracies: Literacy Learning and the Design of Social Futures*, Routledge, London.

Cope, B & Kalantzis, M (eds) 2015, *A Pedagogy of Multiliteracies: Learning by Design*, Palgrave, London.

Coscarelli, CV & Coiro, J 2014, 'Reading multiple sources online', in *Linguagem & Ensino, Pelotas*, vol. 17, no. 3, pp. 751–76.

Courts, PL 1991, *Literacy and Empowerment*, Bergin & Garvey, New York.

Crew, G 1997, *The Viewer*, Lothian, Melbourne.

Crew, G & Woolman, S 1997, *Tagged*, Era, Flinders Park.

Dargusch, J 2014, 'Teachers as mediators: Formative practices with assessment criteria and standards', *Australian Journal of Language and Literacy*, vol. 37, no. 3, pp. 192–204.

Davies, F & Greene, T 1984, *Reading for Learning in the Sciences*, Oliver and Boyd, Edinburgh.

Dawkins, J 1991, *Australia's Language: The Australian Language and Literacy Policy*, Department of Employment, Education and Training, Australian Government Publishing Service, Canberra.

Delpit, L 1988, 'The silenced dialogue: Power and pedagogy in educating other people's children', *Harvard Educational Review*, vol. 58, no. 3, pp. 280–98.

Department for Education and Employment 1999, *The National Curriculum Handbook for Primary Teachers in England*, viewed 18 July 2017, http://www.educationengland.org.uk/documents/pdfs/1999-nc-primary-handbook.pdf.

Derewianka, BM 1990, *Exploring How Texts Work*, Primary English Teaching Association, Rozelle.

Derewianka, BM 2015, 'The contribution of genre theory to literacy education in Australia', in J Turbill, G Barton & C Brock (eds), *Teaching Writing in Today's Classrooms: Looking Back to Looking Forward*, Australian Literary Educators' Association, Norwood, pp. 69–86.

Derewianka, BM & Coffin, C 2008, 'Time visuals in history textbooks: Some pedagogic issues', in L Unsworth (ed), *Multimodal Semiotics: Functional Analysis in Contexts of Education*, Continuum, London, pp. 187–200.

Derewianka, B & Jones, P 2016, *Teaching Language in Context*, 2nd edn, Oxford University Press, South Melbourne.

Dondis, DA 1973, *A Primer of Visual Literacy*, MIT Press, Cambridge.

D'warte, J 2014, 'Exploring linguistic repertoires: Multiple language use and multimodal literacy activity in five classrooms', *Australian Journal of Language and Literacy*, vol. 37, no. 1, pp. 21–30.

Dyson A H 2003, *The Brothers and Sisters Learn to Write: Popular Literacies in Childhood and School Cultures*, Teachers College Press, New York.

Edwards-Groves, C 1998, *Reconceptualisation of Classroom Events as Structured Lessons: Documenting and Changing the Teaching of Literacy in the Primary School*, Unpublished PhD thesis, Griffith University, Queensland.

Edwards-Groves, C 2003a, *On Task: Focused Literacy Learning*, Primary English Teaching Association Australia (PETAA), Sydney.

Edwards-Groves, C 2003b, 'Building an inclusive classroom through explicit pedagogy: A focus on the language of teaching', in G Bull & M Anstey (eds), *The Literacy Lexicon*, 2nd edn, Pearson, Sydney, pp. 83–101.

Edwards-Groves, C, Anstey, M and Bull, G 2014, *Classroom Talk: Understanding Dialogue, Pedagogy and Practice*, PETAA, Newton.

Ellis, ES 1986, 'The role of motivation and pedagogy on the generalization of cognitive strategy training', *Journal of Learning Disabilities*, vol. 19, no. 2, pp. 66–70.

Exley, B, Honan, E, Kervin, L, Simpson, Wells, M & Muspratt, S 2016, 'Surveying the field: Primary school teachers' conceptions of the literacy capabilities of recently graduated primary school teachers', *Practical Literacy: The Early and Primary Years*, vol. 21, no. 2, pp. 39–42.

Fisher, R, Brooks, G & Lewis, M (eds) 2002, *Raising Standards in Literacy*, Routledge, London.

Fleiger, J 1991, *The Purloined Punch Line: Freud's Comic Theory and the Postmodern Text*, The Johns Hopkins University Press, Baltimore.
Foundation for Young Australians 2017, *The New Work Smarts: Thriving in the New Work Order*, The Foundation for Young Australians, Sydney.
Freebody, P 1992, 'A socio-cultural approach: Resourcing four roles as a literacy learner', in A Watson & A Badenhop (eds), *Prevention of Reading Failure*, Ashton-Scholastic, Sydney, pp. 48–60.
Freebody, P & Freiberg, J 2001, 'Re-discovering practical reading activities in schools and homes', *Journal of Research in Reading*, vol. 24, no. 3, pp. 222–34.
Freebody, P & Ludwig, C 1998, *Talk and Literacy in Schools and Homes*, Commonwealth of Australia, Canberra.
Freebody, P, Ludwig, C & Gunn, S 1995, *Everyday Literacy Practices In and Out of Schools in Low Socioeconomic Urban Communities*, Commonwealth of Australia, Canberra.
Freebody, P & Luke, A 1990, 'Literacies programs: Debates and demands in cultural contexts', *Prospect: Australian Journal of TESOL*, vol. 5, no. 7, pp. 7–16.
Freebody, P & Luke, A 2003, 'Literacy as engaging with new forms of life: The Four Roles Model' in G Bull & M Anstey (eds), *The Literacy Lexicon*, 2nd edn, Pearson, Frenchs Forest.
Freebody, S & Freebody, P 2017, 'Australian teachers' literacy levels: Comparisons from OECD international Survey of Adult Skills', *ALEA Hot Topics*, Australian Literacy Educators' Association.
French, P & MacLure, M 1981, 'Teachers' questions, pupils' answers: An investigation of questions and answers in the infant classroom', *First Language*, vol. 3, no. 1, pp. 31–45.
Frey, CB and Osborne, M 2013, *The Future of Employment: How susceptible are jobs to computerisation?* Oxford Martin Programme on Technology and Employment, Oxford viewed 2 March 2017, http://www.oxfordmartin.ox.ac.uk/downloads/academic/The_Future_of_Employment.pdf.
Fullan, M 1993, *Change Forces: Probing the Depths of Educational Reform*, Falmer Press, New York.
Fullan, M 1999, *The Meaning of Educational Change*, Teachers College Press, New York.
Fullan, M 2001, *Leading in a Culture of Change*, Jossey-Bass, San Francisco.
Fullan, M 2007, *The New Meaning of Educational Change*, 4th edn, Teachers College Press, New York.
Fuller, R & Hood, D 2005, 'Utilising community funds of knowledge as resources for school learning', in B Comber & B Kamler, *Turn-around Pedagogies: Literacy Interventions for At-risk Students*, Primary English Teaching Association (PETA), Newtown.
Gardner, P 2017, 'Worlds Apart: A comparative analysis of discourses of English in the curricula of England and Australia.' *English in Education* doi: 10.1111/eie.12138, http://onlinelibrary.wiley.com/journal/10.1111/(ISSN)1754-8845/issues.
Gee, JP 1990, *Social Linguistics and Literacies: Ideology in Discourses*, Falmer Press, London.
Gee, JP 1992, *The Social Mind: Language, Ideology and Social Practice*, Bergin & Garvey, New York.
Gee, JP 2004, *Situated Language and Learning: A Critique of Traditional Schooling*, Routledge, New York.
Gillies, RM & Boyle, M 2010, 'Teachers' Reflections on Cooperative Learning: Issues of Implementation', *Teaching and Teacher Education*, vol. 26, no. 4, pp. 933–40.
Gleeson, L & Blackwood F 2011, *Look, A BOOK!*, Little Hare Books, Richmond.
Goe, L 2007, *The Link Between Teacher Quality and Student Outcomes: A Research Synthesis*, National Comprehensive Center for Teacher Quality, Washington, DC.
Goe, L & Stickler, LM 2008, *Teacher Quality and Student Achievement: Making the most of recent research*, National Comprehensive Center for Teacher Quality, Washington, DC.
Goe, L, Bell, C & Little, O 2008, *Approaches to Evaluating Teacher Effectiveness: A Research Synthesis*, National Comprehensive Center for Teacher Quality, Washington, DC.
Goodman, KS 1967, 'Reading: A psycholinguistic guessing game', *Journal of the Reading Specialist*, vol. 6, pp. 126–35.
Goodman, KS 1986, *What's Whole in Whole Language?* Scholastic, Ontario.
Gordon, SP (ed) 2008, *Collaborative Action Research: Developing Professional Learning Communities*, Teachers College Press, New York.

Gravett, E 2007, *Little Mouse's Big Book of Fears*, Macmillan, London.
Gray, B 1980a, 'Concentrated encounters as a component of functional language literacy teaching', in T Le & M McCausland (eds), *Proceedings of the Conference, Child Language Development: Theory into Practice*, Launceston Teachers' Centre, Launceston.
Gray, B 1980b, *Developing Language and Literacy with Urban Aboriginal Children: A First Report on the Traeger Park Project*, Curriculum Development Centre, Canberra.
Green, J & Weade, G 1990, 'The social construction of classroom reading: Beyond method', *Australian Journal of Reading*, vol. 13, no. 4, pp. 326-36.
Grenny, J, Patterson, K, Maxfield, D, McMillan, R & Switzer A 2013, *Influence: The New Science of Leading Change*, McGraw Hill, New York.
Griffith, RL & Ruan, J 2005, 'What is metacognition and what should be its role in literacy instruction', in SE Israel, CC Block, KI Bauserman & K Kinnucan-Welsch (eds), *Metacognition in Literacy Learning: Theory, Assessment, Instruction and Professional Development*, Lawrence Erlbaum, New Jersey, pp. 3-18.
Gutierrez, K D 2008, 'Developing a sociocritical literacy in the third space', *Reading Research Quarterly*, vol. 43, no. 2, pp. 148-64.
Habermas, J 1970, 'A theory of communicative competence', *Inquiry*, vol. 13, pp. 360-75.
Halliday, MAK 1973, *Explorations in the Functions of Language*, Edward Arnold, London.
Hansen, DT 2014, 'Theme issue: Cosmopolitanism as cultural creativity: New modes of educational practice in globalizing times', *Curriculum Inquiry*, vol. 44, no. 1, pp. 1-14.
Harlen, W 2005, 'Teachers' summative practices and assessment for learning: Tensions and synergies', *The Curriculum Journal*, vol. 16, no. 2, pp. 207-23.
Harste, J 1993, 'Literacy as curricular conversations about knowledge, inquiry and morality,' in RB Ruddell, MR Ruddell & H Singer (eds), *Theoretical Models and Processes of Reading*, International Reading Association, Newark, Delaware, pp. 1025-47.
Hartman, DK, Morsink, PM & Zheng, J 2010, 'From print to pixels: The evolution of cognitive conceptions of reading comprehension' in EA Baker (ed), *The New Literacies, Multiple Perspectives on Research and Practice*, The Guilford Press, New York, pp. 131-64.
Heath, SB 1982, 'Questioning at home and at school: A comparative study', in G Spindler (ed), *Doing the Ethnography of Schooling*, Holt, Rinehart & Winston, New York, pp. 103-31.
Heath, SB 1983, *Ways with Words: Language, Life and Work in Communities and Classrooms*, Cambridge University Press, Cambridge.
Heath, SB 1986, 'The functions and uses of literacy', in S De Castell, A Luke & K Egan (eds), *Literacy, Society and Schooling*, Cambridge University Press, Cambridge.
Hest, A 1997, *When Jessie Came Across the Sea*, Walker Books, London.
Hoh, A 2017, 'Kids now spending more time online than watching television, survey shows', viewed 16 February 2017, http://www.abc.net.au/news/2017-02-15/children-now-spend-more-time-online-than-watching-tv/8272708.
Holman, D, Wall, TD, Clegg, CW, Sparrow, P & Howard, A (eds) 2005, *The Essentials of the New Workplace: A Guide to the Human Impact of Modern Work Practices*, Wiley and Sons, Chichester.
Hull, G & Schultz, K (eds) 2002, *School's Out! Bridging Out-of-school Literacies with Classroom Practices*, Teachers College Press, New York.
Hull, GA & Stornaiulo, A 2010, 'Cosmopolitan literacies, social networks, and 'proper distance': Striving to understand in a global world', *Curriculum Inquiry*, vol. 44, no. 1, pp. 15-44.
Israel, SE, Bauserman, KL & Collins Block, C 2005, 'Metacognitive assessment strategies', *Thinking Classroom*, vol. 6, no. 2, pp. 21-8.
Iyer, R & Luke, C 2010, 'Multimodal, multiliteracies: Texts and Literacies for the 21st century,' in DL Pullen & DR Cole (eds), *Multiliteracies and Technology Enhanced Education: Social Practice and the Global Classroom*, IGI Global, Hershey, New York.

Janks, H 2010, *Literacy and Power*, Routledge, London.
Jewitt, C 2008, *Technology, Literacy and Learning: A Multimodal Approach*, Routledge, Abingdon.
Jewitt, C & Kress, G 2008, *Multimodal Literacy*, Peter Lang, New York.
Jewitt, C, Bezemer, J & O'Halloran, K 2016, *Introducing Multimodality*, Routledge, London.
Jones, A 1986, *At School I've Got a Chance: Ideology and Social Reproduction in a Secondary School*, PhD thesis, University of Auckland, New Zealand.
Kalantzis, M & Cope, B and the Learning by Design Group 2005 *Learning by Design*, Common Ground, Altona.
Kalantzis, M, Cope, B, Chan, E & Dalley-Trim, L 2016, *Literacies*, 2nd edn, Cambridge University Press, Port Melbourne.
Kemmis, S 2005, 'Knowing practice: Searching for saliences', *Pedagogy, Culture and Society*, vol. 13, no. 3, pp. 391-426.
Kress, G 2000, 'Design and transformation: New theories of meaning', in B Cope & M Kalantzis (eds), *Multiliteracies: Literacy Learning and the Design of Social Futures*, Routledge, London.
Kress, G 2003, *Literacy in the New Media Age*, Routledge, London.
Kress, G 2010, *Multimodality: A Social Semiotic Approach to Contemporary Communication*, Routledge, Abingdon.
Kress, G & van Leeuwen, T 2001, *Multimodal Discourse: The Modes and Media of Contemporary Communication*, Arnold, London.
Kress, G & van Leeuwen, T 2006, *Reading Images: The Grammar of Visual Design*, 2nd edn, Routledge, London.
Labov, W 1966, *The Social Stratification of English in New York City*, Center for Applied Linguistics, Washington, DC.
Labov, W 1969a, 'The logic of nonstandard English', in N Keddie (ed), *Tinker, Tailor: The Myth of Cultural Deprivation*, Penguin, Melbourne, pp. 21-66.
Labov, W 1969b, 'A Study of Non-Standard English', *Center for Applied Linguistics*, Washington, DC.
Land, R 2001, *The Queensland School Reform Longitudinal Study: Teachers' Summary*, The State of Queensland Education Department, Brisbane.
Landy, FJ, Shankster-Cawley, L & Moran, SK 1995, 'Advancing personnel selection and placement methods', in A Howard (ed), *Frontiers of Industrial and Organisational Psychology: The Changing Nature of Work*, Jossey-Bass, New York.
Lankshear, C & Knobel, M 2003, *New Literacies: Changing Knowledge and Classroom Practice*, Open University Press, Buckingham.
Lankshear, C & Knobel, M 2006, *New Literacies: Everyday Practices and Classroom Learning* 2nd edn, McGraw Hill/Open University Press, Maidenhead.
Lankshear, C & Lawler, M 1987, *Literacy, Schooling and Revolution*, Falmer Press, London.
Lankshear, C & Lawler, M 1989, *Literacy, Schooling and Revolution*, 2nd edn, Falmer Press, New York.
Lankshear, C with Gee, JP, Knobel, M & Searle, S 1997, *Changing Literacies*, Open University Press, Buckingham.
Lawton, D 1968, *Social Class, Language and Education*, Routledge and Kegan Paul, London.
Laycock, L 1998, 'A way into a new language and culture', in J Evans (ed), *What's in the Picture? Responding to Illustrations in Picture Books*, Paul Chapman Publishing, London, pp. 79-95.
Lenneberg, EH 1967, *Biological Foundations of Language*, Wiley, New York.
Levett, A & Lankshear, C 1990, *Going for Gold: Priorities for Schooling in the Nineties*, Daphne Brasell Associates Press, Wellington.
Lewis, D 2001, *Picturing Text: The Contemporary Children's Picturebook*, Taylor and Francis, London.
Lingard, B, Hayes, D & Mills, M 2003, 'Teachers and productive pedagogies: Contextualising, conceptualising, utilising', *Pedagogy, Culture and Society*, vol. 11, no. 3, pp. 397-422.
Lingard, B, Ladwig, J, Mills, M, Bahr, M, Chant, D & Warry, M 2001, *The Queensland School Reform Longitudinal Study*, Education Queensland, Brisbane.
Little, O, Goe, L & Bell, C 2009, *A Practical Guide to Evaluating Teacher Effectiveness*, National Comprehensive Center for Teacher Quality, Washington, DC.
Littleton, K & Mercer, N 2010, 'The significance of educational dialogues between primary school children', in K Littleton & C Howe (eds), *Educational Dialogues: Understanding and Promoting Productive Interaction*, Routledge, London.

Littleton, K & Mercer, N 2013a, *Interthinking: Putting Talk to Work*, Routledge, London.

Littleton, K & Mercer, N 2013b, 'Educational dialogues', in K Hall, T Cremin, B Comber & L Moll (eds), *The Wiley Blackwell International Handbook of Research on Children's Literacy Learning and Culture*, Wiley Blackwell, Oxford.

Lo Bianco, J 2000, 'Multiliteracies and multilingualism', in B Cope & M Kalantzis (eds), *Multiliteracies: Literacy Learning and the Design of Social Futures*, Routledge, London, pp. 92–105.

Louden, W & Rivalland, J 1995, *Literacy at a Distance: Literacy Learning in Distance Education*, Edith Cowan University, Perth.

Ludwig, C & Herschell, P 1998, 'The power of pedagogy: Routines, school literacy practices and outcomes', *Australian Journal of Language and Literacy*, vol. 21, no. 1, pp. 67–83.

Luke, A 1993, 'The social construction of literacy in the primary school,' in L Unsworth (ed), *Learning and Teaching*, Macmillan, Sydney.

Luke, A 1995, 'When basic skills and information processing just aren't enough: Rethinking reading in new times', *Teachers College Record*, vol. 97, no. 1, pp. 95–115.

Luke, A 2004, 'Teaching after the market: From commodity to cosmopolitanism', *Teachers College Record*, vol. 106, no. 7, pp. 1422–43.

Luke, A & Carrington, V 2004, 'Globalisation, literacy, curriculum practice' in T Grainger (ed), *The Routledge Falmer Reader in Language and Literacy*, Routledge Falmer, New York, pp. 52–66.

Luke, A & Freebody, P 1997, 'Shaping the social practices of reading', in S Muspratt, A Luke & P Freebody (eds), *Constructing Critical Literacies: Teaching and Learning Textual Practices*, Allen & Unwin, St Leonards, pp. 185–225.

Luke, A & Freebody, P 1999a, 'A map of possible practices: Further notes on the four resources model,' *Practically Primary*, vol. 4, no. 2, pp. 5–8.

Luke, A & Freebody, P 1999b, *Further Notes on the Four Resources Model*, viewed 21 March 2017, http://kingstonnetworknumandlitteam.wikispaces.com/file/view/Further+Notes+on+the+Four+Resources+Model-Allan+Luke.pdf.

Luke, A & Freebody, P 2000, *Literate Futures: Report of the Review for Queensland State Schools*, Education Queensland, Brisbane.

Luke, A, Matters, G, Barrett, R & Land, R 2000 'New Basics Project technical paper', viewed 21 March 2017, http://works.bepress.com/gabrielle_matters/30/.

Luke, A, Comber, B & Grant, H 2003, 'Critical literacies and cultural studies', in G Bull & M Anstey (eds), *The Literacy Lexicon*, 2nd edn, Pearson, Frenchs Forest, pp. 15–35.

Macaulay, D 1990, *Black and White*, Houghton Mifflin, New York.

MacNeill, N, Cavanagh, RE & Silcox, S 2003, 'Pedagogic principal leadership', *Management Education*, vol. 17, no. 4, pp. 14–17.

Marriott, S 2009, 'Picture books and the moral imperative', in J Evans (ed), *What's in the Picture? Responding to Illustrations in Picture Books*, Paul Chapman Publishing, London, pp. 1–24.

Marsden, J & Ottley, M 2008, *Home and Away*, Lothian, Melbourne.

Martin, JR 1985, *Factual Writing: Exploring and Challenging Social Reality*, Deakin University Press, Geelong, Victoria.

Martin, JR 1992, *English Text: System and Structure*, Benjamins, Amsterdam.

Martin, JR 1993, 'Literacy in science: Learning to handle text as technology', in MAK Halliday & JR Martin (eds), *Writing Science: Literacy and Discursive Power*, Falmer Press, London.

Martin, JR & Rothery, J 1993, 'Grammar: Making meaning in writing,' in B Cope & M Kalantzis (eds), *The Powers of Literacy*, Falmer Press, London.

Masters, G 2014, 'Towards a growth mindset in assessment' *Practically Primary*, vol. 19, no. 2, pp. 4–7.

McConnell, S 1992, 'Literacy and empowerment', *Australian Journal of Language and Literacy*, vol. 15, no. 2, pp. 123–38.

Medwell, J 2012, 'An Introduction to Assessing English' in R Cox (ed), *Primary English Teaching: An Introduction to Language, Literacy and Learning*, Hawker Brownlow, Moorabbin, Victoria. (English version originally published by SAGE, London, 2011.)

Mercer, N 1995, *The Guided Construction of Knowledge: Talk Amongst Teachers and Learners*, Multilingual Matters, Clevedon.

Mercer, N 2000, *Words and Mind: How We Use Language to Think Together*, Routledge, London.

Mikulecky, L 2010, 'An examination of workplace literacy research from new literacies and sociocultural perspectives,' in EA Baker (ed), *The New Literacies: Multiple Perspectives on Research and Practice*, The Guilford Press, New York.

Mills, KA 2005, 'Deconstructing binary oppositions in literacy discourse and pedagogy', *Australian Journal of Language and Literacy*, vol. 28, no. 1, pp. 67–82.

Mills, KA 2011, *The Multiliteracies Classroom*, Multilingual Matters, Bristol.

Moon, B 2014, 'The literacy skills of secondary teaching undergraduates: Results of diagnostic testing and a discussion of findings', *Australian Journal of Teacher Education*, vol. 39, pp. 111–13.

Morrell, E 2008, *Critical Literacy and Urban Youth: Pedagogies of Access, Dissent and Liberation*, Routledge, London.

Muspratt, S, Luke, A & Freebody, P (eds) 1997, *Constructing Critical Literacies: Teaching and Learning Textual Practice*, Allen & Unwin, Melbourne.

National Board for Professional Teaching Standards, viewed on May 12, 2017 http://www.nbpts.org/sites/default/files/ATLAS/atlas_onepager.pdf.

National Comprehensive Center for Teacher Quality, Washington, DC.

New London Group 1996, 'A pedagogy of multiliteracies: Designing social futures,' *Harvard Educational Review* vol. 66, no. 1, pp. 60–92.

Newfield, D, Andrew, D, Stein, P & Maungedzo, R 2003, 'No number can describe how good it was: Assessment issues in the multimodal classroom', *Assessment in Education*, vol. 10, no. 1, pp. 61–81.

Nicholas, M 2015, 'Informed assessment: Self-doubt and reflecting on practice', *Literacy Learning: The Middle Years*, vol. 23, no. 1, pp. 7–13.

Nikolejava, M & Scott, C 2001, *Words About Pictures: The Narrative Art of Children's Picture Books*, University of Georgia Press, Athens.

Novak, BJ 2014, *The Book with No Pictures*, Penguin, New York.

Nystrand, M 1997, *Opening Dialogue: Understanding the Dynamics of Language and Learning in the English Classroom*, Teachers College Press, New York.

Oliver, N 2006, *Home*, Omnibus Books, Malvern.

Ottley, M 2007, *Requiem for a Beast: A Work for Image, Word and Music*, Lothian, Hachette, Sydney.

Oxenham, J 1980, *Literacy: Writing, Reading and Social Organisation*, Routledge & Kegan Paul, London.

Pantaleo, S & Sipe, LR (eds) 2008, *Postmodern Picturebooks: Play, Parody and Self-Referentiality*, Routledge, New York.

Paris, S & Newman, R 1990, 'Developmental aspects of self-regulated learning.' *Educational Psychologist*, vol. 25, pp. 87–102.

Paris, SG & Paris, AH 2001, 'Classroom applications of research on self-regulated learning', *Educational Psychologist*, vol. 36, no. 2, pp. 89–101.

Paris, SG, Cross, DR & Lipson, MY 1984, 'Informed strategies for learning: A program to improve children's reading awareness and comprehension', *Journal of Educational Psychology*, vol. 76, no. 6, pp. 1239–52.

Paris, SG, Newman, RS & McVey, KA 1981, 'From tricks to strategies: Learning the functional significance of mnemonic actions', unpublished manuscript, University of Michigan, Ann Arbor.

Parker, D and Ottley, M 2013, *Parachute*, Little Hare, Richmond.

Pearson, PD & Gallagher, MC 1983, 'The instruction of reading comprehension', *Contemporary Educational Psychology*, vol. 8, no. 3, pp. 317–345.

Plummer, A 2016, *Playful Texts and the Emergent Reader: Developing Metalinguistic Awareness*, Equinox, Sheffield.

Poole, ME 1972, 'Social class differences in code elaboration: A study of written communication at the tertiary level', in the *Australian and New Zealand Journal of Sociology*, vol. 8, pp. 46–55.

Poulter, JR and Davis, S 2008, *Mending Lucille*, Lothian, Sydney.

Pressley, M & Allington, RL 2015, *Reading Instruction that Works: The Case for Balanced Teaching*, The Guilford Press, New York.

Queensland Curriculum and Assessment Authority, 2014, *Beyond NAPLAN: Using Reading Data to Improve Students' Performance in Higher-order Questioning*, Queensland Curriculum and Assessment Authority, South Brisbane.

Quellmalz, ES & Haertel, GD 2008, 'Assessing new literacies in science and mathematics' in J Coiro, M Knobel, C Lankshear & DJ Leu (eds), *Handbook of Research on New Literacies*, Routledge, New York, pp. 941-72.
Raney, K 1997, *Visual Literacy: Issues and Debates*, Middlesex University Press, London.
Raney, K 1998, 'A matter of survival: On being visually literate', *The English and Media Magazine*, vol. 39, pp. 37-42.
Raney, K 1999, 'Visual literacy and the art curriculum,' *Journal of Art and Education* vol. 18, no. 1, pp. 41-7.
Rennie, J & Patterson, A 2010, 'Young Australians reading in a digital world', in DR Cole & DL Pullen (eds), *Multiliteracies in Motion*, Routledge, Abingdon, pp. 207-23.
Resnick, LB, Michaels, S & O'Connor MC, 2010, 'How (well-structured) talk builds the mind', in DD Press & RJ Sternberg (eds), *Innovations in Educational Psychology*, Springer, New York, pp. 163-94.
Rosenberg, T 2017, 'American Girl: How do you grow up healthy in an era of body shaming and anonymous bullying on social media? You fight back', *National Geographic*, vol. 231, no. 1, pp. 110-27.
Ruhemann, A & Tan, S 2010, *The Lost Thing* (DVD PAL) Madman Entertainment, Australia.
Rymer, R 2012, 'Vanishing voices', *National Geographic*, vol. 222, no. 1, pp. 60-93.
Sanchez, JI 1994, 'From documentation to innovation: Reshaping job analysis to meet emerging business needs', *Human Resource Management Review*, vol. 4, no. 1, pp. 51-74.
Silvers, P & Shorey, M 2012, *Many Texts, Many Voices: Teaching Literacy and Social Justice to Young Learners in the Digital Age*, Stenhouse, Portland.
Sinclair, J & Coulthard, M 1975, *Towards an Analysis of Discourse: The Language of Teachers and Pupils*, Oxford University Press, London.
Smith, F 1978, *Reading*, Cambridge University Press, Cambridge.
Smith, F 1982, *Understanding Reading: A Psycholinguistic Analysis of Reading and Learning to Read*, Holt, Rinehart and Winston, New York.
Smith, F 1983, *Essays into Literacy*, Heinemann, Exeter.
Smith, L 2010, *It's a Book*, Walker Books, Newtown.
Solomon, Y 2008, *Mathematical Literacy: Developing Identities of Inclusion*, Routledge, New York.
Starcevic, V 2013, 'Is Internet addiction a useful concept?' *Australian and New Zealand Journal of Psychiatry*, vol. 47, no. 1, pp. 17-21.
Stoll, L, Bolam, R, McMahon, A, Wallace, M & Thomas, S 2006, 'Professional learning communities: A review of the literature', *Journal of Educational Change*, vol. 7, no. 4, pp. 221-58.
Street, BV 1984, *Literacy in Theory and Practice*, Cambridge University Press, Cambridge.
Street, BV (ed) 1993, *Cross-cultural Approaches to Literacy*, Cambridge University Press, Cambridge.
Styles, M & Noble, K 2009, 'Thinking in action: Analysing children's multimodal responses to multimodal picturebooks', in J Evans (ed), *Talking Beyond the Page: Reading and Responding to Picturebooks*, Routledge, Abingdon, pp. 118-33.
Sutton, M 2017, 'Virtual Reality addiction threat prompts cautious approach as VR nears "smartphone-like" take-off', *ABC News*, 10 February, viewed 11 February, http://www.abc.net.au/news/2017-02-10/addiction-risks-as-vr-gets-set-to-take-the-market-by-storm/8252614.
Tan, S 2000, *The Lost Thing*, Lothian, Port Melbourne.
Tan, S 2001, *The Red Tree*, Lothian, South Melbourne.
Tan, S 2002, *Picture Books. Who are they for?*, viewed 19 June 2017, http://www.shauntan.net/comments1.html.
Tan, S 2006, *The Arrival*, Lothian, Melbourne.
Taylor, D 1983, *Family Literacy: Young Children Learning to Read and Write*, Heinemann, Exeter, New Hampshire.
Tough, J 1976, *Listening to Children Talking*, Ward Lock Educational, London.
UNESCO 1957, *World Illiteracy at Mid-century*, UNESCO, Paris.
UNESCO 2017, *Five Laws of Media and Information Literacy*, viewed 23 March 2017, http://www.unesco.org/new/en/communication-and-information/media-development/media-literacy/five-laws-of-mil/.
Unsworth, L 2001, *Teaching Multiliteracies Across the Curriculum: Changing Contexts of Text and Image and Practice*, Open University Press, Oxenham.

van Kraayenoord, CE 2003, 'Literacy assessment', in G Bull & M Anstey (eds), *The Literacy Lexicon*, 2nd edn, Prentice Hall, Sydney.
Varlander, S 2012, 'Individual flexibility in the workplace: A spatial perspective', *The Journal of Applied Behavioural Science*, vol. 48, no. 1, pp. 33–61.
Vygotsky, LS 1962, *Thought and Language*, MIT Press, Cambridge.
Waber, B, Magnolfi, J & Lindsay, G 2014, 'Workspaces that move people', *Harvard Business Review*, October, viewed 14 March 2017, https://hbr.org/2014/10/workspaces-that-move-people.
Wagner, T 2008, *The Global Achievement Gap: Why Even Our Best Schools Don't Teach the New Survival Skills Our Children Need – and What We Can Do About It*, Basic Books, New York.
Wallace, P 2014, 'Internet addiction disorder and youth', *EMBO Report*, vol. 15, no. 1, pp. 12–16, viewed 20 March 2017, https://www.ncbi.nlm.nih.gov/pmc/articles/PMC4303443/.
Watson, K 2004, 'The postmodern picture book in the secondary classroom', *English in Australia*, no. 140, pp. 55–7.
Wells, G 1993, 'Reevaluating the IRF sequence', *Linguistics and Education*, vol. 5, pp. 1–37.
Wells, G 1999, *Dialogic Inquiry: Towards a Sociocultural Practice and Theory of Education*, Cambridge University Press, Cambridge.
Wells, G (ed) 2001, *Action, Talk and Text: Learning and Teaching Through Inquiry*, Teachers College Press, New York.
Wiggins, G & McTighe, J 2005, *Understanding by Design*, Pearson, New Jersey.
Wiliam, D 2007, 'Once you know what they've learned, what do you do next? Designing curriculum and assessment for growth', in R Lissitz (ed), *Assessing and Modeling Cognitive Development in School*, JAM Press, Maple Grove.
Williams, F & Naremore, RC 1969, 'Social class differences in children's syntactic performance: A quantitative analysis of field study data', *Journal of Speech and Hearing Research*, vol. 12, pp. 777–93.
Williams, M 2007, *Archie's War*, Walker Books, London.
Wolfe, SE & Alexander, RJ 2008, 'Argumentation and dialogic teaching: Alternative pedagogies for a changing world', *Beyond Current Horizons Project*, Department for Children, Schools and Families, UK.
Yamada-Rice, D 2010, 'Beyond words: An enquiry into children's home visual communication practices', *Journal of Early Childhood Literacy*, vol. 10, no. 3, pp. 341–63.
Young, E 2011, *The House that Baba Built: An Artist's Childhood in China*, Little Brown, New York.
Zimmerman, BJ 2000, 'Attaining self-regulation: A social cognitive perspective', in M Boekarts, P Pintrich, & M Zeidner, M (eds), *Self-Regulation: Theory, Research, and Applications*, Academic, Orlando, pp. 13–39.

GLOSSARY

Codes: A terminology that can be used to create meaning in a particular semiotic system.

Communicative competence: Refers to the ability of middle class students to understand when it is appropriate to use standard or non-standard dialects (or elaborate and restricted codes) in formal or less formal contexts. While working class students know both the codes and dialects they are unable to judge when it is appropriate to use them. They are therefore not communicatively competent.

Consuming: Making meaning with multimodal text in order to fulfil a particular purpose, in a particular context. It may involve interaction with others to achieve the purpose. The text may be disseminated via a range of technologies.

Conventions: The agreed upon, or accepted ways, of using the codes. Together the codes and conventions are the tools that come together to enable a reader/viewer to make meaning. There are codes and conventions that are associated with each semiotic system.

Deficiency Hypothesis: A belief that poor performance by students from a working class background can be attributed to factors operating within the home. This 'blame the victim' approach shifts responsibility for educational failure away from the school to families because of deficiencies that are believed to be present within the context of the home.

Design (noun): Refers to the components of meaning, for example the form or structure of a text.

Designing (verb): The process of making meaning as the selected repertoire of resources are combined and recombined to interpret, communicate and represent meaning through a text.

Diagnostic assessment: Assessment, often based on the use of standardised tests, that is designed to find out what students know so that the appropriate skills, strategies and processes can be taught. It is conducted before learning takes place and can provide information to both teachers and students.

Dialogic pedagogies: Those pedagogies that are based on a mutually determined construction between teacher and learner and rely on a shared responsibility for learning.

Dialogic talk: Engages both teachers and students in a genuine dialogue that aims to further the process of inquiry and promote critical thinking and higher order thinking skills. It occurs between teacher and student, student and student and can be initiated by teacher or student.

Difference Hypothesis: Language and literacy practices present in the families of minority groups can be seen as alternative forms of standard English. The differences, termed linguistic relativity, can be interpreted as differences of dialect rather than as some form of penalty or explanation of poor performance at school. It then becomes the responsibility of the school to accommodate these differences rather than blaming the home.

discourses: Refer to selections of language that connect together to make sense. They also refer to how sentences are related to one another in a text to make meaning.

Discourses: The social practices learnt in the home and community that produce characteristic ways of talking that are related to the attitudes, values, ideologies and behaviours that are adopted by individuals.

Elaborate code: Proposed by Bernstein (1961) as almost the direct opposite of the restricted code and having the following characteristics – accurate and complex sentences; a discriminating selection of a range of conjunctions, adjectives, adverbs, prepositions; frequent use of the personal pronoun; use of subordinate clauses; use of generalised statements; complex and explicit meanings; language of possibilities. These characteristics result in a wide range of syntactical alternatives and a flexible approach to syntactic organisation.

Emotional and Social Intelligence: The competencies linked to self-awareness, self-management, social awareness and relationship management, which enable people to understand and manage their own and others' emotions in social interactions. The ability to get along with others and facilitate co-operation.

Environmental scan: An environmental scan is conducted to identify factors that may inform the educational philosophy and pedagogical practices of a school. Data would be collected regarding the physical and geographical environment and characteristics of the community regarding, work, income, social and cultural activities, education levels, attitudes toward, and expectations of education. Questionnaires, interviews, surveys and government information sources can be used to gather data.

Formative assessment: Assessment usually based on teacher judgement or teacher-designed tests that takes place while students are engaged in learning. Because it takes place during learning, it provides feedback to students and also assists in the development of future learning for both students and teachers.

Globalisation: Refers to economic and political trends that take place on the world (or global) stage rather than in one country, local area or within a particular social group. Globalisation can also refer to societal or cultural factors (cultural globalisation) that can impinge on language practices across, or within, societies.

Interthinking: The use of talk by students working in groups by using a collective, rather than an individual approach, to justify their solutions, to engage in problem solving in learning and to develop their reasoning capabilities. Because the approach is inherently social, it enables students to share capabilities and thereby achieve more than they might be able to do individually.

IREs: A question and answer sequence or exchange that consists of a three-part structure. This structure was typically made up of an initiation by the teacher (I), most often a question, followed by a response (R) from a student and ending in some form of evaluation (E) by the teacher.

Literacy Identity: Life experiences provide a repertoire of resources about literacy and literate practices that contribute to an individual's literacy identity. Students bring to school a range of experiences from their social and cultural life that is their lifeworld, that is, everything that happens to them outside of school. Those experiences that take place in classrooms, after careful guidance by a teacher, form the student's school-based world.

Literate Practice: The ways in which literacies (for example speaking, listening, reading or writing) are used in a particular social or cultural group. This includes, the purposes for using literacy, the ways of using literacy and the contexts in which literacy is used. Membership of a particular social or cultural group may influence what aspects of literacy are valued most (for example oral language over written language, images over words).

Metacognition: Knowledge, monitoring and control of one's thinking processes in order to employ the most appropriate strategies to achieve a goal.

Metalanguage: In the context of a multiliterate classroom, metalanguage refers to terminology that enables producers and consumers of multimodal text to clearly articulate and describe all features of a multimodal text, including the codes and conventions of the semiotic systems and technologies used in its construction, together with the processes of consuming and producing the multimodal text.

Monologic talk: Monologic talk resembles a monologue by the teacher. Talk is dominated by the teacher who acts as the source of all knowledge and provides little, or no, opportunity for student-initiated talk.

Multiliteracies: A concept of literacy as being multimodal rather than language dominant, being made up of multiple literacies and multiple literate practices that continuously evolve as local and global society, culture and technology change the contexts in which literacy is practiced. Multiliteracies enable capacities to cope with change and effectively participate and contribute to all aspects of society; workplace, leisure, social, cultural and civic environments.

Pedagogy: The concept of pedagogy explains the relationship between teaching and learning. It defines the conditions necessary for students to fully participate in learning while also describing the teaching practices necessary to support such learning. Literacy pedagogy needs to take account of developments in contemporary society such as cultural and linguistic diversity and also the range of new texts produced by the semiotic systems and the new technologies, the advent of new literacies and consideration of literacy identity.

Personal oriented family: A family where power and status is gained by an individual by virtue of personal competence (a particular talent). Child rearing is accompanied and associated with reasoning language and practices (let's negotiate this).

Phases of lessons: Phases refer to changes in focus or task during a lesson. Phase divisions or changes can be signalled both orally and physically. Two oral signals can be given, either an explicit statement or instruction to move on to another task or change focus (for example 'Our next task is…') or a tag utterance which is known and recognised by all members of the class as a signal of change (for example, OK… All right…). Physical signals can be of three kinds, a change in activity by students, physical reorganisation of the room or students moving (for example from sitting on the floor to their desks) or use of equipment (for example starting a film to be watched).

Positional oriented family: A family where power and status is gained by an individual by virtue of their position in the family (father, mother, child). Child rearing is accompanied and associated with threatening language and practices (do as I tell you).

Postmodern picture book: The postmodern picture book manipulates the characteristics of a traditional picture book (for example, plot, characters, setting, format, sequencing, illustrative material) to interrupt reader expectations and create multiple readings and meanings.

Primary colours: These are red, yellow and blue, and have a pure pigment, that is, no other colour has been mixed with them and they cannot be made by mixing any other colours together. They are the basis of all other colours

Primary Discourses: Those Discourses acquired in the home through oral interaction in natural settings with significant others.

Producing: Engagement in the design and creation of a multimodal text, together with the selection of an appropriate means of dissemination, that will fulfil a particular communicative purpose, for a specific audience and context. May involve collaboration with others to access.

Psycholinguistics: A theory of language and literacy learning and teaching that draws on the fields of psychology and linguistics. As such, it integrates the study of cognition (psychology) and language (linguistics) and focusses on the structure of skills and thinking processes that take place in the mind. It is, therefore, a largely internal, invisible and highly individualistic. According to some theorists, it can sometimes involve a series of developmental stages.

Redesign/Redesigning: The combining, recombining and reworking of the selected resources to consume or produce a unique multimodal text.

Repertoire of Resources: The available designs that may be drawn upon when consuming or producing a text.

Restricted code: Originally described by Bernstein (1960, 1962a, 1962b, 1964) as having the following characteristics – short, simple and often unfinished sentences; limited use of adjectives, adverbs and subordinate clauses; infrequent use of personal pronouns; use of categorical statements; use of repetitive expressions; implicit meanings. These characteristics result in a narrow range of syntactical alternatives and a rigid approach to syntactic organisation.

Secondary colours: These are the next level of colours and result from mixing the primary colours. They are orange (red plus yellow) green (blue plus yellow) and purple (red plus blue).

Secondary Discourses: Those Discourses acquired in settings such as school, church, workplaces and other civic contexts.

Semiotic system: A system of signs and symbols that have agreed upon meanings within a particular group.

Social media: Websites and applications (apps) that enable users to develop online social networks and communities to share ideas, information, personal messages and interests, for example, Facebook, Twitter, Snapchat and LinkedIn. They facilitate user-generated content.

Social practice: The recognised, agreed and accepted behaviour (acting and interacting), talking and valuing among a social or cultural group. The social or cultural group will use these ways of behaving and talking in particular contexts. They may have a shared language (for example, slang) and ways of dressing or ways of wearing clothes. They may also share ways of viewing or acting toward particular social or cultural groups.

Sociolinguistics: A theory of language and literacy learning and teaching that draws on the fields of sociology and linguistics. It focusses on social interaction and inter-personal communication in social settings. It is based on the study of language in use and is therefore able to be observed externally in groups and other social situations.

Summative assessment: Assessment that provides information to students, teachers, parents and the general community after the learning has taken place. It is backward looking because it is designed to measure what students have learned. Various programs of state and national testing are also summative where the focus is sometimes on comparing student with student, school with school or state with state rather than on measuring what learning has taken place.

Synthesising: The ability to engage in the processes necessary to move back and forth among a repertoire of resources, including semiotic systems, to make or represent meaning.

Tertiary colours: These result from one primary colour being mixed with one of its nearest secondary colours, yellow plus orange results in yellow/orange, red plus orange results in red/orange, red plus purple gives a red/purple, blue plus purple results in blue/purple, blue plus green results in blue/green, yellow plus green results in yellow/green. Consult a colour wheel to see a visual rendition of this.

Transformation: The result of the process of design. The consumer will have been transformed by engaging with the available resources and multimodal texts in new ways in order to make meaning. Conversely the production and dissemination of a multimodal text will have transformed those who engage with it.

INDEX

Page numbers and page number spans in *italics* refer to *figures*.
Page number and page number spans in **bold** refer to **tables** and *also* to terms listed in the **glossary** at the end of the book (pp **236-9**).

art 179-81
Alexander, R.J. 150, 158-61
Allen, D. 180
Allington, R.L. 204
Anderson, C. 183
Anderson, L.W. 144
Andrew, D. 204
Anstey, M. 7, 10, 16, 18, 22, 36, 46, 50, 55, 59, 65, 67, 69, 71-3, 75, 89, 91, 99, 116, 130, 132, 134, 137, 140, 142-3, 145-6, 148-55, 158, 173, 178, 184, 198-9, 201, 204-6, 210, 213-15
appearance **121**; see also Gestural Semiotic System
Applebee, A.N. 11
Arizpe, E. 179-80, 183
assessment: auditing instruments 206-8; diagnostic 203; evaluation vs 198-9; evaluation and planning 208-12; formative 203; general principles of 198-203; issues in 200-3; monitoring cycle 199; multiliterate/multimodal school 219; student performance 200-3; summative 203; audience resources 109-11; see also multimodal texts
Au, W. 201
Audio Semiotic System **120**

backward design 208-10, *209*
backward mapping 211-12
Bader, B. 171
Bahr, M. 205
Baker, C.D. 137, 150, 158
Baker, E.A. 16
Balanskat, A. 25-6
Barnes, D. 159-61
Barrett, R. 205
Barton, D. 67
Barton, G. 182-3
Bates, K. 201
Bauserman, K.L. 144
Bean, T.W. 47-8
Bearne, E. 91

Bee, B. 10
Bell, C. 203
Bernstein, B. 49-54, 129, 142
Bezemer, J. 57, 61
Biesta, G. 201
Blackwood, F. 178
Bloch, S. 172
Bloom, B.S. 144
bodily contact **121**; see also Gestural Semiotic System
body position **121**; see also Gestural Semiotic System
Bolam, R. 213
Bondy, E. 143
Boyle, M. 214
Briggs, R. 172
Brown, A.L. 94, 97, 143
Brown, I. 205-6
Bruner, J.S. 159
Buckingham, D. 204
Bull, G. 7, 10, 16, 18, 22, 36, 46, 50, 55, 59, 65, 67, 71-3, 75, 89, 91, 99, 116, 132, 134, 137, 142-3, 145-6, 148-54, 173, 198-9, 204-6, 210, 213-15
Burn, A. 136

Calabrese, R.L. 214
Cali, D. 172
Cambourne, B. 128, 142
Caputi, P. 205-6
Carr, W. 201
Carrington, V. 65
Carson, K.P. 21
Cavanagh, R.E. 136
Cazden, C.B. 53-4, 129, 133, 150, 158
Chan, E. 3, 6, 16, 65, 84, 91-2, 143, 200-3
Chant, D. 205
Charters, J. 172
Chomsky, N. 129
civic change 28-9, 36-8
Clark, K. 179-80
classroom management **151**; see also teacher talk

classroom pedagogy and practice: classroom discourse, functions of 150–4; classroom talk 136–43; lesson structure 147–58; teacher talk and dialogic talk 127–63; functions of teacher talk 147–58
clauses **121**; see also Linguistic Semiotic System
Clegg, C.W. 21
Coats, K. 176
codes 49–52: Audio Semiotic System **120**; breaking 70–1, **185**; definition 60, **236**; elaborate code, definition 49–50; Gestural Semiotic System **121**; Linguistic Semiotic System **121**; restricted code, definition 49–50; semiotic systems 60, **118, 120-1, 123**; Spatial Semiotic System **123**; Visual Semiotic System **118**; see also deficiency hypothesis; personal oriented family; positional oriented family; semiotic systems
Coffin, C. 115
cohesive devices **121**; see also Linguistic Semiotic System
Coiro, J. 114, 204–6
Cole, D.R. 16
Collins Block, C. 144
colour **118**; see also Visual Semiotic System
Comber, B. 65, 144, 213
communication/meaning making 85
communicative competence 49, 53–4, 57: definition 53–4, **236**
community: response to change 40
competence: definition 85
consuming: definition 89, **236**; producing and 89–93; see also multimodal texts
contextual resources 109–11; see also multimodal texts
conventions: definition 98, **236**; see also codes
Cope, B. 3, 6, 15–16, 18, 65, 67, 84, 91–2, 129, 136, 146, 200–4
Coscarelli, C.V. 114
Coulthard, M. 148, 150
Courts, P.L. 14
Cowan, K. 183
Crew, G. 171–2
critical literacy 64–5: cautions about 147; concept of 143–4; critical pedagogy and 187–91; higher order thinking skills 144–6
critical pedagogy 184–91: critical literacy, development of 187–91; see also pedagogy
critical reading practices 184–91
critique: definition 85
Cross, D.R. 94, 143
cultural change 28–9, 36–8
cultural diversity 45–8
cultural resources 111–12; see also multimodal texts
curriculum: pedagogy and 128–35

Dalley-Trim, L. 3, 6, 16, 65, 84, 91–2, 143, 200–3
Dargusch, J. 201
Davies, F. 11
Davis, S. 172
Dawkins, J. 14

deficiency hypothesis 51–3: definition 51, **236**
Delpit, L. 142
Derewianka, B. 115
design: definition 85, 92–3, **236**; understanding by 209; see also multimodal texts
designing: definition 92–3, **236**; see also multimodal texts
diagnostic assessment 200: definition 203, **236**; see also assessment
dialogic pedagogies 160–1: definition 160, **236**
dialogic talk 106, 128, 158–63: definition 159, **236**; dialogic pedagogy 158–61
Difference Hypothesis 52–3, **236**
Discourses 54–7, 129–31, 135, 147: definition 54, **236**; 'discourses', definition 54; Primary 54–5; Secondary 55
distance **123**; see also Spatial Semiotic System
Dondis, D.A. 180
Dunkerly-Bean, J. 47–8
D'warte, J. 54, 142
dynamic pedagogy 161–2
Dyson, A.H. 54

editing **118**: see also Visual Semiotic System
Edwards-Groves, C. 50, 137, 142–3, 146, 148, 152, 158, 198, 204
elaborate code 49–50, 52–3: definition 49–50, **236-7**
emotional and social intelligence 25, 27, 39, **237**
Engelhart, S. 25–6
environmental scan: definition 134, **237**
evaluation see assessment
Exley, B. 204
eye movement **121**; see also Gestural Semiotic System

facial expression **121**; see also Gestural Semiotic System
Five Laws of Media and Information Literacy 36, 38
Fleiger, J. 173
focus **118**: see also Visual Semiotic System
Formative assessment 203, **237**
formative assessment: definition 203; see also assessment
Four Resource Model 69–75: application 75; code breaking 70–1; context 69–70; meaning making 71–2; text analyst practices 73–5; text user practices 72–3
framing: Spatial Semiotic System **123**; Visual Semiotic System **118**
Freebody, P. 6, 52, 54, 65, 69–70, 75, 129, 137, 142, 144–5, 148, 158, 204
Freebody, S. 204
Freiberg, J. 129, 137, 148
French, P. 148
Frey, C.B. 24–5
Fullan, M. 214
Fuller, R. 214
functions of language **7**, 9

Gallagher, M.C. 161
Gardner, P. 3, 170

gaze **121**; *see also* Gestural Semiotic System
Gee, J.P. 11, 13, 51, 54-5, 129-31, 142, 150
Gestural Semiotic System **121**; *see also* semiotic systems
Gillies, R.M. 214
Gleeson, L. 178
globalisation 2, 15, 18, 28, 38, 45-8, 173: definition 45, **237**
Goe, L. 203
Goodman, K.S. 128
Google 19
Gordon, S.P. 213
Grant, H. 65, 144
Gravett, E. 171
Gray, B. 10
Green, J. 129
Greene, T. 11
Grenny, J. 202
Gunn, S. 137, 148
Gutierrez, K.D. 65

Habermas, J. 54
Haertel, G.D. 204
Halliday, M.A.K. 7, 8
Hamilton, M. 67
Hansen, D.T. 48
Harlen, W. 201
Harste, J. 158
Hartman, D.K. 86, 200-1
Hayes, D. 205
head nods **121**; *see also* Gestural Semiotic System
Heath, S.B. 7-8, 54, 130, 142
Herschell, P. 148
Hest, A. 172
higher order thinking skills: critical literacy 144-6; interthinking 146
Hoh, A. 31
Holman, D. 21
Honan, E. 204
Hood, D. 214
Howard, A. 21
Hull, G. 54
Hull, G.A. 48
human resources 113-14; *see also* multimodal texts

identity *see* literacy identity
information management: literacy **151**; *see also* teacher talk
interthinking 20, 146: cautions about 147; definition **237**; higher order thinking skills 146
IREs 148-50, 158: definition 148, **237**; monologic talk 158; use of 148-50
Israel, S.E. 144
Ivanic, R. 67
Iyer, R. 144

Janks, H. 65
Jewitt, C. 46, 61, 84, 136, 145

Jones, A. 133
Jones, P. 115

Kalantzis, M. 3, 6, 15-16, 18, 65, 67, 84, 91-2, 129, 143-4, 146, 200-4
Kamler, B. 213
Kane, M.J. 143
Kauffman, G. 183
Kemmis, S. 201
Kervin, L. 204
kinesics **121**; *see also* Gestural Semiotic System
Knobel, M. 11, 54, 65, 142, 204-6
Krathwohl, D.R. 144
Kress, G. 46, 54, 57, 59, 61, 81, 84, 86, 91-3, 116, 136, 144-5, 171, 200-1

Labov, W. 52-4, 129
Ladwig, J. 205
Land, R. 146, 205
Landy, F.J. 21
language functions **7**, 9
Lankshear, C. 9, 11, 54-5, 65, 133, 142, 204-6
Lawler, M. 9, 55, 133
Lawton, D. 52
Laycock, L. 183
Lenneberg, E.H. 129
lessons: attention **156**; coda **156**; display **156**; focus **156**; guided implementation **156**; mapping phase structure *157*; phases of 154-8; planning and design 208-12; presentation of text **156**; report **156**; review **156**; structure 147-58; transition out **156**; unguided implementation **156**; *see also* backward design; backward mapping
Leu, D.J. 204-6
Lewis, D. 173
lighting **118**: *see also* Visual Semiotic System
Lindsay, G. 19
line **118**: *see also* Visual Semiotic System
Lingard, B. 205
linguistic relativity 52-3
Linguistic Semiotic System **121**; *see also* semiotic systems
Lipson, M.Y. 94, 143
literacy: change 83-7; cognition **152**; definitions of 2-6; 'doing' **151**; information management **151**; learning 'how' and 'when about' **152**; 'literacies' and 7-15; 'neutral' practice of 129-31; political enterprise of 131-2; practice, construction of 133-4; social practice of 15, 128-9, **152**; traditional 15
literacy identity 67-9: conceptual framework *68*; definition 67, **237**; multimodal texts 107-8; resources influenced by **107**
Literate Practice: definition **237**
literate practices: workplaces 18-23
literature: exploration of 169-92
Little, O. 203
Littleton, K. 19-20, 51, 82, 146, 159-61, 214

Lo Bianco, J. 45
Lockyer, L. 205-6
Louden, W. 133
Ludwig, C. 52, 54, 137, 148
Luke, A. 6, 10, 32, 48, 56, 65, 69-70, 75, 129, 142, 144-5, 150, 204-5

Macaulay, D. 177-8
MacLure, M. 148
MacNeill, N. 136
Magnolfi, J. 19
Mallouri, L. 183
Marriott, S. 171
Marsden, J. 172
Martin, J.R. 11, 128
Masters, G. 202-3
Matters, G. 205
Maungedzo, R. 204
Maxfield, D. 202
McConnell, S. 10
McMahon, A. 213
McMillan, R. 202
McTighe, J. 200, 208, 210
McVey, K.A. 97
meaning: construction 64-5; making 71-2, 84-7, **185**
Medwell, J. 198, 200-1
Mercer, N. 19-20, 51, 82, 146, 158-61, 214
metacognition: definition 94, **237**; metacognitive prompts **100-1, 104-5**; multimodal text consumption **100-1**; multimodal text production **104-5**; see also multimodal texts
metalanguage: definition 97, **237**; metacognition and multimodality **100-1, 104-5**; see also multimodal texts
Michaels, S. 158
Mikulecky, L. 18
Mills, K.A. 16, 144, 147
Mills, M. 205
Monologic talk 158-60, **237**
monologic talk: definition 158; IREs and 158
Moon, B. 204
Moran, S.K. 21
Morrell, E. 65
Morsink, P.M. 86, 200-1
multiliteracies: assessment and evaluation 219; 'being' multiliterate 44-76; characteristics of **27, 37**; civic change 28-9, 36-8; cultural change 28-9, 36-8; curriculum and pedagogy 134-5; definition 17, **237**; knowledge and beliefs about 128-35; global trends and practices 13-40; origins of 15-17; postmodern picture books 173-9; relationships among **27, 37**; rise of 13-40; social change 28-9, 36-8; teaching and learning 127-63; technological change 28-9; visual concept of terminological origins 17; workplaces 17-18, 26-8
multimodal texts: assessment and evaluation 219; change in texts and literacy 83-7; consumption 87-93, 91, 98-9; conventions 98; designing 93-4; designing of 93-124; dissemination 91; linguistic semiotic system 81-3; literacy identity 107-8; meaning making 84-7; metacognition 94; metalanguage 97; model for engaging with **185-6**; production of 87-93, 91, 99-102; purpose 91; reading and writing 87-9; redesigning 88; repertoire of resources 92, 97; resources 102-16; semiotic systems and 80-124; static and dynamic approaches to text 84-7; synthesising 91; transformation 93; transparency 98-102; see also resources
music 181-3
Muspratt, S. 142, 204

NAPLAN writing test 86, 116, 173, 200-1
Naremore, R.C. 52
Newfield, D. 204
Newman, R. 97
Nicholas, M. 201
Nikolejava, M. 173
Noble, K. 172
Non-standard English (NSE) **53**
Novak, B.J. 177
Nystrand, M. 158

O'Connor, M.C. 158
O'Halloran, K. 61
Oliver, N. 171
orientation **121**; see also Gestural Semiotic System
Osborne, M. 24-5
Ottley, M. 171-2, 183
Oxenham, J. 3-4

pace **120**; see also Audio Semiotic System
page position **123**; see also Spatial Semiotic System
Palincsar, A.S. 97
Pantaleo, S. 173
Paris, A.H. 94, 106
Paris, S.G. 94, 97, 106, 143
Parker, D. 136, 172
Patterson, A. 83
Patterson, K. 202
Pearson, P.D. 161
pedagogy: approaches to 204-5; critical 184-91; definition 136, **237-8**; dialogic 158-61; dynamic 161; evaluation of pedagogy and practice 203-6; implicit vs explicit 142-3; multiliterate 162; pedagogical change 205-6; practice and planning 197-220; whole school approaches 212-18; see also critical pedagogy
performing arts 183-4
personal oriented family 50-1: definition 50, **238**
phases of lessons 154-8, 163: definition 155, **238**; see also lessons
Photoshop 32-3
phrases **121**; see also Linguistic Semiotic System
pitch **120**; see also Audio Semiotic System
Plummer, A. 176
point of view (POV) **118**: see also Visual Semiotic System
Poole, M.E. 52

positional oriented family 50-1: definition 50, **238**
postmodern picture books 170, 173-9, 183-4, 192: art 179-81; characteristics of **174**; definition 170, **238**; disciplinary approaches 179-84; literature exploring concept of **176-8**; multiliterate practices 173-9; music 181-3; performing arts 183-4; semiotic systems 179-84
posture **121**; see also Gestural Semiotic System
Poulter, J.R. 172
Pressley, M. 204
primary colours 116: definition 116, **238**
Primary Discourses 54-6: definition 54-5, **238**; see also Discourses
producing: consuming and 89-93; definition 88, **238**; see also multimodal texts
proximity **121**; see also Gestural Semiotic System
psycholinguistics: definition 129, **238**
Pullen, D.L. 16
punctuation **121**; see also Linguistic Semiotic System

QR codes: community response to change 40; Five Laws of MIL 38; image composition 183; movies 5, 182; music composition 183; NAPLAN 116; network sites 30; news archives 5; Photoshop 33; postmodern picture books 179, 182-3; websites 99, 114, 182; workplaces 19, 24; YouTube videos 189
Quellmalz, E.S. 204

Raney, K. 180
reading: concept of 87-9; process of 90
redesign/redesigning 46, 89, 93, 102-3, 116, 142, 170: definition 88, **238**; see also multimodal texts
Rennie, J. 83
repertoire of resources 67, 70, 93, 97, 115, 124, 183: definition *91*, 92, **238**; see also multimodal texts
Resnick, L.B. 158
resources 102-16: audience *107*, 109-11; contextual *107*, 109-11; cultural *107*, 111-12; human *107*, 113-14; literacy identity *107*; non-human *107*, 113-14; purpose *107*, 109-11; semiotic *107*, 116; social *107*, 111-12; strategic *107*, 112-13; technological *107*, 114-15; textual *107*, 115-16; see also multimodal texts
restricted code 49, 54: definition 49-50, **238**
Rivalland, J. 133
Robinson, M. 65
Rosenberg, T. 33
Rothery, J. 11
Ruhemann, A. 182-3
Rymer, R. 45

Sanchez, J.I. 21
Schultz, K. 54
Scott, C. 173
screen position **123**; see also Spatial Semiotic System
Searle, S. 11
secondary colours: definition 116, **238**
Secondary Discourses 54-6: definition 55, **238**; see also Discourses

semiotic systems 59-61: Audio Semiotic Systems **120**; definition 59, **238**; Gestural Semiotic System **121**; Linguistic Semiotic System **121**; moving beyond 81-3; multimodal texts and 80-124, **186**; postmodern picture books 179-84; primary colours 116; secondary colours 116; semiotic resources 116; Spatial Semiotic System **123**; tertiary colours 116; Visual Semiotic System **118**; see also codes
sentences **121**; see also Linguistic Semiotic System
Shankster-Cawley, L. 21
shape **118**: see also Visual Semiotic System
Shorey, M. 88
Short, K.G. 183
Silcox, S. 136
Silvers, P. 88
Simpson, A. 204
Sinclair, J. 148, 150
Sipe, L.R. 173
Smith, F. 7, 8, 128
Smith, L. 177
social change 28-9, 36-8
social diversity 45-8
social media 30-5, 37, 75, 81-2: definition 30, **238**
social practice 7-9, 11-12, 14-15, 22, 24, 54, 128-9, 144, **152**, 171, 207, **238-9**
social resources 111-12; see also multimodal texts
sociolinguistics: definition 129, **239**
Solomon, Y. 158
Sparrow, P. 21
Spatial Semiotic System **123**; see also semiotic systems
Standard English (SE) **53**
Starcevic, V. 32
Stein, P. 204
Stewart, G.L. 21
Stickler, L.M. 203
Stoll, L. 213
Stornaiulo, A. 48
strategic resources 112-13; see also multimodal texts
Street, B.V. 8, 129
student performance: approaches to 202-3; monitoring of 200-3; see also assessment
Styles, M. 172, 179-80, 183
summative assessment 201: definition 203, **239**; see also assessment
Sutton, M. 30
Switzer, A. 202
synthesising 86, 93, **105**, 211: definition 91, **239**; multimodal texts *91*; see also multimodal texts

Tan, S. 98-9, 170-2, 182-3
Taylor, D. 130
teacher and student interaction 136-42
teacher discourse 148-50
teacher talk: classroom management **151**; elaboration **151**; functions of 147-58, **151-2**; informative questions **152**; literacy information management **151**; organisation **151**; process questions **152**; projection **151**;

reconstruction **151**; utility questions **152** technology: change 28–9, 36–8; globalisation 45–8; postmodern picture books 179–84; resources 114–15; text structure 170–3

tertiary colours 119: definition 116, **239**

texts: analyst practices 73–5, **186**; conceptions about 62–4; continuous change 83–7; neutrality 34–6; pre-engagement with **185**; representation 85; static and dynamic description of 84–7, 85; technology and 170–3; textual resources 115–16; types 57–8; understanding 58–9; user practices 72–3, **186**

texture **118**: see also Visual Semiotic System

Thomas, S. 213

Tough, J. 130

transformation, 66, 74, 91: definition 93, **239**; see also multimodal texts

Unsworth, L. 16, 182–3

van Kraayenoord, C.E. 200–2
van Leeuwen, T. 54, 59, 61, 91–3, 144
Varlander, S. 19
Visual Semiotic System: codes and conventions **118**
vocabulary **121**; see also Linguistic Semiotic System
volume and audibility **120**; see also Audio Semiotic System
Vygotsky, L.S. 129

Waber, B. 19
Wagner, T. 200
Wall, T.D. 21

Wallace, M. 213
Wallace, P. 32
Warry, M. 205
Watson, K. 173
Weade, G. 129
websites 114
Wells, G. 150, 158–9, 161
Wells, M. 204
whole school approaches: auditing instruments 216–18; pedagogy, practice and planning 212–18; procedural development of 213–16; see also pedagogy
Wiggins, G. 200, 208, 210
Wiliam, D. 202
Williams, F. 52
Williams, M. 172
Wolfe, S.E. 160
Wolpert, M. 183
Wolstencroft, H. 91
Woolman, S. 172
workplaces: creativity 19; future prospects 23–6; literate practices 18–23; multiliteracies 17–18, 26–8; spatial use and organisation 19
writing: concept of 87–9; process of 90

Yamada-Rice, D. 57
YouTube videos 189
Young, E. 172

Zheng, J. 86, 200–1
Zimmerman, B.J. 94